WITHDRAWN
UTSA LIBRARIES

China's New Underclass

This book examines the implications of China's economic reforms for domestic work and domestic workers. The author examines the factors that give rise to paid domestic work in a socialist economy, and goes on to look at the need for social protection of domestic workers within cities in contemporary China.

Using a socialist feminist approach, the book investigates how China's economic restructuring has deliberately crafted a domestic service sector from the top down. Through the analysis of the situation of paid domestic labour, it demonstrates how the changes in socialist ideology under a market economy have justified the state's support for paid domestic labour, the large role of the state in these ideological changes and how domestic labour is related to economic changes and the market economy itself. The book argues that the state's economic reforms have changed gender and class relations in Chinese society.

Based on interviews with domestic workers, their employers, their social advocates and government officials, this book examines the economic and social security of domestic workers and provides information about their precarious working conditions that could be improved through public policy. It also explores women's agency and activism, and the current role of NGOs and trade unions in labour protection.

Xinying Hu is a Chinese scholar who received her PhD from the Department of Women's Studies, Simon Fraser University, Canada.

Routledge Contemporary China Series

1 **Nationalism, Democracy and National Integration in China**
 Leong Liew and Wang Shaoguang

2 **Hong Kong's Tortuous Democratization**
 A comparative analysis
 Ming Sing

3 **China's Business Reforms**
 Institutional challenges in a globalised economy
 Edited by Russell Smyth, On Kit Tam, Malcolm Warner and Cherrie Zhu

4 **Challenges for China's Development**
 An enterprise perspective
 Edited by David H. Brown and Alasdair MacBean

5 **New Crime in China**
 Public order and human rights
 Ron Keith and Zhiqiu Lin

6 **Non-Governmental Organizations in Contemporary China**
 Paving the way to civil society?
 Qiusha Ma

7 **Globalization and the Chinese City**
 Fulong Wu

8 **The Politics of China's Accession to the World Trade Organization**
 The dragon goes global
 Hui Feng

9 **Narrating China**
 Jia Pingwa and his fictional world
 Yiyan Wang

10 **Sex, Science and Morality in China**
 Joanne McMillan

11 **Politics in China Since 1949**
 Legitimizing authoritarian rule
 Robert Weatherley

12 **International Human Resource Management in Chinese Multinationals**
 Jie Shen and Vincent Edwards

13 **Unemployment in China**
 Economy, human resources and labour markets
 Edited by Grace Lee and Malcolm Warner

14 **China and Africa**
Engagement and compromise
Ian Taylor

15 **Gender and Education in China**
Gender discourses and women's schooling in the early twentieth century
Paul J. Bailey

16 **SARS**
Reception and interpretation in three Chinese cities
Edited by Deborah Davis and Helen Siu

17 **Human Security and the Chinese State**
Historical transformations and the modern quest for sovereignty
Robert E. Bedeski

18 **Gender and Work in Urban China**
Women workers of the unlucky generation
Liu Jieyu

19 **China's State Enterprise Reform**
From Marx to the market
John Hassard, Jackie Sheehan, Meixiang Zhou, Jane Terpstra-Tong and Jonathan Morris

20 **Cultural Heritage Management in China**
Preserving the cities of the Pearl River Delta
Edited by Hilary du Cros and Yok-shiu F. Lee

21 **Paying for Progress**
Public finance, human welfare and inequality in china
Edited by Vivienne Shue and Christine Wong

22 **China's Foreign Trade Policy**
The new constituencies
Edited by Ka Zeng

23 **Hong Kong, China**
Learning to belong to a nation
Gordon Mathews, Tai-lok Lui, and Eric Kit-wai Ma

24 **China Turns to Multilateralism**
Foreign policy and regional security
Edited by Guoguang Wu and Helen Lansdowne

25 **Tourism and Tibetan Culture in Transition**
A place called Shangrila
Åshild Kolås

26 **China's Emerging Cities**
The making of new urbanism
Edited by Fulong Wu

27 **China-US Relations Transformed**
Perceptions and strategic interactions
Edited by Suisheng Zhao

28 **The Chinese Party-State in the 21st Century**
Adaptation and the reinvention of legitimacy
Edited by André Laliberté and Marc Lanteigne

29 **Political Change in Macao**
Sonny Shiu-Hing Lo

30 **China's Energy Geopolitics**
The Shanghai Cooperation Organization and Central Asia
Thrassy N. Marketos

31 **Regime Legitimacy in Contemporary China**
Institutional change and stability
Edited by Thomas Heberer and Gunter Schubert

32 **U.S.-China Relations**
China policy on Capitol Hill
Tao Xie

33 **Chinese Kinship**
Contemporary anthropological perspectives
Edited by Susanne Brandtstädter and Gonçalo D. Santos

34 **Politics and Government in Hong Kong**
Crisis under Chinese sovereignty
Edited by Ming Sing

35 **Rethinking Chinese Popular Culture**
Cannibalizations of the canon
Edited by Carlos Rojas and Eileen Cheng-yin Chow

36 **Institutional Balancing in the Asia Pacific**
Economic interdependence and China's rise
Kai He

37 **Rent Seeking in China**
Edited by Tak-Wing Ngo and Yongping Wu

38 **China, Xinjiang and Central Asia**
History, transition and crossborder interaction into the 21st century
Edited by Colin Mackerras and Michael Clarke

39 **Intellectual Property Rights in China**
Politics of piracy, trade and protection
Gordon Cheung

40 **Developing China**
Land, politics and social conditions
George C.S. Lin

41 **State and Society Responses to Social Welfare Needs in China**
Serving the people
Edited by Jonathan Schwartz and Shawn Shieh

42 **Gay and Lesbian Subculture in Urban China**
Loretta Wing Wah Ho

43 **The Politics of Heritage Tourism in China**
A view from lijiang
Xiaobo Su and Peggy Teo

44 **Suicide and Justice**
A Chinese perspective
Wu Fei

45 **Management Training and Development in China**
Educating managers in a globalized economy
Edited by Malcolm Warner and Keith Goodall

46 **Patron-Client Politics and Elections in Hong Kong**
Bruce Kam-kwan Kwong

47 **Chinese Family Business and the Equal Inheritance System**
Unravelling the myth
Victor Zheng

48 **Reconciling State, Market and Civil Society in China**
The long march towards prosperity
Paolo Urio

49 **Innovation in China**
The Chinese software industry
Shang-Ling Jui

50 **Mobility, Migration and the Chinese Scientific Research System**
Koen Jonkers

51 **Chinese Film Stars**
Edited by Mary Farquhar and Yingjin Zhang

52 **Chinese Male Homosexualities**
Memba, Tongzhi and Golden Boy
Travis S.K. Kong

53 **Industrialisation and Rural Livelihoods in China**
Agricultural processing in Sichuan
Susanne Lingohr-Wolf

54 **Law, Policy and Practice on China's Periphery**
Selective adaptation and institutional capacity
Pitman B. Potter

55 **China-Africa Development Relations**
Edited by Christopher M. Dent

56 **Neoliberalism and Culture in China and Hong Kong**
The countdown of time
Hai Ren

57 **China's Higher Education Reform and Internationalisation**
Edited by Janette Ryan

58 **Law, Wealth and Power in China**
Commercial law reforms in context
Edited by John Garrick

59 **Religion in Contemporary China**
Revitalization and innovation
Edited by Adam Yuet Chau

60 **Consumer-Citizens of China**
The role of foreign brands in the imagined future china
Kelly Tian and Lily Dong

61 **The Chinese Communist Party and China's Capitalist Revolution**
The political impact of the market
Lance L. P. Gore

62 **China's Homeless Generation**
Voices from the veterans of the Chinese civil war, 1940s–1990s
Joshua Fan

63 **In Search of China's Development Model**
Beyond the beijing consensus
Edited by S. Philip Hsu, Suisheng Zhao and Yu-Shan Wu

64 **Xinjiang and China's Rise in Central Asia, 1949–2009**
A history
Michael E. Clarke

65 **Trade Unions in China**
The challenge of labour unrest
Tim Pringle

66 **China's Changing Workplace**
Dynamism, diversity and disparity
Edited by Peter Sheldon, Sunghoon Kim, Yiqiong Li and Malcolm Warner

67 **Leisure and Power in Urban China**
Everyday life in a medium-sized Chinese city
Unn Målfrid H. Rolandsen

68 **China, Oil and Global Politics**
Philip Andrews-Speed and Roland Dannreuther

69 **Education Reform in China**
Edited by Janette Ryan

70 **Social Policy and Migration in China**
Lida Fan

71 **China's One Child Policy and Multiple Caregiving**
Raising little Suns in Xiamen
Esther C. L. Goh

72 **Politics and Markets in Rural China**
Edited by Björn Alpermann

73 **China's New Underclass**
Paid Domestic Labour
Xinying Hu

74 **Poverty and Development in China**
Alternative approaches to poverty assessment
Lu Caizhen

China's New Underclass
Paid domestic labour

Xinying Hu

LONDON AND NEW YORK

This edition published 2011
by Routledge
2 Park Square, Milton Park, Abingdon, Oxon, OX14 4RN

Simultaneously published in the USA and Canada
by Routledge
711 Third Avenue. New York, NY 10017

Routledge is an imprint of the Taylor & Francis Group, an informa business

© 2011 Xinying Hu

The right of Xinying Hu to be identified as author of this work has been asserted by him in accordance with sections 77 and 78 of the Copyright, Designs and Patents Act 1988.

All rights reserved. No part of this book may be reprinted or reproduced or utilised in any form or by any electronic, mechanical, or other means, now known or hereafter invented, including photocopying and recording, or in any information storage or retrieval system, without permission in writing from the publishers.

Trademark notice: Product or corporate names may be trademarks or registered trademarks, and are used only for identification and explanation without intent to infringe.

British Library Cataloguing in Publication Data
A catalogue record for this book is available from the British Library

Library of Congress Cataloging in Publication Data
A catalog record has been requested for this book

ISBN: 978–0–415–61765–9 (hbk)
ISBN: 978–0–203–80760–6 (ebk)

Typeset in Times New Roman
by RefineCatch Limited, Bungay, Suffolk

Printed and bound in Great Britain by
CPI Antony Rowe, Chippenham, Wiltshire

To Marjorie
– in thanks for her inspiration

To Yiqing and Bin
– in thanks for their love and support

Contents

List of illustrations	xiii
Acknowledgements	xiv

1 Introduction   1

Theoretical framework 3
Globalization, restructuring and the implications for women's domestic labour 6
Women's domestic labour in China's transition to the socialist market economy 10
Literature review 12
Research methodology 13
Scope of analysis and outline 16

2 Domestic employment regimes in China   18

What is the domestic employment regime? 19
Bondservant regime in feudal society 20
Servants in near-modern history 23
Domestic service under the socialist central-planned economy 27
The domestic service regime after economic reforms 32
Conclusion 35

3 Globalization, economic reforms and paid domestic employment in China   36

Rural economic reforms and rural-to-urban migration 37
Economic restructuring and the rise of precarious employment in cities 46
Conclusion 56

4 Childcare crisis after economic reforms   58

China's social welfare regime in the state-planned economy 59

Childcare policy in the socialist era 63
Market economy and the childcare burden 69
Conclusion 79

5 Domestic labour as precarious work in China   80

Domestic workers' background information 82
Working and living conditions of care workers 85
Precarious working conditions of cleaners 98
Conclusion 104

6 From individual resistance to unionized negotiation   106

Everyday forms of resistance 107
Legal resistance 113
Organizing domestic workers 116
Conclusion 124

7 Establishing domestic workers' rights   126

International frameworks 127
National experiences of labour legislation/regulation on domestic workers 128
What the Chinese government can do 129
Conclusion 138

8 Conclusion   140

Further reflections 141

Appendix 1	Open-ended interview sample questions for domestic workers	144
Appendix 2	Open-ended interview sample questions for employers	146
Appendix 3	Open-ended interview sample questions for domestic agencies	148
Appendix 4	Open-ended interview sample questions for labour authority and support groups	149

Glossary of Chinese words   150
List of acronyms and abbreviations   152
Notes   154
Bibliography   160
Author index   181
Subject index   185

Tables

2.1	Chinese domestic employment regimes	35
3.1	Workers in urban areas and rural areas in China, 2000–05	39
3.2	Income and expenditure of urban and rural residents in China	45
4.1	Various childcare facilities in China from 1949 to 1978	68
4.2	The statistics of childcare development in China, 1979–2007	70
4.3	Number of childcare centres and classes in 2006	73
4.4	The average weekly working time of urban employees (hours)	78

Acknowledgements

Seven years ago, when my family still lived in Beijing and hired a live-in nanny to look after my daughter so that I could pursue a career, I did not anticipate writing a book about domestic workers. Yet, in retrospect, as a researcher in a women's organization whose full-time job was to promote gender equality in China, I wish could have paid attention earlier to this group of people whose work is so significant yet who receive so little attention in the public eye.

This book, originally my Ph.D dissertation, is the result of my studies in the Department of Women's Studies at Simon Fraser University in Canada. Feminist economics theories, labour issues and social policy were my three academic foci. The extensive readings and writings in these three areas fundamentally challenged my thinking and inspired me to study Chinese domestic service labour – the most precarious labour in China's transition process.

Teachers and mentors at Simon Fraser University provided me with critical guidance and support during the course of preparing this book. My deepest thanks go to Dr Marjorie Griffin Cohen, who guided me with great patience throughout my doctoral studies. From my very first assignment to the final revisions of this book – the publication of which was her idea – I had her consistent support and encouragement. I simply could not have asked for a better senior supervisor, and I will benefit forever from her mentorship.

Dr Stephen McBride challenged me to rethink my arguments and theoretical positions and taught me to look at globalization and economic development in critical ways. His insightful comments and suggestions have helped develop the core of the arguments of this book.

Dr Jennifer Marchbank's work has also shaped this book in many ways. She supplied insightful guidance regarding feminist research methods, women's activism, women's care work, childcare policies and welfare typologies as well as how welfare restructuring impacts women's care work and gender regimes.

Dr Fiona MacPhail, an economist from the University of Northern British Columbia, Canada, was extremely helpful. I met her in Beijing when she was invited to a feminist economics workshop at the Peking University. In my first year's study, she hired me as a research assistant to help her and Dr Paul Bowles to investigate casual labour in British Columbia, Canada. Through interviews with casual workers, I gained understanding about these workers' working and living conditions. These experiences led me to think about precarious labour in China, which eventually became my Ph.D research project. Dr MacPhail carefully read every draft of my dissertation, and provided many precious suggestions and comments.

In addition to my advisors, many other people have offered helpful comments and suggestions on the manuscript. I thank Dr Xiao-Yuan Dong, an economist and expert in Chinese studies at the University of Winnipeg, Canada, for her consistent support. Her questions, comments and suggestions have greatly improved the quality of this research. Dr John Calvert also read my dissertation and provided valuable suggestions. I thank Dr Jie Yang for her always insightful advice regarding my reading and writing.

Fellow students at Simon Fraser University have also supported and shaped this project. My thanks go especially to Renji Chen, Guoxin Xing, and their families for their intellectual and emotional support. Thanks also go to Dr. Benjamin Ong.

I wish to thank my other friends in Vancouver: Joanne and John, Pat and Peter, Pilar and Nestor, Jacqueline and Brian, Jiefei, Judy, Angela, and Phyllis and Jo. Alfreda and Gerda have helped me edit various drafts of this book. I thank Margaret for her careful editing, formatting and indexing of this book.

My sincere appreciation goes to my friends in Beijing. Their helpfulness and unfailing support will always be remembered. I would like to thank friends in labour departments: Mo Rong, Wang Yadong, Tian Guangzhe, Zhang Libin, Li Xiangwei and Li Yansong; friends and colleagues at the Women's Studies Institute of China: Tan Lin, Bai Mei, Jiang Yongping, Wu Jing, Jiang Xiuhua, Ji Zhongyun, He Yanrong, Li Yani, Yang Yujing, Xu Guoping, Wang Qinghong, and all others who I cannot list one by one. My special thanks go to Liu Bohong whose support and encouragement have accompanied me throughout my Ph.D study and the completion of this book.

Thanks must also be extended to my friends at the Migrant Women's Club, Han Huimin and Fang Qingxia, who have helped me learn about their organization and their work for domestic workers. I thank Wang Zhuqing and my friends at the Centre for Women's Law Studies and Legal Services of Peking University who kindly invited me to attend their project conference on domestic workers. Her presentation at the conference supplied important information for this book. I am grateful to Wang Li, the organizer of the domestic workers' support group at Fuping Domestic Service School, for allowing me to participate in one of the group's activities. I am also grateful to the managers in the agencies for their generous support of my field study.

I owe a tremendous debt to the domestic workers who shared their experiences with me. Their trust and genuineness have made the research possible and I will always remember them.

Finally, I owe the successful completion of this work to my family: my parents, my husband and my wonderful daughter, without whose unconditional love and support this book would not have been possible.

1 Introduction

Although paid domestic labour is a kind of work arrangement that has continued for centuries and has survived the transformations of various economic systems, such as feudalism, capitalism and even socialism, openly providing and hiring domestic help is a new social phenomenon for the majority of the Chinese people. For both the current generation of domestic workers and their employers who have grown up in the socialist era, paid domestic help is a new experience (Yan 2003b; 2008). In China, paid domestic labour was identified historically with the pre-Mao era as class exploitation. After the foundation of new China in 1949, the government declared its main objective to be the achievement of an egalitarian socialism. This egalitarianism aimed at eliminating class divisions in three areas: the differences between peasant and worker, differences between urban and rural areas, and differences between mental labour and manual labour in society. Hiring domestic help was seen as a 'bourgeois' lifestyle and was assumed not to exist before the economic reforms. However, even before the economic reforms there were always a small number of rural women who worked in cities as maids or nannies for wealthier households. These were usually the households of high-level cadres and intellectuals (Jacka 1997; Yan 2003b). This type of employment, however, was never openly incorporated into state or collective employment relationships and it was kept invisible from the public domain (Jacka 1997; Yan 2003b).

Domestic service in China revived in the early 1980s after the state began its transition from a centrally planned economy to a market-oriented economy. Poor women from rural areas were the first cohorts to move into cities in search of caregiving and cleaning jobs. After the mid-1990s, the laid-off female workers from the state-owned enterprises (SOEs) joined this labour pool. While many domestic workers are employed through agencies and cleaning services, a large portion of the labour market is employed through informal kinship or networks. This means there are no precise national statistics on the size of the domestic labour force. It is estimated that there are about 15 million domestic workers now working in households throughout China, but this may be an underestimation of the total because of problems with labour statistics. Some observers estimate that it is possible the number is close to 20 million (Z. Q. Wang 2007). This is now a major area of employment in China and accounts for over ten times the employment in major sections of the formal economy, such as the steel industry (with 2 million workers) and textiles (with 2–3 million workers). Despite the huge number of domestic workers already working, the demand is escalating. In Beijing, the 2006 statistical data show that out of the 3,257,000 households in the eight city districts, 340,000 households, or 10.7 per cent, hire domestic workers. This is an increase over the 7.7 per cent of Beijing households that hired domestic service workers in 2002. There was a net increase of 152,000 households in 2006 compared with 188,000 households that hired domestic helpers in 2002, while there was an average demand gap of 20,000–30,000 that could not be filled each year (D. J. Li 2007). According to a survey of 1,600 households by the former Ministry of Labour and Social Security (MOLSS 2000)[1] in Shenyang, Qingdao, Changsha and Chengdu, 40 per cent of these surveyed households need domestic service. The survey data show that Shenyang needs 96,000 domestic service workers with a gap of 40,000; the demand in Wuhan is 100,000 with a gap of 90,000; in Nanjing the domestic worker demand is 360,000, and there are 240,000 jobs that need to be filled; and the demand in Tianjin is increasing by 20 per cent every year (China Employment Training Technical Instruction Centre (CETTIC) 2004). These various numbers reflect that domestic service has become an industry in high demand in China and that the supply does not match the demand. The decline in state support for vital services such as childcare and medical care means the work of social reproduction is now marketized, which in turn leads to the increase in the demand for domestic work.

Unlike in previous eras, domestic service has become an industry that is actively nurtured by the Chinese government in order to deal with the huge numbers of rural migrant women workers and those urban women who lost jobs and remain unemployed as a result of the economic reforms. To solve the serious unemployment problem among women, domestic labour has been recognized officially as a form of government-promoted 'flexible' employment. In 2000, MOLSS set up the national occupational standards for domestic workers. According to the China National Occupational Standards of Domestic Workers, a domestic worker is a 'person managing household affairs as required for the household they serve, including taking care of children, the elderly, and sick persons', and domestic workers are divided into three levels – beginner, intermediate and senior – according to their working skills (MOLSS 2000: 1). At the same time, the China Employment Training Technical Instruction Centre (CETTIC), MOLSS, published training materials for each level. Since then, domestic service has formally become an occupation. The following paragraph was taken from the preface of the Domestic Service White Paper by CETTIC, MOLSS:

> The development of the domestic service industry plays an important role in improving people's lives. It also has a positive effect on opening up employment opportunities, and particularly by solving the women's employment issue. . . . Domestic service can be regarded as the main way to increase employment positions in urban areas currently and in the future.
>
> (CETTIC 2004: 1)

Although there are also a significant number of unemployed males, they have not been targeted as potential domestic labourers. According to the above-mentioned survey of domestic service industry by MOLSS, there were about 14.9 per cent male and 85.1 per cent female domestic workers respectively in this sector (CETTIC 2004).

Nevertheless, domestic labour has become a rapid development industry and an inseparable part of urban people's daily life. Paid domestic labour tasks include a wide range of housework known as the three Cs – cooking, cleaning and caring (Anderson 2000). Live-in domestic workers are in the highest demand, as this kind of labour is particularly well adapted to the needs of families with children and elderly members needing care. House cleaning is also an increasing form of waged domestic labour. It was estimated that in 2006, in Beijing, among all the domestic workers, live-in domestic workers accounted for 50.3 per cent, house cleaners whose work is calculated on an hourly basis accounted for 46.1 per cent and other workers were 3.6 per cent (D. J. Li 2007).

Although domestic labour is a government-recognized form of employment, it belongs to the flexible employment category, which has risen substantially in the wake of the marketization of labour. Compared with a full-time, permanent job, domestic labour is a form of precarious work in which there is rarely job security. It is characterized by few statutory protections, low wages and no benefits (International Labour Organization (ILO) 2002). Domestic workers' rights remain limited and their basic welfare benefits are considerably inferior to those of other categories of wage-earners who work in the public production domain. Little attention has been paid to the economic security and social security of the emergence of such a precarious form of work. The lack of legal protection leaves female domestic workers open to the abuse of employers as well as employment agencies.

Dealing with formal and legal protection for domestic workers is critical because domestic service has now become a booming industry that is fostered by state policy. It is also meaningful for forging a harmonious 'well off' society,[2] a collective goal that is officially advocated by the Chinese government. Therefore, it becomes necessary to develop an analysis of what has contributed to the current precarious situation of domestic workers and what can be done to alleviate the situation. The aim of this book is to analyse the ways in which domestic workers have been alienated in the economic reform period and to uncover the hiddeFFn and unknown realities of domestic workers living under the complexities of both state socialist and capitalist labour market relations. Based on this investigation of the economic and social security of domestic workers, I hope to be able to contribute to public policy solutions to paid domestic labour issues.

Theoretical framework

The analytical frameworks employed in this study emanate from a socialist feminist approach to women's oppression. This general socialist feminist approach will be supported with insights from feminist theories related to gender, care work and social reproduction, and feminist economic development theories. In China, as elsewhere, domestic labour, whether paid or unpaid, is primarily women's work and any change in this work has an impact on the gender relations within the society. The current official promotion of paid domestic service in China and the precarious nature of the work in a socialist country in economic transition indicate a substantial change in both gender relations and the gender order in this country.

A socialist feminist approach to women's oppression contends that women's subordination originates from both capitalism and patriarchy. In a socialist feminist analysis, capitalism and male dominance are intertwined in women's subordination under capitalist economic relations. These intertwined social relations define the particular activity a woman engages in at a given moment, or, in Rubin's (1975) words:

> A woman is a woman. She only becomes a domestic, a wife, a chattel, a playboy bunny, a prostitute, or a human Dictaphone in certain relations. Torn from these relationships, she is no more the helpmate of a man than gold in itself is money.
>
> (Rubin 1975: 158)

Socialist feminists argue that women's alienation may take many forms and the various forms are interrelated. For instance, women's oppression in the home is linked with gendered and occupational differences in waged labour (Cockburn 1983; Hartmann 1979, 1981). For socialist feminists there are no individual solutions to women's oppression because life under capitalism and male dominance will always be alienating and it would require socialist relations of production to avoid oppression.

Socialist feminism focuses on the ways in which the labour done by women in the household, that is domestic labour, helps to sustain the capitalist system. Women's domestic labour contributes to the reproduction of labour power by having and rearing children and by looking after husbands who work in the production sphere, but this domestic labour is undervalued. Socialist feminism analyses the interconnections between the public sphere of capitalist and state relations on one hand and the private sphere of the family/household on the other. Socialist feminists argue that not only does women's domestic labour in the home prop up the capitalist edifice and allow the system to function with considerable low labour costs, but they also note that 'in many ways the distinction between private and public created and sustained the unequal relations between men and women throughout society' (Hamilton 2005: 17).

The socialist feminist approach makes it possible to point to a wide range of complex reasons for the rise of paid domestic labour and its precarious nature in China. To employ such a framework, I consider the current situation of domestic labour as related to global capitalism and the reconfigured nature of patriarchy under neoliberal governance in the globalization process. The condition of Chinese domestic labour is situated in this global context. However, the rise of capitalist institutions alone does not explain what is happening in China. Although ideas about labour migration and global economic development theory may partially explain the current Chinese situation by shedding light on the capitalist labour market and other economic approaches associated with capitalism, these theories do not fully capture the whole picture. This is mainly because the focus on capitalist institutions in China tends to overlook the role of state patriarchy in both labour and gender relations. For example, world system theory represented by Wallerstein (1974; 1979) uses capital as the only factor to explain the world order which consists of three types of countries – the dominant core, the semi-periphery and the dependent periphery. This approach is based on the idea that capitalism has created an increasingly integrated world economy, in which it has generated 'excluded, marginal, dispossessed and poor people' (Cohen and Kennedy 2007: 196). By the same token the new international division of labour theory argues that by locating some manufacturing process in cheap labour countries, the only winners are the transnational companies (Frobel, Heinrichs and Kreye 2007 [1980]; Gilbert 2008; International Gender and Trade Network 2009). These theories are significant for understanding the shift in power structures and the marginalization of many developing countries in the global economy. However, the focus on marginalization of developing nations tends to undervalue the capacity of the national state's political power in transforming their situations in the world order (Cohen and Kennedy 2007: 197–8). Equally significant is the underestimation of established power structures within societies. In the case of China, the global shifts in power are intricately tied to patriarchal power in the private sphere as well as the patriarchy of the state. To understand the current market-oriented labour system and specifically the situation of paid domestic workers' in China, the integral nature of capitalist institutions, state patriarchy and familial patriarchy have to be understood.

Examining changes in China within the system of global capitalism is necessary because China has become integral to the global capitalist economy through its economic reforms and its open door to global capital. The global economic neoliberal approaches to economic and social issues have had a powerful impact on the reshaping of Chinese society. Since the state socialist regime of contemporary China launched the shift from a rigidly planned economy to a market economy, Chinese society has been open to the full impact of private and global capital. The lives of Chinese workers, whether they are in the formal production domain or in the private domestic sphere, have to be understood in the context of the increasing capitalization or marketization of a socialist society.

In addition to the pressures exerted by the interests of domestic and international capital, China's socialist system's incorporation into global capitalism is embroidered with the state's shift in ideology. This is shaped by a search for modernity and a desire for closer ties with the capitalist world (*yu shijie jiegui*), a transformation process in which state power plays a pivotal role. Some scholars use the idea of 'state neoliberalism' as a key dimension to analyse China's economic development associated with the party-state's leadership interest in inserting China into the global capitalist order (Chu and So 2010). As Ngai argues,

> The hybrid marriage of state power and global capital generates new forms of control on both the societal and individual levels . . . land and labor, nature

and human life are all marketed as commodities for sale, not merely by the capitalist market, but by the socialist party-state.

(Ngai 2005: 4)

Therefore, the Chinese government's persevering support for socialism has shifted into 'a new order' that means 'in all its behaviours, including economic, political, and cultural – even in governmental behaviour – China has completely conformed to the dictates of capital and the activities of the market' (Y. P. Wang 2003: 141).

Women's labour has always been regarded as an inseparable part of state development strategy in China; therefore, state ideology has played a major role in reforming women's position in the transformation of Chinese society. To understand the rapid expansion of domestic service and paid domestic workers' situation, one needs to analyse the role of state patriarchy as a major force in the process. 'State patriarchy' in this book refers to the ways in which the state exerts power that are typically associated with patriarchy in feminist analysis. This term relates to the relative significance of forces shaping women's work and lives at a specific historical economic period. In this book, the term 'state patriarchy' is appropriate because it highlights the way in which the state has consciously focused on women's traditional work that in China was associated with the pre-socialist era (specifically paid domestic work), to advance market-oriented economic development. Through its power to promulgate a paid domestic service industry, the state has reinforced a traditional gender order through its patriarchal power. Equally significant is the way in which state patriarchy is a part of the very fabric of the Chinese state's shift towards a market-oriented economy. State patriarchy becomes a significant feature in the defining gender order in the marketization process.

Familial patriarchy is another element that shapes both the nature of gender relations and the shift in domestic labour regimes in China. Although the Chinese Communist Party worked at eliminating the feudal residual that 'men are superior, women are inferior' (*nan zun nü bei*), familial patriarchy has always existed in Chinese society. The patriarchal family was maintained throughout Mao's socialist era by patrilocal and patrilineal marriage practices[3] and the gendered division of labour in the realm of work and household. The current development of paid domestic service is not seriously disrupting gender norms within families in China. There is no doubt that the shift in the political support for this type of paid work is supported by the patriarchal family structure. In China, capitalist institutions and patriarchy have worked hand in hand to produce the particular exploitation experienced by paid domestic workers, an exploitation that is experienced by gender, class and rural–urban disparity.

Globalization, restructuring and the implications for women's domestic labour

During the last thirty years the development of a global economy, namely globalization and the spread of neoliberalism, has supported the growth of domestic employment on a global scale. Economic processes and political policies underpin the income inequalities that feed demand for domestic help and create people looking for domestic employment.

Economic globalization refers to 'the dramatic increase both in the mobility of capital and in the international organization of production and distribution' (Cohen 1997: 30). Along with economic globalization are 'cultural and ideological changes which support the spread of global economic systems' (1997: 30). The dominant ideology that is driving the current economic globalization is neoliberalism. Based on the tenets of free-market neoclassical economic theory, neoliberalism emphasizes market efficiency, which requires increased international competition between countries for investment and production, a greater emphasis on trade, and less government spending and regulation of the economy (Cohen 1994, 1996; Cohen *et al.* 2000; McBride 1992, 2001; McBride and Wiseman 2000). This means that economic growth is the focus of state governments' policies and, whatever state governments may do, the starting point should not deviate from economic development. The decline of the Keynesian welfare state in many nations in Europe, throughout North America, and the imposition of social adjustment programmes in developing countries mean national governments have greatly weakened their historical commitments to the poor and vulnerable. State policy all too frequently places the needs of transnational capital above all others. As many scholars (Cohen 1994, 1996, 2000; McBride 1992, 2001; McBride and Wiseman 2000; Jackson *et al.* 2000; Sassen 1996; Clarkson 2002) have pointed out, free trade entrenches corporate values at the epicentre of public policy through the international and national structures that facilitate the mobility of capital and speculative finance. State restructuring associated with globalization does not promise anything substantial to the disadvantaged groups in the society who are usually expected to have their conditions improved only through the normal workings of the market.

Governments' attitudes that legitimized neoliberal trends had at their heart a reimposition of inequality and an intensification of women's oppression (NAC 1995; Luxton 2006). Specifically, while governments allow international corporations to organize their production process freely, they also increasingly download social reproduction responsibilities – such as childcare and health care, which to some extent were previously provided by the state and were thus considered capital costs – onto individuals and families. This process increased women's unpaid labour (Day and Brodsky 1998; Bezanson 2006) and brought about the rise of precarious paid domestic labour.

The concept of social reproduction refers to 'the processes involved in maintaining and reproducing people, specifically the labouring population, and their labour power on a daily and generational basis' (Bezanson and Luxton 2006: 1). Accordingly, it involves the activities of 'provision of food, clothing, shelter, basic safety, and health care, along with the development and transmission of knowledge, social values, and cultural practices and the construction of individual and collective identities' (Bezanson and Luxton 2006: 1). Since social reproduction domain deals with the care of human beings and women are main caregivers in any society, feminist political economists use the concept of social reproduction to analyse women's domestic labour and economic roles in welfare states. Specific types of economic and social policies related to regimes of capital accumulation, are defined also by regimes of social reproduction, or how society goes about reproducing itself. This interrelation among policies, capital accumulation and social reproduction, in turn, is based on specific notions of appropriate gender relations or gender regimes. This is to say that under gender regimes, there are different types of economic and social policies. To understand it, one has to understand the idea of gender regime. Feminists define a gender regime as 'a set of social relations characterized by a sexual division of labour and a gender discourse that support that division' (Cameron 2006: 46–7). A particular gender regime or gender order reflects state policies in mediating the relationship between social reproduction and production within the process of capital accumulation in a certain period (Cameron 2006). Feminist literature has explored how certain welfare state regimes are related to corresponding gender order. For example, Sainsbury (1994; 1996) constructs two contrasting ideal types: the malebreadwinner and the individual earning models to analyse gender relations in welfare states. For Sainsbury, the male-breadwinner model is one where 'the familial ideology celebrates marriage and a strict division of labour between husband and wife' (Sainsbury 1996: 41). In this model, the husband is the head of the household, and it is his duty to provide material needs for all members of his family – his wife and children – through full-time employment. The wife is expected to make and maintain a good home and provide care for her husband and children. The state recognizes the family as an economic unit. Benefits are paid and taxes are collected to support this unit, not the individuals within it. In the male-breadwinner model the boundary between the private and public sphere is strictly enforced. Caring and reproductive work are confined to the family and are largely unpaid. Contrary to this model, Sainsbury suggests an individual earner model, in which each adult is individually responsible for his or her own maintenance, and both men and women are earners and carers. The unit of benefit, contributions and taxation is the individual with little attention to the presence of dependants. Labour market policies are targeted at both men and women, and much caring work is paid and provided publicly. Sainsbury's earnings framework highlights whether social rights are familialized or individualized. Her analysis provides a perspective on consideration of the principle of care as a basis of entitlement in a welfare state[4] and it is important to see how a capitalist welfare state supports women: as wives, mothers or workers (Sainsbury 1996). Some other studies, such as those by Fraser (1997) and O'Connor, Orloff and Shaver (1999), also analyse how gender equality could be established in existing welfare models and recognizes the family and women's unpaid caring and domestic work as a variation in social provision. Overall, the entire line of approaching gender issues in these studies indicates that state policies in social reproduction and production domain are closely related to gender order in a national state.

The current forces of global restructuring are dramatically restructuring the nature of social reproduction and gender regimes within national states (Cameron 2006; Broomhill and Sharp 2007). Feminist debates in Western societies have indicated that government policy changes can exert significant power in changing the dynamic of gender regimes and that the marketization of social reproduction is very much a concern of Western socialist feminism. Feminist theories related to gender, care work and social reproduction have revealed how the state ideology reforms related to care policies affect the gender order (Marchbank 2000; Kremer 2005). As Marchbank's study has shown, gender equality is always the last consideration in the justification for national states' childcare policies (Marchbank 2000). Therefore, it is not surprising that the costs of caring from current changes are largely paid by women, both inside and outside the money economy (Folbre 1994). States have not addressed the challenges of meeting social reproduction needs and frequently remove the social supports that do exist. The governments' assumptions appear to be that women could intensify their subsistence and domestic labour to offset the cutbacks to the more collective provision of services to meet the needs of social reproduction (Bezanson and Luxton 2006). Ideology and policy changes not only reinforce women's household care responsibility, but also create a new hierarchy between women because some women can hire other women to do care work and housework for them. As feminist political economists argue, the more responsibility for social reproduction is imposed on private households, where it is accomplished through unpaid household labour or purchased labour, the more uneven are its impact, standards and material practices, resulting in growing inequalities of gender, race and class (Chang and Ling 2000; Luxton 2002, 2006; Neysmith, Bezanson and O'Connell 2005). As Brodie pointed out, the governing strategy by national states under the reconfigured nature of patriarchy 'disregards both claims making on the state by structurally disadvantaged groups and the broad goal of social citizenship equality' (Brodie 2007: 181).

Huge economic disparities accumulated under these economic efficiency policies in different countries and national areas have created a mass of people who live in or near poverty and are ready to do domestic service and to migrate to do it. Often the poorest do not have the resources to migrate, so migration is not available for all. On the demand side, the growing demand for female paid work and the lack of social supports for families increase demand for domestic workers on a global scale. Domestic service in the contemporary world has become a globalized occupation available for both impoverished women without skills and better-trained women who work at levels below their skills level. Poor women are called either to emigrate abroad to earn foreign currency in the form of remittances or to migrate to cities inside the country to contribute to the domestic economic development initiated by their governments. Domestic workers migrate not only internally and to the developed world but also within regions in the developing world. For instance, women domestic workers migrate from one area of Asia to another: from the Philippines to Singapore, Malaysia and Hong Kong; or from Bangladesh to Saudi Arabia, etc. (Huang, Yeoh and Rahman 2005). It is not always the most impoverished who migrate. Some women migrants may have high qualifications in their country of origin; however, due to lack of opportunities where they live, they enter domestic service in developed countries and areas. For example, Filipino nurses enter Canada on the Live-in Care Program (Cheung 2006; Pratt 2003; McKay 2002). Large new migrations of women workers from the Third World countries must leave their own children in the care of others to care for households in the developed areas of the world (Cohen and Brodie 2007; Cox 2006; Huang, Yeoh and and Rahman 2005; Yeates 2005; Parrenas 2001; Hochschild 2000). This phenomenon, called the 'global care chain' by Hochschild, refers to 'a series of personal links between people across the globe based on the paid or unpaid work of caring' (Hochschild 2000: 131). The term 'global care chain' is widely used in feminist literature in explaining the international nanny and maid trade in domestic care services, but it has also been used to refer to other migrant care workers (health care, sexual care, educational care, etc.) in both individualized domestic/household settings and institutionalized settings (hospitals, schools, and so on) (Yeates 2005: 4–5). The expansion of global care chains reveals the problems of uneven development and major social divisions of class, gender, race/ethnicity and caste (Yeates 2005). There is also literature which recognizes that women from disadvantaged groups (by race, ethnicity, class, etc.) within countries tend to provide domestic services to meet the needs of more powerful social groups (Glenn 1992; 2010).

Women's domestic labour in China's transition to the socialist market economy

The economic transition in China has been reinforced by the global trend towards neoliberal economic approaches to economic and social issues. Although the transition to socialism in the Mao era did not resolve women's subordination, important changes did occur that make the comparison between that era and the current one significant (Croll 1983). The recent period of market reforms have witnessed a deterioration in women's position, relative to the previous period: Women have suffered more unequal treatment in labour protections and employment rights, and social reproduction responsibilities that have been downloaded from the state have largely fallen upon women's shoulders. These care responsibilities are further increased due to the aging population of the Chinese society (see Chapter 4). Given these reasons, in China's transition to a socialist market economy, the gender order in Chinese society has reverted, in many respects, to an older form of gender expectations and relations.

Since the economic reforms, Chinese governments have favoured policies that make business more competitive on the global stage through a shift to private production. In addition to welcoming international capital, the government has fostered domestic capital by nurturing private enterprises and reforming state-owned and collectively owned enterprises. Compared to the centrally planned era where workers could almost find employment only in public-owned enterprises, workers began to find opportunities for employment in Chinese–foreign joint ventures (enterprises funded by foreign funds or foreign technology), enterprises operated exclusively with foreign capital, enterprises funded by residents from Hong Kong, Macao and Taiwan, and Chinese shareholding companies (Chow and Xu 2001). The government also began to allow state- and collectively owned enterprises employment freedom through economic reforms. Since 1991, all enterprises have been allowed to recruit workers on contractual, temporary or seasonal bases according to their needs. Flexible employment is the official definition of new labour market relations promoted by the Chinese government. Flexible employment refers to a variety of employment forms that are different from the permanent, stable employment under the planned economy era. These various types of flexible employment officially are not by any means equivalent to formal waged employment in terms of pay, job security and opportunities for advancement in labour markets. Through the introduction of a genuine market for labour, and in accordance with the logic of capitalist flexible accumulation, labour standards and labour rights have been greatly subordinated to economic development.

The repercussions for women are significant. State-owned enterprise reforms have greatly increased unemployment and have driven unemployed women workers to work in the informal economy as domestic workers. Also, the uneven development between rural and urban areas and between agriculture and industry has created a pool of cheap female labourers willing to leave the countryside to work for urban families.

Restructuring has inevitably reduced public provision for a variety of welfare-related institutions, such as health care, education and childcare. In so doing, the government expects that private households and markets will meet these needs and that the government should not be primarily responsible for social reproduction under a market economy. Although even the socialist social system did not succeed in solving the problems of gender inequality in the division of labour, the state did take on some of the tasks that were previously performed by women privately in the household under semi-feudalism and semi-colonialism China. Many of these tasks were organized collectively and publicly, and women were encouraged to participate in production work (see Chapter 2). As might have been anticipated, after market-oriented economic reforms, much of the care work has fallen back on women, who are still the primary caregivers for both the young and the old in China. The Second Women's Status Survey data in China in 2000 show that compared with 1990, while men's unpaid work time as a proportion of their overall daily work time has reduced by 3 per cent, women spent 1.7 per cent more work time on unpaid housework (S. M. Wang 2006). The women who keep their jobs in the growing competitive labour market have to use other women's domestic labour to be able to fulfil their job commitment at a time when the state has reduced its childcare commitments. Therefore, government policy changes, either to marketize social reproduction responsibilities or to force responsibilities back onto individual households, have not achieved a new or more equitable gender regime under a market economy with socialist characteristics: on the contrary, the dual-breadwinner/state carer model under a state-planned economy era has been changed into a dual-breadwinner/ market carer or informal carer model under a market economy, where those in relatively better income households and professional women who can afford market-provided care can do so while other working-class women use informal unpaid family networks. In either circumstance, the increasingly privatized childcare, health care and elder care services have increased the demand of women's care work.

In fact, the private sphere of family has become a way to absorb labour excess and supplies a flexible army of women labourers as a result of the economic reforms. When there are not enough jobs in the formal production process, women are expected to find a job within the household economy.

In addition, through targeting certain particular groups of women – rural migrant women and urban unemployed women – for domestic service, the government is actually fostering class divisions based on gender, and social and economic status as well. That is, it is not only a gender issue, but also the divide between those who are educated, from wealthy households, and those who are less educated, from poor families.

The rise of domestic service globally as well as in China has made it clear that capitalism and patriarchy are intertwined and they may take new forms in oppressing women in contemporary society; unchanged is the sexual division of labour that assigns domestic work to women and absolves men from that responsibility. As some feminist economics scholarship has shown, economic development cannot automatically empower women and the current sexual division of labour is likely to disadvantage women in the development process (Beneria 2003; Elson 1999; Koggel 2003; MacPhail and Dong 2007). The inequalities and practices that support the growth of domestic employment should no doubt be challenged and the realities of domestic work in contemporary China need to be exposed.

Literature review

In recent years, a multitude of feminist studies on paid domestic labour has been conducted worldwide. Despite the national states' invariably engineering and facilitating paid domestic service under globalization, many feminist scholars have noticed the unjust treatment of women, especially those in the Third World. There has been a notable shift in Western feminist scholarship regarding women's labour in the home over the last three decades. While research in the 1960s and 1970s focused on the significance of unpaid domestic labour for women's oppression, since the 1980s feminist scholars have devoted more attention to the role of paid domestic service in oppressing minority and working-class women. The growing interest in paid domestic labour reflects a common sense among some feminists that the employment of domestic workers in private households is a crucial means through which asymmetrical gender, race and class relations among women are structured. The feminist literature ranges from developed countries, such as the United States of America (Romero 1992; Hondagneu-Sotelo 2001), Canada (Schecter 1998; Pratt 1999; Stiell and England 1999) and Britain (Gregson and Lowe 1994; Cox 2006), to new economically developed countries, such as Singapore (Yeoh and Huang 1999) and Malaysia (Chin 1998), to developing countries such as Tanzania (Bujra 2000). These feminist studies have explored the nature and characteristics of waged domestic work and domestic workers, the question of occupational mobility, employer-employee relations, questions of status, domestic workers' struggles to organize politically, and the question of the persistence of waged domestic labour from different study perspectives.

However, the study of Chinese paid domestic labour is still in its early stages. Although ever since China's economic reforms started, a large body of feminist studies – inside and outside China – has emerged to investigate the gendered impact of economic transition, the existing studies focus on discrimination and segregation in the public production domain and treat women more or less as a homogenous group. The changing gender order in the private sphere and the conflicting interests between different women groups are often overlooked. The academic literature in China on domestic employment is extremely rare. The *China Journal Article Database*, which covers almost all formal Chinese journals from 1994 until the present, indicates that few academic articles dealt with domestic workers' rights. Only three papers based on two surveys explore issues related to wages, benefits, statutory holidays and sexual harassment (H. F. Wang 2006; Wang and Lan 2006; Han 2006). One author discusses socialization and professionalization of domestic service industry and the legal protection of domestic workers (Qin 2006a; 2006b). Recently, a case study by Wang Jufen, Si Min and Chen Yuexin explored domestic workers' access to social security in Shanghai (J. F. Wang, Si and Chen 2010). Yan Hairong's study (2003a; 2003b; 2007; 2008) focused on the rural-to-urban migration of young women to work as domestic workers in urban China. From a cultural anthropology perspective, she analysed the discursive power relations of employers and domestic workers after post-Mao modernity. Wanning Sun used rural migrant live-in domestic workers who live and work for urban middle-class households as a study focus to explore how post-Mao domestic workers become a figure of crossing boundaries as rural versus urban attributes, work versus non-work, and the domestic versus the public through a cultural politics perspective (Sun 2009a). A very few studies by Western scholars, such as Gaetano (2004) and Jacka (1997), also involve rural migrant domestic workers. It is safe to say that overall, the information about female domestic workers and their work is sparse. Little is concretely known about the issue. For example, little is known about laid-off workers transitioning into domestic workers, the role of the agencies and other intermediaries, or the workers' working conditions. No study has taken on a socialist feminist approach and used feminist political economic analysis to fully investigate domestic workers' economic and social security circumstances in China. In contrast to other occupations that have been investigated during the economic transition, there is little information and research concerning domestic women workers.

To be truly comprehensive in reflecting the circumstances of paid domestic labour and the nature of paid domestic work in contemporary China, this book tries to use theoretical and empirical analysis to encompass these topics, such as how China's economic transition has shaped the domestic service industry, the current working and living conditions of domestic workers and individual as well as organized action by domestic workers. By investigating paid domestic workers and their work, this book makes an effort to fill an important knowledge gap in the general literature of labour, gender and economic transition.

Research methodology

While feminist researchers have a history of debating the use of quantitative and qualitative methods and while feminist research was once equated with qualitative interviewing in the early 1980s (Letherby 2003), the feminist research methodology literature now seems to agree that there is no distinctive feminist method, but rather a plurality in applications of methods (Harding 1987; Reinharz 1992; Berik 1997; Letherby 2003). The choice of method(s) depends on the topic and research question (Reinharz 1992; Kelly, Burton and Regan 1994; Berik 1997; Letherby 2003). However, feminists argue that to understand the critical issues in women's lives, women do need to be the centre of the enquiry – whatever method is used. When possible, gathering primary data is as important in feminist research as it is in other types of research (Berik 1997; Letherby 2003).

Following a feminist approach, which puts women at the centre of the analysis, this research project employs a combination of methods. It relies on the textual examination of government documents, published and unpublished materials, and interviews mainly with domestic workers, but also with employers, key government officials, local authorities and advocates for domestic workers. Interviews were conducted in Beijing, which draws domestic workers from all over the country because of its unique position as the capital city and a political, economic, communication and cultural centre of China. In addition, Beijing is at the forefront of the domestic service industry in China. Not only was the first domestic service company in China opened in Beijing, but it was also the first city in China to establish municipal regulations for domestic service. Beijing's experiences can represent China because its conditions are being replicated, with minor differences, in other cities.

I made two field trips to Beijing from July to August 2007, and from October 2007 to January 2008. While the two most important forms of waged domestic labour in contemporary China – the nanny and the cleaner – are the main interview participants in my study, in an effort to better understand domestic workers' working conditions, I also interviewed employers, agency managers and members of advocacy interest groups. Interviews with labour officials were conducted with the aim of gaining greater insight into how and why government chooses the policies it does. In total, there were 62 participants in this study.

An open-ended in-depth interview methodology was chosen in order to capture diverse subjective experiences and perspectives of working as a domestic worker. In feminist methodology literature, the use of qualitative in-depth interviews is considered one of the most effective ways to find out about the experiences of 'silenced women' or other silenced groups (Geiger 1986: 335; Letherby 2003: 89). Questions in this research focused on the economic circumstances that are associated with both migrant women workers and urban unemployed workers, namely their choice of work, the mechanisms that were used to find work and the working conditions that they experience. This examination of working conditions focuses on wages, hours of work, workplace safety, social benefits and job stability. A key intention in this study is to capture, as much as possible, the effect of the recent economic reforms on the lives of domestic workers. The open-ended interview method allowed domestic workers the right to speak about any issue that concerned them, and through this method, I gained a wealth of information on the ways in which they understood the nature of their work and how the economic reforms have affected them and their lives.

While some recruitment of domestic workers was through agencies, some was undertaken through posters, and the snowball method – 44 domestic workers were interviewed individually, although 12 participants were interviewed in groups of two to four people either because of scheduling difficulties or because they felt more comfortable to talk to a stranger in a group. Group interviews allowed for very free-ranging discussions of work that were stimulated by the revelations of the experiences of peers, which enriched the information. There were 29 nannies and 15 cleaners who participated in the interviews, which covered diverse experiences among rural and urban, live-in and live-out, agency and non-agency domestic workers. Although I did make efforts to look for male care workers and cleaners, all respondents were female, reflecting the fact that domestic work is still by and large women's work.

Feminists have argued that giving respondents control over the interview and breaking down the hierarchy between researcher and respondent are important (Letherby 2003). When doing research on personal or sensitive issues, holding interviews in a respondent's own space will usually make them feel more in control (Letherby 2003). Therefore, in this research, interviews often were conducted while domestic workers were working. For example, I interviewed them while they were supervising children in neighbourhood parks or shopping, but many were also undertaken during their free time after work, or while they were looking for new employment. To protect the workers from any repercussions that might have accrued from attending the interviews, I did not interview domestic workers and employers involved with the same household; the interviews were anonymous; and I am using pseudonyms throughout the research. The interviews lasted from 40 minutes to two hours, depending on the worker's schedule. The interviews were tape-recorded and notes were taken either during the interview or immediately afterwards.

Interviews with employers, employment agencies, key government authorities, and non-government organizations such as trade unions, women's federations, and domestic workers' support groups like the Migrant Women's Club (*dagongmei zhi jia*) were recruited through my former work network at the Women's Studies Institute of China and through personal networks in Beijing.

While the interview materials provide the most crucial source of information for this study, it is also supplemented by several other methods of qualitative study. I conducted participant observation in two domestic service agencies and I attended two workshops, one dealing with the healthy development of domestic service industry in China and the other focusing on the protection of domestic workers' rights in Beijing. I also used archival and statistical documents related to relevant government regulations and labour force statistics from MOLSS, the National Statistics Bureau and Beijing municipal regulations. I also used documents related to non-official policies, such as regulations from agencies and the Beijing Home Service Association (BHSA), court judgments of some law cases, documents on policies about domestic workers in Asian, and European and North American literature.

The interview guide questions are included in Appendices 1–4. Both the interviews and the textual materials were in Mandarin, and I have done the entire translation throughout the book.

Scope of analysis and outline

The main objective of this book is to analyse how and why the economic reforms have affected paid domestic labour. It will also analyse ways in which public policy changes could bring about an improvement in the economic security and labour protection for female domestic workers.

This book contains eight chapters in total. The introductory chapter explains the background information of the development of paid domestic work in China and analyses the theoretical framework and research methodology of this research, with a focus on the role of the state and the contradictions that arise with the growth and dominance of markets in a socialist economy.

Chapter 2 analyses domestic employment regimes in China along a historical trajectory. By reviewing the different domestic service regimes in China, the chapter shows how paid domestic work was valued in different historical periods and how the current system of paid domestic labour is rooted in Chinese history. In order to show the contrast between paid domestic labour before economic reforms and the centrally planned era, this chapter highlights the way in which social reproduction was treated during the centrally planned, pre-market-oriented economy. Since so much has changed with the shift from a centrally planned economy to a market-based economy, this chapter is central to the development of the book's analysis.

Chapter 3 sets the Chinese situation in a global context, and analyses both the political and market forces that contribute to the supply of paid domestic work. This chapter reviews the feminist analysis of economic reforms in China – particularly with regard to the changes in labour and labour market for women. It investigates economic reforms and structural adjustment policies in rural and urban China and explains how women in both rural and urban areas have been pushed into domestic service labour markets. Especially important here is the role of public policy in specifically designating paid domestic work as a solution to the dual problems of female unemployment and the growing need for private household labour associated with economic reforms.

Chapter 4 explains the driving forces behind the demand for domestic work. Using childcare policy as a case, this chapter illustrates the effect of globalization and neoliberalism restructuring on the social reproduction domain. After tracing the childcare policy changes for the last sixty years in China, this chapter aims to explain the current care crisis in childcare after the government's retreat in this area. This chapter will stress that domestic workers' and employers' voices are significant for understanding the tremendous rise in the need for paid domestic workers (even in households which have very modest means). The withdrawal of social services (i.e., a change in the state's responsibility for social reproduction) creates a huge demand for this type of work.

Chapter 5 gives a portrait of the precarious nature of domestic employment in China. Drawing from extensive interviews in which I explored the experiences of the women themselves, this chapter focuses on two main types of domestic work (childcare and cleaning) to analyse the working conditions and experiences of domestic workers. It explains the normal pay ranges, different types of working arrangements and access to social security for domestic workers. This chapter also distinguishes between the experiences of migrant and urban laid-off workers with the intent of highlighting the continuity of the type of treatment that rural migrant workers receive.

Despite the difficult working conditions of paid domestic workers in China, these domestic workers are not merely passive victims in dealing with their relationship with employers. They often try to create a survival space for themselves. Chapter 6 looks at the resistance strategies that workers adopt by examining either their everyday resistance or the legal means though which domestic workers resist and negotiate with their employers. This chapter also explores the possibilities of organized resistance based on domestic workers' identity and different roles that NGOs have played in organizing them. The potential role of trade unions in the protection of domestic workers is also explored.

Based on the analysis of the situation of paid domestic labour in the above chapters, Chapter 7 deals with policy solutions to improve domestic labour's working conditions. This chapter aims to examine the policy implications of this study as the Chinese government works towards its goal of developing a 'harmonious society'. It explores various types of avenues that can be taken to improve domestic workers' economic and social security.

This book concludes with some reflections on the overall findings of this study, with the overarching objective of understanding ways in which social reproduction can be reconciled with market production in contemporary China.

2 Domestic employment regimes in China

> Domestic service is brought about by the social division of labour ... and is based on differences established by the market. Domestic service is a type of work, and there is no work which can be seen as high-end or low-end, or as noble or degrading (*gao di gui jian*).[1] What kind of work is categorized as high-end or low-end, or noble or degrading in the 360 occupation scheme[2] – can you tell me? There should be no high or low status work (under socialism), right? I would say that, nowadays, a good domestic service worker (*jia zheng fu wu yuan*)[3] might be very respected by people.
>
> (Interview with a labour officer, 7 November 2007)

> I have been doing this work (domestic service) for about four years.... I feel that we are not respected or understood by people. Even we domestic workers ourselves have a sense of inferiority. But in general, we are looked down upon by other people. This is the main problem.
>
> (Interview with a worker, 27 November 2007)

After decades of economic reforms, the logic of the market has largely dictated the character of the Chinese economy, not only in the relations of production but also in how domestic service is viewed and treated. In contemporary China, the official state ideology has now indicated that paid domestic employment is a result of a natural social division of labour that arises from a stage of economic development. It is no longer interpreted as something that is related to historical gender subordination and class exploitation, which was the traditional socialist interpretation of private paid domestic work. A contradiction arises, however, in the theory and practice of socialism in connection with domestic work. While the government accepts the effects of economic liberalization and market-oriented reforms on the emergence of paid domestic employment, it also preaches its socialist rhetoric of equality in all forms of employment. This means that private paid domestic work is now to be interpreted as worthwhile work. Unlike in earlier socialist eras, jobs are no longer classified as 'noble or mean occupations', and every job is considered a service for other people in the society.

However, the mechanisms of the market economy and the government's rhetoric can neither erase the precarious nature of paid domestic employment nor hide its indication of greater class stratification and patriarchal oppression that arises from the unequal power relationship between private employers and the domestic workers they employ. Domestic workers' feeling of 'not being respected by people' and being 'looked down upon by others' is indicative of the disparity in the value of occupations – despite the state's rhetoric of the equal worth of all work. State programmes that bring ever greater numbers of women into domestic service reflect the particular ways in which the market interacts with patriarchy.

The devaluation of female domestic work in the Chinese market system could not occur without deeply rooted patriarchal relations within China. As feminist analyses of capitalism have shown, the value of domestic work in any society is conditioned by both historical and contemporary forces, and women's subordination is mutually decided by patriarchy and capitalism (Young 1981; Hartmann, 1981). This insight of the interaction of patriarchy and the productive relations within the economic system can also be applied to socialist systems. In China, the existence of domestic service at different historical periods exhibited distinct Chinese characteristics, whether through the bondservant system in feudal times or domestic service under socialism. In each period, the devaluation of women's domestic work was closely related to both the ruling class ideology and the particular nature of patriarchy at the time. I intend to show that the development of a market economy and private property in China and the subsequent precarious situation of domestic workers is not only a feature of the capitalist features of China's economy, but is also related to the historical devaluation of domestic labour and the historical characteristics of patriarchy in China.

In this chapter, I will present a feminist historical materialist analysis of paid domestic employment regimes, and by so doing, I will analyse the ways in which patriarchy and capitalism (or private ownership) work together to create the contemporary domestic service system. I will attempt to trace the historical development of domestic employment regimes by the bondservant system in feudal society till the middle of the Qing dynasty (1840–1911), the Republican era (1912–49) and the People's Republic of China, which includes the central planned economy era (1949–78) and the market economy era (1978–present). As a work arrangement, paid domestic service has always been situated in the broader social, economic and political context of its period. It is my view that, in the context of China, it will be difficult – if not impossible – to improve the status of domestic workers unless the root and causes of their exploitation are fully explored.

To begin with, I will explain the concept of a domestic employment regime and its relation to analysis of gender regimes and other employment regimes in China.

What is the domestic employment regime?

The term 'regime' has been widely employed by scholars in social sciences. While this concept is not always applied with consistent meaning across disciplines, there is a consensus that a regime is a management system in an issue area (Henderson 1988). The most widely used definition of a regime is that of Krasner (1982) in international political economy 'sets of implicit or explicit principles, norms, rules, and decision-making procedures around which actors' expectations converge in a given area of international relations' (Krasner 1982: 186). In this chapter, the given area is domestic employment. By using regime analysis, I aim at exploration of the sets of ruling factors in domestic employment. I consider domestic employment regime as structured within a number of contexts: government ideology and policies, cultural or social norms, and mode of production. Domestic employment regimes, therefore, incorporate the defining mode of production and the social relations associated with it. For example, the regime associated with the bondservant existed only under a feudal society, and similarly, a paid servant is associated with a capitalist society and each correlates to a particular manifestation of patriarchy with feudal or capitalist or socialist society characteristics. Also associated with each system are the cultural, policy and legal relations that govern domestic work and workers.

Domestic employment regimes are closely linked to employment regimes in the production domain and, as government policy changes in the labour market affect general labour regimes, they also have an impact on domestic labour. For example, workers from the formal production domain laid-off during government economic reforms in China shift to employment in the domestic sphere. Domestic employment regimes as well as other regimes in the production sphere all reflect how state policies and economic development affect labour. The literature on employment regimes in contemporary China has shown how labour has been subordinated to ideas about growth through the market during the economic transition. For instance, Ngai's study on factory dormitory regimes in south China investigated factory workers' employment changes that resulted from specific government policy (Ngai 2009). One point of this discussion of the changes in domestic employment regimes is to contribute to the overall understanding of the nature of the working class in contemporary China.

As a kind of work arrangement, paid domestic labour is closely related to gender regimes. In the first chapter, I introduced the concept of gender regimes and described how feminists in Western society use it to analyse different welfare state regimes. In different societies, even within a specific type of broad capitalist of socialist system, state policies and cultural or social norms vary, and these variations affect gender relations. Therefore, the analysis of domestic employment regimes in Chinese history will reveal the power relations between men and women in different historical periods in China. I will argue that domestic employment regimes and gender regimes are integrally related and mutually reinforcing.

Bondservant regime in feudal society

In China, the feudal society started with the Qin dynasty (221 BC). Therefore, the bondservant system can be traced back to more than 2,000 years. It lasted until the end of the Qing dynasty (1644–1911). Although there had been appeals to abolish the exploitative bondservant regime in near-modern society since 1840, it was only officially abolished in 1909 (Yan 2007). Bondservants were both males and females who worked for their owners without the personal freedom to leave.

However, unlike slaves, although bondservants were bound to their owners, they had the right to buy back their personal freedom and the right to live: their owners could not kill them at will.

The bondservant regime was a system that arose from slavery; therefore, it inevitably inherited its class exploitation nature from the slave epoch. The nature of gender hierarchy under feudal patriarchal Confucian society also contributed to the characteristics of the feudal and brutal bondservant regime. Private land holding was the material basis of social status in Chinese feudal society. As the ruling class, the landlords profited from the land they owned and many gained possession of very large estates. Their extravagant lives included acquiring and using bondservants, especially beautiful female servants for both domestic service and sexual pleasure and entertainment. Under feudalism, peasants did have more freedom than slaves did, but they were subject to their landlords' rules and to landlords' rent and government taxes, both of which were often unreasonable, considering the meagre lives they led. It was therefore not unusual for bankrupt peasants to sell their children or wives to be bondservants. Most bondservants were women and daughters of poor peasant families. The number of these bondservants increased in times of depression and national calamities (Lang 1968).

The feudal patriarchal government supported and secured the bondservant regime by its Confucian ideology and policy apparatuses. Confucianism, which had been established as the ideal philosophy by the end of the Han dynasty (206 BC–220 AD), endorsed a strict gender hierarchy and class stratification. Confucianism not only aligned the female with the cosmic force of *yin* and the male with *yang* with a hierarchical relationship of *yang* presiding over *yin*, it also set the inner-outer (*nei-wai*) distinction, in which females were assigned to the inner, and males to the outer sphere. *Nei* referred to the private/domestic sphere and *wai* referred to the public/social sphere. As a division of labour, the idea was that males were primary in the outer; females were primary in the inner spheres (*nan zhu wai, nü zhu nei*). Women were assigned to handle domestic affairs, such as nurturing children, cooking, weaving and other household work, while men handled public and social affairs, such as farming, commerce and government affairs. Due to *nei-wai* being a functional distinction and a regulative ideal, women of all classes were assigned the domestic role. In addition, they were required to be subordinate to family patriarchs even in the realm of *nei*. Throughout their lives, women were called upon to obey the Three Bonds of Obedience (*san cong*): to obey fathers when young, husbands when married and adult sons when widowed (Johnson 1983; Lang 1968; Li-Hsiang 2006). This philosophy was supported by the ideal traditional family, which was patriarchal, patrilineal and patrilocal, and was embedded in an extended male kinship network. Women were not allowed to enter the realm of *wai* legitimately since 'a woman without talent is virtuous (*nüzi wu cai bian shi de*)' (Ming saying). As Lang (1968) argued, obedience, timidity, reticence and adaptability were considered the main virtues of women.

Women's low status in both the family and society made them 'only slightly more than chattel, routinely bought and sold in marriage, concubinage or outright slavery' (Johnson 1983: 1). Therefore, Chinese women's systematic oppression and subordination in their gendered role by the patriarchal family and society were supported by the feudal ideology of Confucianism and secured by feudal governments. Confucianism insisted on strict class stratification and endorsed the domination of a ruling class over inferior classes. For Confucianism, the art of government was to 'let the sovereign do his duty as a sovereign, the subject his duty as a subject, the father his duty as a father, and the son his duty as a son' (Cranmer-Byng 1958: 41). Therefore, proper order and hierarchy in the political realm of the state directly related to the proper order and hierarchy of the family. The family's proper order was to be obedient and filial subjects to the Chinese rulers. Symbolically, the entire political system was based on the ideal Confucian family and its moral code. It was the patriarchal state ideology and those norms that upheld the bondservant system as successive feudal governments tried to support and secure the bondservant system through laws and regulations. For example, government officials from the Qin dynasty to the Qing dynasty were routinely assigned land and bondservants according to their ranks. War captives were official bondservants who were controlled by the feudal governments (Wei, Wu and Lu 1982).

The contemporary historian Chu mentioned in his study in 1995 that while people became bondservants as captives from war or through being indentured either by birth or by debt, some were also bought from human markets where bankrupt peasants sold either themselves or their children (Chu 1995; Yan 2007). Formed in the Northern Wei dynasty (386–534) and having matured in the Tang dynasty (618–907), the *liangjian* class division in feudal society regarded bondservants, together with actors, prostitutes and beggars, as mean people (*jianmin*), the opposite of good people (*liangmin*), which included the literati, farmers, craftsmen and merchants (and women in households). However, bondservants were different from prostitutes and beggars (other classes with no social dignity) because they were a special social class who had no freedom and were bound to their masters. Although they were human beings, their status was similar to that of their masters' other private property. For instance, in the Tang dynasty (618–907), the law clearly stated, 'bondservants were the equals of livestock' (Chu 1995: 4). In the Northern Wei dynasty (386–534) and the Tang dynasty (618–907), bondservants were subsumed under the masters' households and were thus not entitled to land distribution, while prostitutes and beggars, at least theoretically, could own land (Chu 1995). Upon becoming bondservants, the women would also lose their own family names and would be given their masters' surnames. Bondservants also had to dress in a way that identified them as servants. Generally, female bondservants were allowed to wear only black clothes, which declared their low social status. Bondservants could get out of bond service either by being set free by their masters or by government acts – which was rare – or by buying themselves out. Unless already out of bond service and having become free people, neither bondservants themselves nor even their offspring could legally take imperial exams, which was the common route to civil service and a change in social identity (Chu 1995).

From the Northern Wei dynasty (386–534) to the last feudal dynasty, Qing (1644–1911), legal codes not only differentiated between *liangmin* and *jianmin*, but also imposed different legal codes for masters and servants. Servants were most severely punished for offences against their masters. In addition to these rules, there were a variety of rules upheld by local gentries to compel domestic discipline (*jiafa*) and clan conventions (*zugui*) that further subjugated bondservants (Chu 1995; Yan 2007). There is no question that bondservants were at the bottom of the social hierarchy. They had to bear inhumane working conditions and both physical and psychological mistreatment. Female bondservants' destiny was even worse than male bondservants due to the patriarchal social system. They were routinely considered to be their rulers' sexual objects – rape was common, and there was no law to punish masters who raped their servants. During the Yuan dynasty, the law made it clear that raping of servants by their masters was not a criminal act. Overall, the bondservant system was a form of mutated slavery linked with private land ownership and its highly elaborate social hierarchy (Chu 1995); the only difference with slavery was that theoretically bondservants could buy back their freedom.

The long period of more than 2,000 years of state power and support no doubt helped to encourage actual bondservant practices throughout society. By the middle of the Qing dynasty, when the first rumblings of modern reform for women began to be faintly heard, bondservants were embedded in the most exploitive system in Chinese feudal history. Although the bondservant system was officially abolished at the end of the Qing dynasty in 1909, its influence has been long-lasting, and the degrading image of serving people has affected the idea of domestic work in China even today (Yan 2007).

Servants in near-modern history

Since the mid-nineteenth century, which was the beginning of near-modern history in China, waged servant labour gradually replaced the bondservant system (Yan 2007). Although servants' social position was still very low, they were hired to perform domestic work and were legally no longer their employers' private property. To some extent, they enjoyed a small amount of personal freedom. These changes occurred with the invasion of Western colonialism, the weakening power of feudal patriarchy and the development of capitalism.

Chinese near-modern history witnessed the decaying power of the Chinese government and the growing colonial power of Europe. Driven by industrialization and the need for new markets, European colonists tried to open the door of China during the first Opium War (1840–2), which the British won in 1842.[4] In 1860, after the second Opium War (1856–60), China had to submit to Britain and France. In the following years, China suffered from great territorial losses, not only to Western countries, but also to Japan and Russia. China became a semi-colony under foreign control (Lang 1968).

The colonial power that represented capitalism brought both economic development and capitalist ideologies, such as ideas about equality and individualism, into Chinese society. At the same time, the inability of Confucian values and social structures to meet the challenges of technological progress, foreign incursion and ruthless international competition led some Chinese elite to seek solutions to save the country from foreign control and to make the transition to capitalism more secure. Colonialism and the rise of the indigenous capitalist class sought to destroy the old Confucian order and create a new world order. Under such circumstances, the feudal structure that oppressed women in the domestic sphere was criticized, and the Chinese capitalist class became increasingly aware of the importance of the role of women in overturning the feudal powers. Western liberal capitalist ideology's support for equality, democracy and individual freedom was, therefore, imported into China to free Chinese women from feudal oppression and strengthen capitalists' influence. Western ideas and selected works expressing women's rights were translated. For example, John Stuart Mill's *The Subjection of Women* was translated into Chinese and published in China in 1903.[5] In addition to the translation and introduction of Western feminist thoughts, some Chinese scholars also wrote and published books, such as *Nü Jie Zhong* (*Feminine World's Bell*), *Nü Jie Lei* (*Feminine World's Tears*), and *Nüzi Xin Shijie* (*The New World for Women*), among which *Nü Jie Zhong* has the most effect. *Nü Jie Zhong* was published in 1903 in Shanghai. It was the first work to study women's issues and promote women's rights in China. In the book, author Jin Tianhe argued that women should call for a feminist revolution, which ought to be combined with national liberation (Lü et al. 2008).

While the importation of the concept and the vocabulary of 'women's rights' can be seen as a by-product of China's emulating a Western-style nation state in order to resist Western colonialism (M. X. Wang 2001), it was also inseparable from Western rulers' attempts to force their culture and values upon China. It is, of course, worth mentioning that European colonists may have had a different view than the Chinese people about women but Europe, and especially Britain, was far from liberal on the issue of women's rights. For example, at the beginning of the twentieth century, women in Britain only had limited property rights and limited rights to their children. Only a very few were able to vote, and then only in local politics.[6] But the idea of equality, and specifically gender equality, was a powerful force that had a lasting impact.

Despite the colonists' ambiguous concept of women's rights, while Chinese men wanted to use womanpower against foreign aggression, women were urged to liberate themselves from their traditional role of domestic labour and become involved in saving the nation from foreign oppression. The traditional Confucian 'women inside and men outside' division of labour shifted. Women began to work outside the home and became waged labourers. However, male Chinese capitalists were interested in liberating women only to benefit China as a nation; they were not interested in women's equal rights with men. Therefore, for male capitalist elite, women were mothers to the nation; if the female situation could not be transformed, there was no way that China would be strong enough to compete with Western powers. Based on this point, it is not hard to understand why, after the capitalist revolution successfully broke down the last imperial dynasty, the Qing dynasty in 1911, women were not legally granted the same rights as men in the new Republic of China.

Chinese feminists, awakened by the women's movement in the Western countries, realized that to acquire freedom they had to fight against persistent patriarchal ideology: They fully realized that male capitalists and the capitalist system's ideas of equality would not lift them out of gender inequality. In 1912, the women's suffrage movement was launched. Among the movement's eleven objectives was the clearly stated prohibition of the sale of girl servants.[7] This was listed as an objective because selling servants was still popular, even after the bondservant system was officially abolished at the end of the Qing dynasty. The suffrage movement also challenged the traditional division of labour by claiming women's access to the public domain of activities and, more specifically, to the institutions of political decision-making. It marked 'the beginnings of a long debate on the foundations of the sexual division of labour and long struggle by female solidarity groups to redefine the role and status of women in the public and domestic spheres' (Croll 1978: 79).

After the May Fourth New Culture Movement (1915–24),[8] which was initiated by the capitalist class aiming to defeat the old Confucian ideology, the women's movement began to have an opportunity to interact with communist ideology. This was because Chinese elites were always actively searching for alternative values and ideals to revitalize China and create a more just society. Introduced into China in 1917 after the victory of Russia's October Socialist Revolution, Marxism was widely accepted and spread throughout China during the May Fourth Movement. The Chinese Communist Party (CCP), formed in 1921, endorsed from its inception the May Fourth feminist demand for equal rights for women with an emphasis on the elimination of private ownership and the class system. The Chinese bourgeois government's inability to either unify colonized China or grant women equality with men was the catalyst that led the feminist movement to socialist programmes. The domestic servant problem began to be seen as part of class exploitation of women workers and the poor masses.

The bondservant system's gradual replacement by waged servant labour clearly had economic foundations. At the economic level, China's acceptance of the open door policy demanded by the West stimulated the growth of the Chinese capitalist class. The rise of new modes of production meant that there was an increased need for cheap labour and resources, but the new capitalist class had to fight with feudal patriarchal power; therefore, women were urged to liberate themselves from their traditional domestic role and become involved in production. In addition, the rise of modern industry provided a vast market for female labour that was not utilized in the old economy. Instead of becoming bondservants, poor peasant girls could now work in factories. In China, as elsewhere, the textile industry employed a considerable number of women: 72.3 per cent of the cotton-spinning workers in the Shanghai factories were women in 1927 (Lang 1968). The factory labour system undoubtedly affected the domestic service sphere. In addition, by accelerating the disintegration of the self-sufficient peasant economy, industrialization gradually deprived the family of its role as a productive unit and, consequently, the family patriarch lost his position as leader of the work of family members. The development of better transportation facilities increased the mobility of the population and made it possible for young men and women to get work far from their homes, a factor that further weakened family control and encouraged women to leave the home. These economic factors all deeply challenged the bondservant system and led to the transformation of the bondservant regime to waged servant labour.

Domestic servants not only became waged labourers, but they also gained some new titles in the 1930s. Besides 'servant' and 'domestic,' female servants were also called *ayi* (aunt) and *baomu* (nanny), which conferred some measure of respect (Yan 2007). Depending on their age and marital status, older or married women servants were called old *ayi*; younger or unmarried servants were called little *ayi*. Originally, *baomu* was used to refer to women who were in charge of protecting, nursing and educating children in royal courts. The term was later adopted to refer to women in other households who took care of children, did housekeeping and worked in nurseries (Yan 2007). In the 1930s and 1940s, rural poverty and urban industrialization caused many women to migrate from the countryside to cities for domestic work. However, because of traditional low social status, these women had few practical protections and mistreatment was not uncommon; thus, their situation gained attention.

Concerns about improving servants' working conditions and prohibiting the mistreatment of servants began to surface. For example, in 1936, a magazine called *Women's Life* published an article entitled 'Employed Women's Movement' by Luo Lai. The article explicitly stated that:

> ... here, the employed women referred to are female servants. ... They are unlimitedly exploited women slaves, and their work nature makes it very hard to get them organized. However, at least, the following requirements for them must be addressed:
>
> 1) Limit working time, for instance, to 8–10 hours a day.
> 2) Set certain pay standards, namely the minimum wage.
> 3) Cancel the intermediary fee, and where the intermediary fee should be paid, it should be done by employers.
> 4) One month advance notice should be given for the termination of work.
> 5) Medical treatment should be paid by employers and sick workers should not be fired, but should receive their usual pay.
>
> (Lu and Wang 2004: 278)

Some of the elite even called for the termination of the use of servants altogether. For instance, in January 1936, the *Women's Special Issue of Shenbao* (a Shanghai local newspaper) published a talk, encouraging the people to '... abolish the concubine, ban prostitutes, save female beggars, forbid retaining servants, and help unemployed women. ...' (Lu and Wang 2004: 275). These outpourings of public requests for employers to respect servants' human dignity, to care about servants' life, and to reduce servants' work intensity and working time showed a progressive social development in terms of workers' rights. Some discussions directly related to socialism since *Women's Life* was a left-wing journal influenced by the CCP. For instance, also in the volume of *Women's Life* mentioned above in 1936, an author named Hu Gang published 'Where Should Concubine, Servants, Prostitutes, Women Beggars and Unemployed Women Go', arguing that the above-mentioned women could be liberated only if all oppressed people unite to build a new society. This new society, in which all people were masters, was eventually achieved in 1949 as the socialist country was founded.

Domestic service under the socialist central-planned economy

Domestic service did not disappear immediately along with the foundation of a new socialist society. As waged labour, it survived the early years of the socialist era (although in much smaller numbers than existed in the pre-socialist era). In the 1950s and 1960s, a small number of rural women continued to work in cities as maids or nannies. Their employers were wealthier households, usually headed by high-level cadres and the intellectual elite. Domestic service's existence continued for two main reasons. One was because of the simple practical reason that no work, no matter how objectionable ideologically, could wither away in a very short time and a certain level of domestic work itself was essential work. But also there existed the problem of consequence of the call for women's mass entry into public production before the adequate development of public services to support this new labour force. Paid domestic service can be said to have finally disappeared only in the 1960s. The end of this type of work was a logical development of the Cultural Revolution (1966–76), which focused on suppressing all evidence of the capitalist market and manifestations of the bourgeois class.

Domestic service under socialism is not supposed to exist: this type of work, associated with capitalism in a capitalist society, is characterized as class exploitation associated within Chinese culture with residual feudalism. Within socialism, women were to be treated as equal to men and equality would be manifested partly through the liberation they would experience through production activities. Marx and Engels argued in *The Communist Manifesto* that after turning over the old social order, entirely revolutionizing the mode of production was necessary: 'all instruments of production should be centralized in the hands of the state' and it would be necessary to 'increase the total of productive forces as rapidly as possible' (Marx and Engels 1999: 84). They also proposed measures such as 'equal liability of all to labour. Establishment of industrial armies, especially for agriculture' (Marx and Engels 1999: 84). These ideas were strictly carried out in socialist China with the implementation of public ownership and centrally planned production and distribution. A crucial part of this regime was the idea that everyone in the working class was a master of the new country and both men and women should participate in socialist production equally. This participation in socialist production referred explicitly to the kinds of paid work that occurred outside the household.

Under socialism, state ideology supported women's equality. Women's 'taking part in socialist production on a large scale' was considered 'the direction of the advancement of women's liberation after the victory of the socialist revolution' (Gao 2007: 183). As the chair of new China, Mao insisted on women's equal social status with men and was clear about the path leading to women's liberation. In a 1955 speech, he said:

> In order to construct a great socialist society, it is extraordinarily meaningful to motivate masses of women to participate in production activities. In the production process, equal pay for work of equal value for both men and women must be enforced. The true equality for men and women can only come true through socialist transformation in the whole society.
> (Mao 1955, as cited by All-China Women's Federation 1988: 64)

The ideology was deeply influenced by Marxism-Leninism. Engels's view on abolishing private property and bringing women into public production in his work, *The Origins of the Family, Private Property and the State*, became central to the Party's official view of how to build a socialist society with equality for men and women. Engels's classic passage was frequently quoted in discussions of women's liberation in China (Davin 1975; Johnson 1983):

> The emancipation of women and their equality with men are impossible, and remain so, as long as women are excluded from social production and restricted to domestic labour. The emancipation of women becomes feasible only when women are enabled to take part extensively in social production.
> (Engels 1972: 221)

To promote gender equality, the government's main policies centred on the mobilization of women's labour into public production and liberating women from domestic labour. Therefore, women were organized into the labour force in both urban and rural areas. This was the basic practice during the 1950s, especially in the Great Leap Forward (1958–60).[9] According to available statistics, at the end of 1952, the number of female workers in state-owned enterprises was 1.8 million; at the end of 1958, this number was 8.1 million; and by the end of 1960, the number of female workers in state-owned enterprises reached 100 million (Tao and Gao 1991). If women workers in collectively owned enterprises were counted, the total number of women in what was considered the 'productive sphere' was much higher. The ever-increasing numbers of women working for pay only decreased for a short time after the Great Leap Forward. This occurred because of a general increase in unemployment, which caused large numbers of women to lose their jobs. When this job loss for women happened, families resumed the traditional pattern of husband as breadwinner and wife as caregiver. However, by the time of the Cultural Revolution (1966–76), in the fall of 1971, 90 per cent of working-age women were working for pay in both urban and rural areas (Sidel 1972). Women's jobs included those normally associated with women's work, but also included work typically associated with males. Women were glorified as 'Iron Girls,' who 'defied conventional notions of biological weakness and physiological limitations' (Honig 2000: 98). They crossed the gender border and joined 'fishing teams, drilling teams, oil teams, well-sinking teams' (Honig: 98). They could be anything, including 'factory workers, police, doctors, teachers, nurses, airplane pilots, bus drivers, cadres (political workers), and members of the People's Liberation Army' (Sidel 1972: 24).

While women were draw into the labour force, to complement the socialist accumulation and economic collectivization, the Chinese government also tried to take up new responsibilities associated with social reproduction. This usually occurred through work units in urban areas and people's communes or brigades in rural areas. The task was to develop a system of public services and welfare, in order to socialize domestic work and relieve workers' domestic burden. With fewer women within the household to carry out social reproduction tasks, the state needed to find other ways to organize social reproduction tasks. For example, the state ordered the work units in the country to set up social service facilities, such as childcare centres and cafeterias (Song 2007). The former domestic work performed by women at home began to be replaced by public nurseries and kindergartens, public medical system and communal dining halls (see Chapter 4). Many work units had their own cafeterias, boiled water rooms, baths, clinics (or small hospital), elementary (and high) schools and even movie theatres (Liu, Zhang and Li 2010: 152–3). Work units also built apartments near the workplace to provide welfare housing for workers. In Sidel's study (1972), for example, the Third Textile Mill of Beijing, where women workers accounted for 70 per cent, had housing for over 2,000 families near the factory, and had nurseries, primary and middle schools, barbershops and a dining hall that could seat 2,000–3,000 people. For ¥12 to ¥13 a month, which only accounted for one fifth of the average factory worker's monthly salary, one could have three meals a day, and most workers ate most of their meals in the dining hall (Sidel 1972). Some work units also provided free commuter buses for workers, with special seats reserved for pregnant women and mothers with young children; mothers could carry their young children and go off to work (Liu, Zhang and Li 2010). A married woman with children can:

> Go to the dining hall for breakfast, drop her child at the nursery, walk to work, return to the dining hall for lunch, work the rest of the day, pick up the child at the nursery, and then either eat with her family in the dining hall or make dinner for them at home.
>
> (Sidel 1972: 32)

In rural areas, people's communes and brigades also had nurseries, kindergartens, and primary and middle schools to meet the daycare needs of working mothers and the educational needs of the children. Communal dining halls were first opened during the Great Leap Forward movement.

These measures have undoubtedly played an effective role in promoting women's equal and full participation in the workforce. While women were encouraged to enter into public production, the state tried, at the same time, to liberate women from traditional family patriarchy in the domestic sphere. The first new law passed by the Chinese government in the socialist era was the Marriage Law. It was published in May 1950. The law deemed:

> the relationship between husband and wife as a full and equal partnership based on the recognition that women have an equal right with men to develop their knowledge and skills, an equal right to independence, and freedom for full participation in economic, social and political life.
>
> (Croll 1978: 230–1)

Through the implementation of the new law, the Chinese government abolished the feudal marriage system, which was based on the ideal of superiority of men over women. Women's equal rights in their families were granted by law. The emancipation of women within the domestic sphere was directly linked to women's involvement in social production (Croll 1978); hence, women's positions in society and at home were both advanced. As Sidel's (1972) study indicates, the attitude of husbands had to change to mark the liberation of women, and husbands did help with the housework, child rearing and cooking. However, women still did more housework than men (Sidel 1972) and the 'liberation of women through public labour' (Johnson 1983: 166) approach to gender equality brought only partial liberation to women because while great emphasis was placed on encouraging women to work outside the home, little effort was made to encourage men to take greater responsibility for housework. Although women were legally equal with men, the old feudal thoughts and ideas that women were inferior died hard. It was not a smooth way to enforce the new Marriage Law even if the Women's Federation put great effort into assisting women to exercise their new rights.[10] Therefore, the fundamentals of patriarchal family structure were not challenged: men's attitudes towards work inside the home shifted little and public expectations of women's responsibility for home and children endured. Women were still seen as natural caregivers. They still had to deal with most of their domestic responsibilities as 'private' problems. Although there was outside support such as public childcare facilities to help women meet the demands of their expected roles as wives and mothers, these public services were still limited because of the overall material scarcity in China. Under a socialist planned economy, the liberation of women from the burden of housework was expected to be realized through the eventual socialization and mechanization of domestic labour. One more reason why the domestic workload remained heavy for women was partly because the state's accumulation strategy called for investment in heavy industry rather than the production of consumer goods such as clothing and shoes to relieve women's domestic work (Hershatter, 2007). As Croll (1983) argued, 'the government had to a certain extent come to rely upon female unpaid labour to subsidize economic development programmes' (Croll: 9). Therefore, official egalitarian ideology imposed double burdens on some women. In addition, some liberated women were still segregated in jobs that were suitable for traditional women's roles. For example, all nursery and kindergarten teachers were women (Sidel 1972; Emerson 1968); no effort was made to recruit men into fields that would deal with small children and 'there seems to be no concern for breaking down the traditional sex roles in professions such as teaching and nursing, both of which are virtually all female' (Sidel 1972: 25). This was also the case in light industry such as textiles and food processing, where women comprised as much as 70 per cent of the workforce (Emerson 1968).

Since women had to work inside and outside their households, not surprisingly, paid domestic service was still in demand in city, although very few wealthier families, usually high-level cadres and the intellectual elite, could afford this service. Most people could use only unpaid female relatives. Throughout this era, domestic responsibilities were simply passed on to different women's shoulders, from younger to older and from urban women to rural women. Gender inequality and class divisions still existed despite the Chinese government's endeavour to break down these walls.

Domestic workers mostly consisted of middle-aged women who left their husbands and children in search of work in order to overcome economic difficulties resulting from the effects of natural disasters or from the loss of a male breadwinner in the family (Jacka 1997). The party branch in their village and county normally recommended them, and employers hired them also through party arrangements in cities. This was mainly because, under the planned economy, migration was strictly controlled (see Chapter 3). The harsh restriction on rural-to-city migration also stopped these women from staying in cities permanently; therefore, after working in the city for several years, these women usually returned to their hometown. Only a few who had had some education (although they were mostly illiterate or semi-literate), found factory jobs with their employer's help, and managed to become a legal city resident and change their peasant identity. Getting a job in the public sphere was the only way to change one's peasant identity.

To distinguish overtly subjected servants in previous eras, the terms of respect, *baomu* and *ayi*, were widely used to represent all domestic workers regardless of their specific responsibilities. During my interview with an officer from the labour authority who is now responsible for making policy about domestic workers, he explained that,

> although there were very few *baomu* in number at that time (1950s –1960s), that did not mean there were no *baomu*. I was raised by *baomu* when I was little. My family has used several *baomu*. . . . My parents were intellectuals – they were both doctors.
> (Interview, November 7, 2007)

Because of the widespread socialist moral standard and the doctrine of universal equality, domestic workers under the centrally planned economic era were generally treated relatively as equal to employers and enjoyed certain autonomy in the employer's homes as a workplace. This does not mean that class inequality did not exist between domestic workers and their employers. Yan's study (2007) found that the older domestic workers often described the abundance of food available at the employers' homes compared with its scarcity in the countryside, and they talked about various forms of hardships that they endured while working in the city for elite families. Through these narratives, the unequal power relationship was revealed (Yan 2007).

Although an actual employment relationship existed between the domestic worker and her employer, the government never accepted domestic service as an employment arrangement, nor did it acknowledge the role domestic service played in the economy. There were two reasons for the reluctance to accept domestic service as paid work. First, the government had a 'productionist bias' (Elson 1988: 6). That is, it promoted more formal wage workplace relations and did not recognize activities that connected the workplace and households. Second, because of the long history of the exploitation and oppression of domestic workers in previous Chinese eras, it was assumed that, in an egalitarian socialist state, domestic workers should not exist as a class. The government's reluctance to openly incorporate domestic employment into state or collective employment relationships reflected, in part, the government's unease with the whole image of domestic service.

During the Great Proletarian Cultural Revolution at the end of the 1960s and in the 1970s, the reassertion of issues of class and class struggle as the primary categories for understanding all social problems led to the complete abolishment of domestic workers. Many domestic workers either quit their jobs or were dismissed and went back to their hometowns. However, the elimination of domestic service did not mean that the women's double burden was solved; on the contrary, the issues of women's double burden were treated as entirely a matter of personal political consciousness (Johnson 1983). As Johnson argued, the assumption under state patriarchal thinking, in the name of socialism, was that a woman who had a true revolutionary proletarian consciousness should be able to handle all of her responsibilities as a worker, a mother and a wife without complaint; if she could not fulfil her domestic responsibilities, she was called bourgeois, which would place her in a problematic political situation (Johnson 1983). Therefore, in a socialist country, the identity of 'a worker' was not only economic but also political (Song 2007). The question of whether a woman could deal with domestic work determined whether she was qualified to be a worker and thus gained her a political position in the state.

The domestic service regime after economic reforms

Government-led economic reforms started at the end of 1970s and paid domestic service gradually became part of the government-recognized economy through first being part of the informal economy. Work in the informal economy is different from public sector employment in pay, benefits and employment stability. However, paid domestic work has become an officially recognized and promoted employment type, although it is still subordinate to public production. In addition, its value to the increase of the GDP and general economic development is not acknowledged.

State policies are crucial in determining the contours of the domestic service regime. After the economic reforms, the state's ideology relating to gender and class equality – the official rules under the socialist central-planned economy – shifted considerably with the increase in the market as the economic organizing principle. Legions of rural women labourers – with the aid of the new state policy that legitimates their movement – entered cities to fill the demand for domestic labour. At the same time, the government's economic development strategies in cities added to the domestic service supply by allowing the state sector to lay off women workers. Women were laid off on a large scale because they were considered low on the hierarchy of human capital accumulation (*suzhi di*)[11] and therefore, economically inefficient under the demands of market competition. Rural migrant women and urban laid-off women have been 'housewived' to take care of domestic matters. It is estimated that in Beijing at least 90 per cent of domestic workers are rural migrants, with laid-off and unemployed workers accounting for less than 10 per cent (D. J. Li 2007). Furthermore, over 96 per cent of domestic workers are female (Z. Q. Wang 2007).

Patriarchy takes different forms in different eras. In the socialist central-planned economy era, government strategies encouraged women into public production by freeing women from household work through providing public childcare service. These policies intentionally and objectively promoted gender equality and class justice. Today, government-encouraged commercialization of domestic service is actually fostering class divisions based on gender, social and economic status. Familial patriarchy is now grounded in state sanctions and low-income women in the domestic service sector are bearing an increasing share of the domestic work of middle- and upper-income families. Not only does the patriarchal gendered hierarchy of men over women remain unchallenged, but also the power of more-privileged women over less-privileged ones is reconstructed and rationalized. With the domestication of socially subordinated women, patriarchal power and market forces have transformed the private patriarchal family into a workplace, which is radically different from a traditional production domain, as it had been understood in China.

To legitimatize domestic service under a socialist market economy, the state has tried to extend the definition of worker to include domestic service workers. It justifies this with the socialist doctrine that everyone is equal under socialism even though the work may vary. This change in the state concept of what constitutes legitimate work has been accomplished in incremental steps. In 1983, the first domestic service company, San Ba Family Service Centre (SBFSC), which is affiliated with the Beijing Women's Federation, was opened in Beijing. The company directly imports migrant labourers from rural areas to serve city residents. In recent years, various private domestic service agencies have opened in cities. Over time, domestic service has been gradually accepted in the public eye. In the early stages, when only rural women were involved in domestic service, this work arrangement was not really connected with official employment. It was not until the mid-1990s, when laid-off women workers were encouraged to find work in domestic service, that the Chinese government changed its employment policy to accommodate domestic service as an official occupation. Even from this policy change, we can see the hierarchical relationship between rural workers and city workers. From 1995 to 2000, domestic service was classified as an occupation in which a worker was called family service worker (*jiating fuwu yuan*). In May 2000, family service worker was officially renamed domestic service worker (*jiazheng fuwu yuan*), which is used not only to distinguish itself from *ayi* and *baomu*, the traditional terms inherited from the old society, but also to extend the workers' responsibility to help manage or run someone's home. In August 2000, the MOLSS published domestic service worker national occupation standards (see Chapter 1).

This 'renaming movement' reveals two purposes of the government: to empower household work's positive value and to erase its inferior side, and to make the domestic service worker theoretically one of the working class. The new official term also stresses the 'service' aspect of this work and builds upon the socialist doctrine that all work is service for people. The textbook *The Basic Knowledge for Domestic Service Workers* issued by the CETTIC, MOLSS (2006), defines the professional ethics in a socialist society:

> People are masters of the country, the relationship between person and person, industry and industry is equal and mutually helpful. Although there are different divisions of labour and high and low posts, there is no high or low, noble or inferior personality in a socialist country. Although employees in every industry have their special professional interests and personal interests, they all serve the country, and their interests are in accordance with the society's integral interests.
>
> (CETTIC 2006: 5)

The main point is that all work is service for people and domestic service is no different in nature from other types of work:

> In a socialist country, a labourer in any industry is one of the people. Everyone serves other people and is served by other people. It is the common rule for every labourer to think from the standpoint of the people.
>
> (CETTIC 2006: 5)

We can see that the state ascribes the emergence of domestic service in the market economy to a social division of labour. The government also assumes that domestic service workers are equal to anyone within the working class, including the domestic workers' employers. However, in reality, because of the historical inferior position of domestic workers and the concentration of the occupation to disadvantaged women's groups, discrimination and exploitation is a defining feature of the occupation.

It is not that the work in itself is necessarily bad, but exploitative working conditions have been created because of the unequal power relationships created by patriarchy and market power. As long as the domestic employment relationship is confined to the informal economy that is situated between public production and the domestic realm, domestic workers receive neither the full legal protection accorded to employees nor the emotional and affective benefits of family membership. Arat-Koc (1989) describes immigrant domestic workers in Canada: 'Squeezed between the private and public spheres, she belongs to neither one, and probably combines the worst aspects of both' (Arat-Koc 1989: 39).

Table 2.1 Chinese domestic employment regimes

The defining model of production:	Domestic employment regime:	Characteristics of employment relationship:
Feudal	Bondservant	Very limited personal freedom; similar to private property
Capitalist	Servant	Waged labour; member of working class
Socialist (central planned economy)	*Baomu* or *ayi*	Invisible family-like relationship
Socialist (market economy)	Domestic service worker	New occupation; employer–employee relationship

Source: Table prepared by author.

Conclusion

From the historical development of domestic employment regimes, we can see that under different economic forms, whether feudal society or socialist society alike, it is always women from disadvantaged groups who take on domestic work. Migrant women from the impoverished countryside have historically consisted of the main body of domestic workers. The current low status of domestic service and its workers has historical ties with the bondservant and the servant regimes in history.

This chapter has demonstrated that patriarchy and private property ownership or capitalism have intersected with regard to domestic work in various eras of Chinese history. Domestic service is not a new, natural social division of labour that has happened along with China's economic reform, but is an old occupation that has been given new meaning by current government policies. A relatively new character of socialism, with a major role for the market economy, tends to submerge the objectives of gender and class equality in the interests of market mechanisms. Paid domestic service reflects not only the relations between the sphere of 'unproductive' domesticity and that of paid work in the production domain, but also gender relations and the role of the state in these relationships.

3 Globalization, economic reforms and paid domestic employment in China

In China, the economic reforms of the last thirty years to bring about rapid industrialization and the transition from a planned economy to an open market system have brought unprecedented levels of rural migration, urban unemployment, and wage and income disparities between rural and urban areas and within cities. These changes have contributed to the rise of precarious employment that does not offer the stability and security of former work arrangements.

Work in the domestic service domain is among the most precarious form of new work arrangements in China. This is related to not only the rise of new forms of labour arrangements, but also the continuity of occupational segregation in the labour market, the gendered division of unpaid work and state ideology that perpetuates ideas of what is appropriate men's and women's work. National care chains, in which women from different provinces, such as Sichuan, Henan and Liaoning, must leave their children behind to look after other families in China, characterize the new domestic arrangements. Many women travel to different areas around the country to work in the homes of families they have never met. Some cannot even communicate with employers properly because of their strong local accent. This migration resembles the global trend of migrant women travelling from developing countries to developed countries in pursuit of domestic work. The existing global studies have shown that most migration associated with globalization is not international but internal (Cohen and Kennedy 2007). This internal migration in China is considered to be the largest migration of women in Chinese history because neither paid domestic work nor rural to urban migration was encouraged by the Chinese government in the past.

In this chapter, I will analyse the factors leading to the recent economic reform policies in both rural and urban China and show how government policy changes have brought a large number of women to work in the domestic service industry. Through this analysis I will argue that the pressure economic globalization has exerted on the Chinese government has transformed it's policy directions. While the government is intentionally making a new working class in domestic service for economic development purposes, it has put a great deal of faith in the power of capital and markets to meet its economic and social goals. This shift to the market mechanism has given preference to capital over workers' rights and interests.

Rural economic reforms and rural-to-urban migration

China's economic reforms to provide a greater role for the market started in rural areas in the late 1970s.[1] Before the economic reforms, there had not been any large-scale voluntary rural-to-urban labour migration. While the introduction of the Household Responsibility System (HRS) in rural areas and the eased restrictions of population movement provided the possibility of labour migration, the long-standing, continuing inequalities and ever-widening post-economic-reform income gap after economic reforms between the city and the countryside are mainly responsibility for rural to urban migration. As Whyte (2010) argued, 'for China's farmers the combination of market reforms, agricultural decollectivization, and the loosening of migration restrictions provided potential for genuine "liberation" from socialist serfdom' (Whyte: 150).

In rural areas, under the socialist system prior to the reform, land was publicly owned and agricultural labourers were grouped into production teams, brigades and people's communes to work collectively. From 1958 to 1982, the people's commune system was the administration system in rural areas in China. It was a three-level administration in a commune. The commune was the highest-level organization that was responsible for profit and loss, and managed large-scale production such as enterprises, mines, the supply and sales departments (these were state-operated basic commercial unit in rural areas), and credit departments (state-operated basic financial offices in rural areas). The production brigade, which was also known as the administrative group, was the second level. It was the basic unit of economic accounting in a village and it was in charge of all village affairs, including production and welfare. The production team was the fundamental unit organizing peasants directly for production and distribution, and assigning where peasants worked collectively and obtained grain and income. Besides this three-level administrative system in rural areas, agricultural labourers were bound to the land by a strict dual system of rural and urban household registration – the Hukou System – that was introduced in the late 1950s. It is one of the social control/administration systems set up on a household basis, whose members, whether in rural or urban areas, have to register at the local public security office as legal residents. After registration, each household is issued a Hukou Certificate, on which all members of the family are listed as legal residents. Through this system, they are closely controlled by the local government. It was extremely difficult to transfer one's registration from agricultural to non-agricultural status, from rural to urban areas or even from a small town to a larger city office in urban areas or by the village committees in rural areas (Huang 2000). A person's *hukou* was usually inherited from the mother, and urban migration was strictly controlled, especially for women and children who have agricultural registration: the registration system did not grant non-agricultural registration to the children of a man with a non-agricultural registration unless their mother had non-agricultural registration (Judd 1994). As a result of the controls instituted through this system, there been no large-scale voluntary rural-to-urban labour migration. A little over two-thirds of the Chinese population was rural until the economic reforms in the late 1970s (Naughton 1995).

In 1978, after the economic reforms began, a Household Responsibility System (HRS) was implemented in the villages, and the production brigades of the Peoples' Commune System were dissolved. The land use system of HRS was introduced in 1978. Under this system, collective land has been allocated to peasants for use in agricultural production. Each rural household is allocated a certain amount of land based on the number of family members. In addition, some peasants can also ask for more land according to the ability of the household to engage in agricultural production. In exchange for use rights of land, rural households are required to sell fixed portions of harvested crops and other products at prices set by the government as agricultural tax. Once the fixed amount has been sold to the state, peasants can grow crops of their own choice, sell their products freely on the market and keep the income earned by selling extra production. The Household Responsibility System is a way of distributing part of the user right to land and the right to earn income from the collective village body to individual households (Judd 1994). In the HRS, individual rural households were granted more freedom in managing production, and agricultural productivity and efficiency greatly improved. For example, since the HRS, rural grain productivity has significantly increased and it reached 5.28 hundred million tons in 2009, almost five times the amount of grain produced in 1949, and per capita share of grain increased from 210 kilos in 1949 to 406 kilos in 2009, sufficiently supplying 13 hundred million population with food (C. G. Wang and Liu 2009). The continuous increase of agricultural productivity has meant that fewer workers were needed on the land, and more and more peasant labourers had opportunities to look for jobs outside agriculture. However, some scholars have argued that the land use system of HRS is gender-biased because men are natural household heads and more preferential concerning land allocation than women are. Furthermore, since men's external agricultural opportunities are greater than those of women, women's labour has become the major component of ordinary agricultural work. While agricultural work has been feminized, women are at a continuing disadvantage in managing household relations with outside sources of supplies and markets for their products; in addition, because of traditional division of labour, rural women are also responsible for domestic labour and childcare (Judd 1994).

After economic reforms, the once-rigid control of population movement by the planned economy also eased. One change was *hukou* control. In 1984, after the promulgation of the Notice of Peasants Entering and Settling down in Towns by the State Council, rural labourers who moved to towns and ran small businesses were officially permitted to have non-agricultural residency (Party History Research Centre of the CCP Central Committee 2009). The government began to officially allow rural labourers to migrate and work in cities. Although the *Hukou* System has not been eliminated yet and migrant workers still need temporary resident's permits issued by the city police departments to legally work and live in cities, it has been gradually adjusted and reformed. The loose constriction of *hukou* enabled agricultural population transfers and migration.

Another change was that the Chinese government relaxed the regulations governing the distribution of food and other daily necessities (Naughton 1995;

Wen 2008). During the central planned era, food rationing was a supplementary system to the *Hukou* System. Under such a system, while agricultural labourers were directly assigned grain from brigades, people with non-agricultural *hukou* were issued a certain amount of food coupons each month and they could buy grain in state-owned grain shops in cities and towns. There were no free markets in food. This system greatly restrained rural-to-urban mobility. It became possible for people to move from rural areas to cities after the abolishment of food rationing and the rationing of other daily basic commodities, such as soup and cloth,[2] as a free market in food and basic consumer goods emerged during economic reforms. By the end of 1992, only a few counties in the northwest had yet to abolish the grain provision ration coupons (Wen 2008).

The dearth of jobs in the countryside, the eased restriction of rural-to-urban migration and also the reduction in state-supported programmes for health care and childcare (see Chapter 4) in cities are all 'push' factors that have greatly motivated rural-to-urban migration. At the same time, employment possibilities with much higher incomes in cities largely 'pull' agricultural labour into urban areas (Ray 1998; Ha, Yi and Zhang 2009). Other factors of life opportunities such as education, health and civil liberty in cities also attract rural-to-urban migration (Ha, Yi and Zhang 2009). Since the mid-1980s, rural migrant workers have increasingly left agriculture and their hometowns in favour of entering factories and cities (X. Y. Lu 2003). They began to migrate to urban and costal areas in large numbers after 1992 when China accelerated its market-oriented economic reforms (Wen 2008). It is estimated that the migration of rural workers led to a 278 million increase in the permanent urban population between 1979 and 2003 (Lu and Wang 2006; Ha, Yi and Zhang 2009). The 2000 Census data indicate that rural migration is 144 million and that one in nine Chinese are movers in intercounty or intra-county (Fan 2008; Ha *et al.* 2009). The China Yearly Macro-Economics National Statistics show that there were 498,76 million workers in rural areas in 2000, a number that decreased to 484,94 million in 2005. During the same period, the number of workers in urban areas has increased dramatically – from 212,74 million in 2000 to 273,31 million in 2005. Rural migrants to cities now account for 11.6 per cent of China's total population.

Table 3.1 Workers in urban areas and rural areas in China 2000–05, unit: per 10,000 persons

Year	Total number of employed persons	Employed persons by urban and rural areas	
		Urban areas	Rural areas
2000	71,150	21,274	49,876
2001	73,025	23,940	49,085
2002	73,740	24,780	48,960
2003	74,432	25,639	48,793
2004	75,200	26,476	48,724
2005	75,825	27,331	48,494

Source: China Yearly Macro-Economics Statistics (National), China Data Online (accessed through Simon Fraser University Library Database).

Feminist scholars in China have been particularly interested in the impact of economic reforms on rural women and rural women's migration. For example, Gao Xiaoxian, a researcher in Shaanxi Women's Federation, divided the practice of women and development in China into two historical periods: 1950s to the end of 1970s, rural women's collective participation in development by social mobilization; 1980s to onwards, the development motivated by the market (Gao 1999). As she acknowledged, the top-down social mobilization in the 1950s did not change the gendered division of labour: women's traditional role has been sustained and patriarchal authority over the household has been maintained. The economic reform in the late 1970s and the enforcement of the HRS in rural areas reduced the state and collectives' control over peasants, which allowed peasants to enjoy more freedom in agricultural production. This change also affected rural women's labour market participation by increasing it (Gao 1999).

Some feminist writers dealing with recent economic changes tend to focus on analysing the effect of the migration on rural women within local areas. In her study, Jin Yihong, a professor of Ginling College, Nanjing Normal University, concludes that the rural non-agriculturalization process, such as working in township enterprises, has, to a certain extent, improved women's living conditions and allowed women to be more independent. But she is careful to note that gendered differences still exist and is actually increasing as women's occupations are poorly paid and the upward mobility rate for women is smaller than it is for men (Jin 1998).

Those feminist scholars who investigate the rural-to-urban migration mainly focus on factory workers, who are called *dagong mei* (working sisters) since they are young and usually unmarried. For example, Tan Shen, a researcher in the Chinese Academy of Social Sciences who studies *dagong mei* in the Pearl River delta – an export processing zone in Guangdong province – says that the rise of the *dagong mei* is the result of a combination of international investment and cheap female labour. She shows that the *dagong mei* are discriminated against by the local government and are excluded from the labour protection because of their peasant identity. As female workers, the *dagong mei* group is different from both urban women and rural male labour (Tan 1998). This group is normally less educated than urban women workers and migrant rural male labour and there are no specific protections for these workers. In recent years, as a part of the continuing of rural-to-urban migration, many women have migrated to cities to seek employment. Some feminists argue that rural women's migration is gradually increasing and not all of it is related to economic desperation, but that some women migrate in order to seek a better future for themselves. That is, some migration is due to women's self-advancement needs rather than pure survival strategy (Pan and Huang 2005). In this sense, the title *dagong mei* fails to represent the current female migrant group. In the earlier years it was primarily young, unmarried women who migrated, but now, married women and women with children also migrate, and some of them migrate together with their husbands as well as children (Zheng and Xie 2004).

Women now account for almost half of the floating population (*liudong renkou*).[3] The 2000 Chinese census data show that 43.1 per cent of migrants who looked for employment or were self-employed were women (Liang and Chen 2004). However, although rural workers are permitted to work in cities without an urban *hukou* (or household) registration, it is impossible for them to find employment that offers job security, advancement or benefits. Also, rural migrants are willing to do the dirty jobs that are rejected by local residents.

In general, there is a distinct occupational difference between male and female migrants. The Chinese studies which analyse the workforce indicate that in general women are more clustered in the service industry than men are (Hou 2005). English-language studies of labour in China also show that while male migrants gravitate to construction jobs, female migrants tend to seek domestic service jobs (Meng 2000). The reason why female migrants are more likely to do domestic service work is because although domestic service pays relatively low wages compared with other jobs available to migrant women, it appears convenient to many female migrants who have newly arrived in cities. Live-in domestic service requires relatively little initial capital outlay yet resolves the immediate crisis of finding shelter. Additionally, because domestic work is regarded by workers and employers alike as unskilled labour, and as an extension of women's social roles as mothers and wives, it is wide open to new arrivals with no prior work experience or with low education levels.

Although the motivation of women coming to the cities is varied, as was noted earlier, the push factor of poverty is significant. In general, rural migrant workers have flooded into cities to do precarious work because of rural poverty and the huge income inequality between the city and the countryside. Even the income from precarious work in urban areas is much higher than the income received from agricultural work in the rural areas. Therefore, once peasants have the opportunity to move out of the countryside, they are relentless in transforming themselves into 'a new urban working class' (H. Wang 2009: xxiii).

Rural poverty

The explosive growth of a migrant labour underclass is related to two factors: poverty in rural areas and the ability of people to change their location of work. While the reform agenda has accelerated economic growth in both rural and urban areas, it has also worked to the advantage of urban over rural citizens. The result, therefore, has been a dramatic increase in both spatial and class inequalities (Selden and Perry 2010).

To better describe the situation of rural poverty in China, it is important to clarify the definition of poverty and how it is used in this chapter. There is no universal or international definition of poverty, but it is widely accepted that poverty is multidimensional. Rather than focusing solely on economic measures such as income or basic needs, since the 1990s, poverty is also identified as being related to capabilities[4] and rights.[5] The UN Millennium Development Goals incorporate indicators for income poverty, including education and gender inequality in education, and health care and environmental poverty (United Nations (UN) 2000). In China, poverty used to refer only to economic measures: lack of income and lack of basic living needs. The Chinese official poverty line is very low – ¥627 per person per year in 2002. This is considerably lower than the $1 per day poverty line established by the World Bank, which would have amounted to ¥850 per person in China in 2002 (Naughton 2007). In addition, the definition of poverty as it is used in China is too narrow in meaning to cover the multiple dimensions of poverty. To reflect rural poverty in a comprehensive way, I will use the term 'poverty' in this chapter to include the relative deprivation of resources and rights with a focus on inequalities of income and other social welfare services in the countryside compared with urban areas.

During the socialist era China used to be one of the poorest countries and even in the 1980s China ranked among the poorest third of all countries (Naughton 1995). However, it was also one of the most equal countries in the world. Social equality was once an important objective of socialism and in the pre-reform planned economy. China was generally an egalitarian society where income differences were small. China's overall Gini coefficient was 0.28 in 1983, which made China one of the most equal countries in the world, comparable to Sweden, 0.25, Japan, 0.25 and Germany 0.28.[6] Urban society in China was especially equal, and the intra-urban Gini coefficient was only 0.166 (Naughton 2007).

The relatively high level of formal equality was primarily related to the urban sector, with substantial differences continuing to exist between the urban and the rural sectors. Even in the socialist period there was an obvious 'urban-rural divide' (Naughton 2007: 114). As Chinese scholar Wang Hui argues, 'the guise of equality the socialist state maintained in the areas of ideology and benefit allocation belied its dependence upon coercion and planning for the protection of systemic inequality' (H. Wang 2009: 30). In the pre-reform period, peasants still suffered from poverty created by inequality that was related to the dual economic system purposefully designed by the policymakers. Under the dual economic system, the industrial sector was deliberately separated from the traditional agricultural sector by making industrialization the economic priority. Low prices for agricultural products were regarded as a means to accumulate funds for industrialization. Urban workers were considered to be the vanguard of socialism and enjoyed permanent employment and various social benefits, while rural labourers were organized collectively to deliver low-cost grain and other agricultural products to urban areas. The whole dualistic system therefore worked as an implicit tax on farmers, who had lower incomes since they were compelled by the government to sell grain at artificially low prices (Naughton 2007). Furthermore, the rural collectives could provide social services and public goods to rural residents only after they generated a surplus from the sale of agricultural produce (Naughton 2007). The household registration system introduced after the Great Leap Forward movement (1958–60) restricted rural-urban migration, which ensured the relatively high subsidies and benefits for urban residents. Hence, the rural population has never had the same income guarantees that were implicitly extended to the urban population and they were in a more precarious economic position under the old system (Naughton 1995). Therefore, there was a long-standing and continuing inequality between the city and the countryside before the economic reforms of the 1970s. As the World Bank statistics show, the Chinese urban-to-rural income ratio in 1979 was 2.5:1, higher than in other low-income countries in Asia (where the average ratio was 1.5:1) and also higher than in middle-income countries (average 2.2:1) (R. W. Zhao 2001). Under reform conditions, this systemic inequality quickly translated into income differences between classes and social strata, which gave rise to social polarization (H. Wang 2009).

Market reforms at first did not enlarge the urban-rural gap; on the contrary, this gap narrowed at first because the economic reforms started in rural areas and economically benefited peasants first. But ultimately, market reforms contributed to urban-rural inequality because they led to the acceleration of urban economic growth (Naughton 2007). Poverty alleviation in rural areas has been a major goal of China's government during the reform period. 'The desire to strength an enfeebled agricultural sector' and to increase peasants' living standard shaped the course of rural reform efforts (Naughton 1995: 53). With the broad reform-driven economic growth, after the adoption of the household responsibility system and other economic reforms in 1978, the government-advocated poverty alleviation programmes succeeded in reducing absolute poverty in the countryside. According to data from the China National Statistics Bureau, from 1978 to 2004, the number living in poverty has decreased from 250 million to 26.1 million (Zhao 2009 [2005]). However, this dramatic reduction of rural poverty did not prevent the widening income gap between rural and urban areas. In fact, only during the early part of the reform period – from 1978 up to about 1985 – did rural households benefit, and inequality between the rural and urban areas decrease. Official data in China show that rural income soared between 1978 and 1985, growing about 15 per cent per year, while urban household incomes increased by 7 per cent per year; therefore, the urban-rural gap narrowed significantly during this period, and it reached its lowest period even since the economic reforms (Naughton 2007). Although some scholars note that the official data overstate the real growth of rural incomes in this early period, rural incomes did indeed grow rapidly, and certainly faster than urban incomes (Naughton 2007). As the urban reforms were being promoted in 1984, the rural-urban divide started to grow, and by the period between 1988 and 1991, peasant incomes had basically stagnated, and the income gap between urban and rural areas had reached pre-1978 levels (H. Wang 2009). Most observers believe that the plight of the poor in both poor and non-poor regions increased in various ways between 1988 and 1995. This is not poverty in the narrow sense of low income *per se*, but poverty that takes into consideration the economic welfare of the peasants grounded in income-based estimates and social indicator-based estimates, such as rural infrastructure and education opportunities.

Since the mid-1990s, the gap between urban and rural income, consumption and savings has continued to widen. Rural per capita income has consistently grown at half the rate of urban income. In 2002, the average rural per capita income was ¥2476, compared with ¥7703 in the cities.[7] In 2003, official estimates suggested that urban residents earned, on average, three times as much as those in the countryside, although some analysts in China estimated that, in real terms, the urban-rural gap was as high as five or six to one (Croll 2006). This gap, which takes into account the subsidies and services exclusively available to urban residents and the fact that the rural population pays more in taxes than they receive in subsidies and welfare, is very high by international standards. For example, per capita education expenditure provided by the government for urban residents is higher than for rural residents (Chow 2009). Peasants also were subject to extra levies after the tax reform of 1994. This was accompanied by an increase in the proportion of government revenue paid to the central government (from 22 per cent in 1993 to 55.7 per cent in 2004) at the expense of provincial and local governments. At the same time the central government compounded the issue by assigning the responsibility of providing children with a nine-year mandatory education and adequate health care to local governments (Chow 2009). The new levies for peasants included the increase in reported acreage of the peasant's land that is subject to tax over the acreage actually used, a special tax for growing commercial crops other than grain and crops for livestock, fees for schools, road construction and other services provided by the local government (Chow 2009).

These tax changes, occurring at the same time that the availability of social services declined, meant that many peasants and their families exist around or just above the official poverty line. In some sense this poverty is not as visible as it should be because China has an official poverty line that is lower than the international standard. If calculated by the Chinese poverty standard, the percentage of rural peasants in poverty was 3.2 per cent of the rural population, while by the $1 per day international poverty standard, the percentage of rural poor would be 12.5 per cent, and the total number of rural people living in poverty would jump from 29 million to 114 million (Naughton 2007). The World Bank $1 per day poverty line is established in order to capture the number of people who do not have enough food to provide adequate nutrition for their families. After adjustment for differences in local prices, those people living under the poverty line are unable to achieve an adequate caloric intake even when they spend half their income on food. Therefore, the households falling between the Chinese official poverty line and the World Bank poverty line likely suffer from chronic malnutrition (Naughton 2007).

The vulnerability of low-income households has increased substantially over the reform period, as greater economic insecurity and reduced access to health care have made the position of the poor more precarious. As Riskin and Li's study has shown, basic social services, especially education and health care, have become more inaccessible. While the percentage of poor people with five or more years of education has dropped substantially, the percentage of total income they have spent on medical care rose sharply to almost 25 per cent, which by any standard is extremely high (Riskin and Li 2001).

It has been especially difficult for all peasants who rely solely on the land to make a living or to expand their income through agricultural activities (Croll 2006). Rural poverty has been and still is concentrated in the remote, ecologically disadvantaged areas of the northwest and southwest. There are obvious divergences between the developed coastal (or eastern) provinces and the remote interior (or western) regions. For example, basic infrastructure in the interior rural

Table 3.2 Income and expenditure of urban and rural residents in China

Items	Years			
	1989	1997	2001	2002
Annual per capita disposable income of city residents (yuan)	1,374	5,160	6,860	7,703
Annual per capita disposable income of rural residents (yuan)	602	2,090	2,366	2,476
Annual per capita consumption expenditure of city (yuan)	1,211	4,186	5,309	6,030
Household annual per capita living expenditure of rural (yuan)	535	1,617	1,741	1,834

Source: China Statistical Yearbook 2003 (National Bureau of Statistics of China 2003).

areas is far behind what is normal for other areas. In particular, basic services like the supply of running water is far from universal and more than 60 per cent of rural households do not have access to flush toilets. About 6 per cent of the villages are not accessible by roads, 2 per cent of the villages have no electricity supply at all, 6 per cent do not have telephones, and about 250 million rural households face problems with an adequate fuel supply (Chow 2009). But even outside these regions, poverty issues still exist and the slow growth in peasants' incomes relate to the serious social problem known as *san nong* (the three rural problems). San nong refers to problems related to farming, rural areas and farmers (Chow 2009).

Poverty in rural areas is also a gendered phenomenon, as has been noted by feminist scholars who investigate the feminization of rural poverty. For instance, researchers from the College of Humanities and Development Studies, China Agricultural University, argued that in rural areas, female poverty is more severe than male poverty. This is evidenced by not only the higher rate of poverty for females, but also by the fewer employment opportunities and lower education levels of females (Li, Zhang and Tang 2005). They concluded that this situation is likely to continue in the long term because girls have fewer opportunities than boys to get an education (Li, Zhang and Tang 2005).

Given rural poverty and inequalities in rural areas, the result has been a massive migration of people, many from poorer rural regions of central and western China, to the cities and towns of the eastern seaboard in search of lucrative work opportunities. The domestic service industry in cities also echoes this pattern. Female migrant domestic workers are normally from remote rural areas that are less developed. According to the director of the Beijing Home Service Association (BHSA): '. . .we category those areas as *lao shao bian qiong*[8] areas. In other words, if there were no poverty there would be no domestic service workers, and no poverty no domestic service' (D. J. Li 2007: N.p.). In Beijing, the earliest *baomu* after the economic reforms were from Wuwei county of Anhui province and Liyang county of Jiangsu province. Although there was already a tradition of women being domestic workers in these two areas both in revolutionary times before 1949 and during the socialist era, the main reason that they now do domestic service work is related not to tradition but rather to poverty. One of my interviewees who came to Beijing in 1982 told me: 'At that time, it was so poor at home. We had no hope, because we were bound to the land. I desperately wanted to leave my hometown. It didn't matter where I went' (Interview 12 October 2007). Another worker also mentioned rural poverty: she said that in remote mountain areas in Gansu, some poor families only have one set of decent clothes for all their children and whoever goes outside would put them on (Interview 12 October 2007). While the last story may be a little exaggerated, it did mean some people who live in remote rural areas live in desperate poverty. In recent years, more workers come from Gansu, Sichuan, Henan and Chongqing than other areas and this is related to government programmes themselves: most of the workers from these areas are exported to cities by their local government poverty alleviation offices or women's federations.

The manager of SBFSC, who has 25 years experience in this industry, said:

> Although there have been some changes during the last thirty years, rural life is still quite poor. I feel that they come to the city mainly for money. If the living standard in the countryside were to be substantially increased in the future, almost something approximating what it is in the cities, we wouldn't get any women to do this (domestic service). Currently, domestic service workers have these jobs not because of personal preference, but because of some kind of financial difficulty, or to save money for their children's education or to renovate or build new houses.
>
> (Interview, 17 October 2007)

Some of this is changing. In recent years, the government has announced a number of dramatic policy changes aimed at alleviating rural poverty (Whyte 2010). For instance, many rural taxes and fees were reduced and the grain tax was entirely phased out. Also rural school tuition is being eliminated and nine years of education for rural children is now required. A new medical insurance system, which replaced the cooperative medical insurance plans that collapsed early in the reform era, has been enforced in all rural areas (see Chapter 5). In 2007, a minimum livelihood guarantee system was implemented in rural areas (Whyte 2010). Although most of those who are still engaged in agricultural labour in China today remain at the bottom of income hierarchy, it is clear that through these particular measures the government hopes to begin to reduce the rural-urban divide and promote greater equality in China.

Economic restructuring and the rise of precarious employment in cities

The economic restructuring process in cities has affected the very notion of employment itself. The pre-reform 'iron rice bowl (*tie fan wan*)', which is a traditional name for permanent employment, that provided lifetime employment with guaranteed welfare benefits, such as housing, health care, training, pensions, recreation and amenities,[9] has been completely broken and replaced by a genuine labour market (World Bank 2002). Under the government's promotion, the labour market is increasingly characterized by contractual, temporary and informal sector employment, including domestic service work that does not enjoy the same social protection that was found in the central-planned economy era. In this sense, the economic restructuring process is also the process of the subordination of labour protection to economic efficiency.

When China's economy and labour force were based on a socialist planning system, the labour force in the state sector was a permanent labour force. Very little employment – only about 15 per cent of the total employment – was on a casual basis (Naughton 1995). Workers were assigned by the state to enterprises on a permanent basis according to state plans, and they could remain in the same work unit (*danwei*)[10] until they retired. Not only could they stay in a single enterprise for life, but also they could often pass their jobs to their children when they retired (Naughton 1995). Under the system of public ownership and planning of the economy, workers were respected as masters of the country and enjoyed high social and economic security. The work units not only guaranteed lifetime employment, but also provided services such as housing and health care in addition to wages and retirement pensions. This is not to say that the system was perfect for labourers or for economic efficiency. Under the central-planned economy, workers had no freedom to change jobs because each job was considered a contribution to the state, and all occupations were considered equally important. Similarly, enterprises had no right to employ or dismiss workers for efficiency purposes. Workers were assigned to a specific job classification, and enterprises had no authority to reclassify their workers. As Naughton argued, 'it was illegal in principle and impossible in practice' for enterprises to fire workers, and 'quits were almost unknown' (1995: 44). As neither labourers nor employers could choose each other by mutual consent, labour mobility was extremely constrained (Tomba 2002). In 1979, there were only 22,000 total quits and firing of state employees in China, and this number accounted for only 0.03 per cent of the labour force (Naughton 1995). As a result, there was no genuine labour market under such a system. This absence of a genuine labour market is generally associated with problems of low productivity and poor levels of economic efficiency (Tomba 2002). This relatively low productivity reduced the enterprises' ability to create employment opportunities, but since the labour supply increased every year, the number of workers assigned to SOEs and collectives increased accordingly. The redundant worker problem was a serious problem when China began its economic reforms (Institute for Labour Science Studies (MOLSS) 2001).

China's economic reforms are closely linked with its economic development or growth. To promote economic efficiency and attract the flow of foreign capital, the state started restructuring the economy through privatization and deregulation of the labour market. Labour mobility and flexibility become accepted features in the restructuring process. In the 1980s, the state began fostering the growth of the private domestic sector and opening China to international competition through the introduction of foreign-owned enterprises. Later the government gradually granted employment freedom to state and collectively owned enterprises. In 1986, the State Council introduced a contract labour system, under which workers were no longer declared permanent members of state-owned enterprises. Although no mass lay-offs or unemployment occurred until the mid-1990s, enterprises shed large numbers of surplus employees to rectify the drawbacks of the permanent labour system by measures known as 'contractual administration (*hetongzhi guanli*),'[11] 'optimizing regrouping (*youhua zuhe*)'[12] and 'merit employment (*ze you shang gang*)'[13] (Liu 2007). In 1992, under the decision to establish a socialist market economy at its fourteenth National Congress, the CCP officially allowed both the state sector and collective enterprises to lay off surplus workers to enable state-run enterprises to compete more efficiently with non-state ones (Liu 2007).[14]

In 1995 permanent employment was abolished when the Labour Law was enacted. The law stipulated that all workers (whether old or newly recruited) in all types of enterprises had to be employed on a contract basis. Since then all workers have become contractual, and enterprises are now allowed to recruit workers on a contractual, temporary or seasonal basis according to employers' needs. Once again, at its Fifteenth National Congress in 1997, the Party confirmed the decision to reform state-run enterprises by reducing employees.[15] Therefore, since the mid 1990s, enterprises have laid off a great number of workers. In addition, in the face of competition, many state-owned and collective enterprises either closed or privatized, and city workers in state-owned enterprises have been laid-off (*xiagang*) and become unemployed on a large scale (Appleton *et al.* 2002).

As many feminist scholars have argued, throughout these changes women workers experienced a harder time than male workers and were more highly represented among the unemployed (Appleton *et al.* 2002; Du and Dong 2008). This became known among Chinese feminists as the feminization of redundancy. For example, in a survey by the Jiangsu Women's Institute, the researchers uncovered the co-existence of both the feminization of the laid-off workforce and the unlikelihood of women being re-employed (Jin 2004). Studies also show that many laid-off women workers were older in age and had low levels of education. A Hong Kong scholar argued that the lay-off situation of 'older working women who had little skills and had no qualifications beyond high school' was even worse (Yuen-Tsang 1997: 187). These workers faced the triple disadvantage of gender, age and education, and were easily laid off and pushed out of the labour market by state-owned and collective enterprises. A 1987 survey by the Women Workers Committee of the All-China Federation of Trade Unions (ACFTU) found that women accounted for 64 per cent of laid-off workers. Later surveys by the ACFTU found similar figures in the 1990s, demonstrating clearly that the situation had not improved. Official statistics indicate that in 1998, some 48 females were laid off for every 40 males.[16] More recent unemployment figures released by MOLSS indicate that 50 per cent of laid-off workers are women[17] – still a disproportionate amount considering women form roughly 38 per cent of the formal workforce.[18] In 2001, the female registered unemployment rate[19] was 6.4 per cent, which was

1.6 per cent higher than the male's at 4.8 per cent, and accounted for 40 per cent of the registered unemployed population (ILO 2004).

The expansion of unemployment that has affected workers' living conditions and poverty is now no longer solely a rural phenomenon (Gustafsson, Li and Sicular 2008). Once laid off, these workers quickly become the new urban poor. Two main factors contribute to their poverty: They are either only partially paid or not paid at all by their former state sector employers, and government public policy does not provide an adequate safety net to deal with the large amount of unemployment that was the result of the state enterprise reforms (Gustafsson, Li and Sicular 2008). In 1998, Re-employment Service Centres were set up by enterprises to provide laid-off workers with job search services, vocational guidance, training for re-employment and a basic living allowance for a term of three years – the time period when they are in centres (L. Y. Chen 2008; Lee 2010). These centres were financed by enterprises, individuals and society, and the government covered any shortfalls (L. Y. Chen 2008). According to Lee, when this policy ended in 2001, as many as 22.3 million workers were pushed out of enterprises into society without much prospect of finding jobs (Lee 2010). Since 2001, the social security reform allowed enterprises to give a one-off payment to workers deemed redundant, and enterprises would no longer be financially responsible for their laid-off workers' welfare or pensions (Lee 2010). Many laid-off workers were left with a low rate of compensation or no compensation at all (Lee 2010). According to investigations by the State Statistical Bureau, the State Council Research Office, and other units, by 2001 between 20 million and 30 million staff and workers had fallen into poverty nationwide (Solinger 2010). It was estimated that in 2001 between 40 million and 50 million people were living in poverty, accounting for almost 13 per cent of the urban population (Solinger 2010).

To solve their personal economic crisis, laid-off workers have had to resort to various forms of precarious work – the primary form of work available after the economic reforms – since the opportunity of re-employment in public sectors rapidly declined. The Re-Employment Project[20] launched by the government in 1993 and other various retraining programmes have all served to help laid-off workers find jobs in the informal sector as soon as possible. These were primarily jobs of a precarious nature, such as self-employment, subcontracting, part-time and casual labour. While recognizing that employment in the informal sector would absorb many of the retrenched workers during the industrial restructuring, the policymakers advocated strengthening the informal sector in China (L. Y. Chen 2008). Zhu Junyi, an official at the Shanghai Bureau of Labour and Social Security, pointed out, at the China Employment Forum in April 2004, that informal sector employment helped alleviate urban poverty and that for the unemployed, having employment opportunities was more effective than relying on social assistance (as cited in L. Y. Chen 2008). Furthermore, the development of informal sector employment expanded employment opportunities and met the large and growing demands for service in cities. Through the development of the informal sector employment based in neighbourhood communities, service industries can be developed and more jobs created (L. Y. Chen 2008). Zhu also mentioned that the growing of informal sector employment could also develop into more small businesses that would contribute to economic growth and job creation (as cited in L. Y. Chen 2008).

To explain the Chinese government's promotion of informal sector employment, it is necessary to expand upon the various uses of the concept of the informal sector, since China has had different ideas about it in different periods. The term 'informal sector' concept was first used by the ILO in 1972 in a report entitled *Employment, Income and Equality: Strategies to Increase Productive Employment in Kenya* (ILO 1972). According to some other later ILO reports, the term informal sector refers to production units that 'typically operate at a low level of organization, with little or no division between labour and capital ... and on a small scale. ... Labour relations – where they exist – are based mostly on casual employment, kinship or personal and social relations rather than contractual arrangements with formal guarantees' (ILO 1993: N.p.). The ILO/ICFTU (International Confederations of Free Trade Unions) international symposium on the informal sector in 1999 categorized the informal sector workforce into three broad groups: (a) owner-employers of micro-enterprises, which employ a few paid workers, with or without apprentices; (b) own-account workers, who own and operate a one-person business, who work alone or with the help of unpaid workers, generally family members and apprentices; and (c) dependent workers, paid or unpaid, including wage workers in micro-enterprises, unpaid family workers, apprentices, contract labourers, homeworkers and paid domestic workers (ILO 2002). The definition of 'informal sector employment' has been employed in different countries in the world ever since it was introduced. The term was introduced to China in 1980s (Peng and Yao 2004). At that time, in the eyes of Chinese people, only work in the state sectors and collective enterprises was seen as employment. The informality and negative meaning of the term 'informal sector' was generally unacceptable as a term of use by the Chinese government. Considering that the economic reforms were just beginning in the 1980s, in order to avoid the negative impression and resistance of workers to labour market reform, it is understandable that the definition of this form of labour was not formerly recognized by the Chinese government. The Chinese version of 'informal sector employment' mainly refers to the employment in private sectors where there is: (a) a lack of supervision and support from government, no official registration, or is an illegal business; (b) own-account self-employment, or household enterprises, partnership organizations, individual enterprises whose number of workers is less than seven; (c) self-supported production organizations or public welfare labour organizations which aim at creating employment and income and maintaining sustenance for laid-offs and unemployed, supported by local governments; (d) small-scale and low-level organization with basically no division of labour and capital and in low labour productivity; (e) no formal labour contracts, low fringe benefits (Institute for Labour Science Studies, MOLSS 2005).

The difference between the ILO definition and its Chinese use is that the informal sector in China includes both legally registered enterprises and businesses with no legal registration.[21] To erase the negative aspect of informal sector employment, flexible employment is the official definition of new labour market relations recommended and used by the Chinese government. It is a general term for a variety of employment forms that are different from the permanent, stable employment in state enterprises and collective enterprises. Flexible employment includes both informal sector employment and informal employment in the formal sector. Informal employment in the formal sector refers to flexible work arrangements, including short-term temporary employment, part-time employment, dispatching or outsourcing employment, etc. The point of introducing the terminology of 'informal sector employment' particularly as defined by the ILO was to distinguish 'the working poor' from other more stable employed workers and to make their contribution to the economy visible. In contrast, the term 'flexible employment' is used by the Chinese government to identify the newly emerging non-traditional employment forms that have arisen since economic reforms. In China, while 'flexible employment' is the official term used by the government, 'informal sector employment' is mainly used by scholars in academia.

Overall, the government's main purpose is to increase employment, no matter what kind of job it is, and through government promotion many more flexible employment arrangements have emerged in China. The MOLSS survey in 66 cities in 2002 shows that 90 per cent of the re-employment of laid-off workers is characterized as temporary work or hourly work (similar to temporary part-time work in Western countries) (Wang 2004).

Many feminists have focused on the rise of flexible employment and its gendered impact. For instance, based on the Second Chinese Women's Social Status Survey, Jiang Yongping (2005a) argued that women are more likely than men to get into flexible employment. She further pointed out that due to a lack of policy protection there is a huge difference in occupation, income, social security and organization between flexible female labourers and women who have a permanent position; this difference is also obvious between male and female flexibly employed workers. Tan Lin and Li Junfeng's study (2003) also found that there is industry and occupation segregation between male and female flexible employed workers and this segregation is largely reflected in income differences. As some scholars noted, the 'no choice, get a job right away' re-employment approach has led to the decline in women's chances for moving up the occupational ladder and has had an effect on lowering their income and standard of living (Xu 2000: N.p.).

Women workers are called into domestic service

Foucault described the modern capitalist era as 'an era of "biopower"' that is characterized by 'an explosion of numerous and diverse techniques for achieving the subjugation of bodies and the control of population' (1978: 140). What is remarkable in Foucault's notion of biopower is that it defines a state's ability to regulate people's lives. Physical health, hygiene, birth rate and life expectancy become central to state politics and are carefully studied and controlled by the state. Governmental practices attempt to rationalize people's activities. In neoliberal economic logic, people's life should be regulated for the purpose of economic development. Neoliberal economic rationality recognizes that disadvantaged people lack value within the system. The remedy, then, is to find ways so that these people can insert themselves into the system, even if it means as agents to serve the body of people who have value (Anagnost 2004). With this kind of basis for thinking about roles, and perhaps even rights and duties, government facilitates ways for the unprivileged to take care of the privileged. As a result, unprivileged bodies become sites of exploitation for (social) reproduction and, because their labour conditions cannot be guaranteed, their labour is exploited (Anagnost 2004).

Under neoliberal restructuring in China, governmental practice discursively defines laid-off and unemployed workers as appropriate candidates for paid domestic labour, making the current promotion of domestic service a means to help these workers become employed and be an agent in solving their own problems. This market solution to unemployment rests on the idea of 'choice'. The decision to work in the domestic service industry is a choice that women will make to rectify their specific disadvantages. That is, it is their own choice rather than the coercive power of the government authority that leads them to domestic employment. While facilitating laid-off workers' moving into domestic service, the state also simultaneously and paradoxically preserves its power to control these workers' movements by maximizing their flexibility as disposable labourers.

The deployment of unprivileged workers in the paid domestic labour market is gender-specific: while both male and female workers are encouraged to look for precarious employment in the service sector by the government, female laid-off workers are especially encouraged to go back to the private sphere – that is, the home. China's economic reforms have led to an 'inverse migration of women from the public to the private sphere' (Woo 2002: 313). In the 1980s, the mainstream economists' prescription was to 'let women return home' (Zhong 1998: 2) and leave the limited work opportunities to 'the most excellent and most efficient group' (Chen 1999), which was understood to be men. Some mainstream Chinese economists promoted the idea of a single breadwinner model where only one family member in a household would work for pay. This would be accompanied by a 'periodic employment'[22] system for women (Z. Li and Chen 1999; Yu and Liu 1999). Since this prescription was against the gender equality rule under socialism, it was subject to serious objections from the All-China Women's Federation (ACWF) and did not eventually become policy.[23] Against the promotion of periodic employment agenda, the Women's Studies Institute of ACWF specifically established a research project to investigate urban women's employment motivation and their employment needs after giving birth. This project investigated the issue in six cities in 1996.[24] The research results indicated that 88 per cent of women with higher education were strongly against periodic employment and they insisted that women should be respected in their ability to freely make choices. Most interviewees, including both male and female, agreed with the legitimate 90-day maternity leave and they strongly disagreed about the risk of losing their jobs as a consequence of having a longer maternity or paternity leave. Even though some interviewees could accept longer maternity with government or work units providing allowance, only 20 per cent of them agreed to do so if they risked losing their jobs after a longer leave. The main reason for workers' refusal of periodic employment is because they are afraid of losing their jobs, something that would seriously affect their family's standard of living (S. M. Wang and Hu 1997). This research provided first-hand data to ACWF in arguing for women's employment rights. Mainstream economists' promotion of 'women returning home' was temporarily set aside. However, at the end of 2000 and early in 2001, once again to relieve employment pressures, the Chinese government began another round of discussions on adopting a 'periodic employment' system for women (Jiang 2005b). The proposed employment arrangement would allow women to quit the labour force when they got married and gave birth, and to return to the labour market to look for new jobs after their children reached school age. Because of the appeal from women representatives' of the National People's Congress and the National Committee of the Chinese People's Political Consultative Conference, this policy failed to be written into the Tenth Five-Year Plan of National Economy and Social Development (Jiang 2005b; Liu, Zhang and Li 2008). Throughout the discussions, feminists in China clearly insisted on equal employment opportunities for women (Ge 1997; Zhang 1999).

These two open and extensive discussions of the issue of 'women's return to the home' indicate the long-standing policy of the Chinese government regarding women: it would sacrifice women's equal employment rights for what it perceived to be economic necessity, and in the process ignore its international commitment of gender equality.[25] This is in stark contrast to the famous propaganda slogan: 'women hold up half the sky,' which was used to encourage women to move into public production in the socialist Mao era.

Though the government failed to push laid-off and unemployed women back into their own homes to be housewives, current government policies certainly facilitate them being housewives in somebody else's home. Now the government accepts mainstream economists' claim that there is a bright future for women who work in the informal service sector and also their suggestion that women's employment form should vary considerably from past practices. This means the government sees increased part-time employment and household employment as solutions to women's labour problems (Hu 2000). The Chinese government uses specific discourses to glorify what are essentially poor jobs. Slogans such as 'home service is fit for unemployed women workers', and 'community service benefits the nation and the people', are used in an attempt to get unemployed women to change their ideas about employment. The minister of the MOLSS, Zhang Zuoji, states at a nationwide job training and employment conference in 2000 that re-employment would make a breakthrough if a Chinese domestic service market was formed (X. D. Liu 2000). According to the minister, this would be a breakthrough not only because domestic service is a large market, but also because unemployed workers' education levels and ages match the profile for home service work (Liu 2000). Many training programmes for women are designed to get them into occupations such as domestic service and childcare or to encourage them to set up small businesses in the service sector, such as a grocery store or a beauty salon (Fang, Granrose and Kong 2006). According to Chen's study, Shanghai was the first to open Re-employment Service Centres in China. Through these centres the Shanghai government emphasized gender-specific training. The training that was specifically targeted at women included 'in-homework, beauty and hair dressing, image design, costume design and costume making, jewellery design, flower arrangement and tea performance' (L. Y. Chen 2008).

In helping unemployed and laid-off women workers get relief from poverty and become re-employed, the ACWF and local women's federations have done a lot of work, such as providing training and micro-credit loans.[26] However, despite all their efforts, women's federations have also helped unemployed women become re-employed in the domestic service sector. In 1999, together with the Ministry of Civil Affairs, the MOLSS, the Ministry of Urban-rural Development, the State Administration of Taxation and the State Internal Trade Bureau, the ACWF started a nationwide programme – 'Women's Community Services Program' – to help laid-off women get re-employed and meet urban residents' demand.[27] The ACWF currently runs 465 domestic service agencies in 16 provinces and cities (ACWF and ILO 2009). It has created an online internet platform to share supply and demand information for domestic service agencies and domestic workers; and it also organizes national conferences to facilitate communication among the affiliated domestic service agencies. ACWF cooperates with labour bureaus at different levels to provide vocational training and issue certificates to trained domestic workers. In so doing, ACWF aims to improve the quality of service offered by these agencies, and to create a domestic service brand image in the industry. Through these programmes, many unemployed and laid-off women workers have been trained to become domestic service workers. Big Sister Liu is such an example (Interview, 8 November 2007). She is from Liaoning province, an old industrial base in the northeastern part of China. Because her work unit was not making profits, she and many other co-workers were laid off in the late 1990s. She said that there were few employment opportunities because of her age (early 40s), and because she did not have much education it is very hard for her to learn new skills. Her family has been experiencing financial difficulty since she was laid off, so she desperately needs money. But she also wants to be able to pay for her son's high school tuition fees in hopes that her son would have a different fate from hers. She knows that going to a university is the only way that he will have a better life. To ensure her child goes to a university, the family is now investing money in him to take extra lessons in maths, physics and English. All of this is very costly. Following the recommendation of her local women's federation, she came to Beijing in 2003 to do domestic service work. Many women like big sister Liu who are still relatively young, only in their early 40s, need work to be able to pay for their children's education. In addition, they have to pay social insurance such as pensions and medical insurance on their own.

Because of the income differences between different provinces and between big cities and small cities or towns, more and more unemployed and laid-off women workers choose to leave their hometown and migrate to big cities such as Beijing and Shanghai to do domestic service work. This trend is growing. In the last few years, some laid-off workers from Hebei and the northeast provinces, such as Jilin and Liaoning, have come to Beijing. A staff member who works for the Migrant Women's Club (MWC), an NGO that serves migrant women workers in Beijing, explained the phenomenon:

> Since the wages of domestic workers are increasing bit by bit, and also because these laid-off workers have to pay for their children to go to high school or universities, they choose to do domestic service, which can pay them a little better, for example, ¥1,000 or ¥1,500 (per month).[28] Some of them choose to do *yuesao*,[29] since the wage of *yuesao* is even higher (¥3,000–3,500 per month).
>
> (Interview, 12 October 2007)

It appears that the government propaganda has worked and many women have entered domestic service. Those laid-off women workers who do not respond to the government's call and remain unemployed are blamed as having backward notions of employment and are told that their notion of waiting for (*deng*), relying on (*kao*) and asking from (*yao*) government need to be abandoned. The message from the mass media is that the workers should clearly understand that the 'iron rice bowl' is gone forever in this era of global competition and that they should be thankful for any jobs that the government may have created for them.

The pressure laid-off women experience can be intense, particularly during periods of economic crisis. With unemployment rates high, many fear that if they do not take up the domestic service work opportunities now, they may not even be able to keep their 'mud rice bowl' in the future. In my interviews with some laid-off workers they all expressed a sense of loss at losing their 'iron rice bowl' during the planned economy era, but they also indicated that even this work was not secure. In particular, they worried that university students and Filipino domestic workers might compete with them in the domestic service industry. These worries are not groundless. In recent years, the field of Home Economics has been developing in China. To satisfy some employers' high tastes, some universities and colleges such as Jilin Agricultural University and Hebei College of Industry and Technology have established a Home Economics department to train high-level domestic service personnel.[30] This means there will be university graduates joining this market in the near future. In addition, Filipino domestic workers have appeared in big cities such as Beijing[31] and Shanghai (Sun 2002). More than one interviewee admired the Filipino domestic workers' English fluency.

Because of economic globalization, after China's entry into the World Trade Organization (WTO), more and more transnational corporations have started businesses in China. The domestic service industry in China is now aiming to provide services for the representatives of international capital. Being able to speak English and work in foreigners' homes leads to better pay. Filipino domestic workers' professional attitude and English fluency have now become models that are used to educate Chinese domestic workers. Xiao Hong, a domestic worker from Sichuan province, told me that she had seen many Filipino domestic workers in her former employer's community, which is a high-end international apartment. She said:

> The Filipino domestic workers are all registered in Hong Kong and brought to Beijing from there. I have seen many of them. Ai ya! They speak English very well. I admire them so much! They can make 2,000 to 3,000 dollars a month! US dollars! We Chinese domestic workers, whether laid-off workers or university students, cannot catch up with them. First, they are capable in every aspect. Second, they have a good attitude about work, for instance, [Filipino domestic workers think] 'If I do it I must do it well, otherwise I will not do it. I have to be responsible to my employer.'
>
> (Interview, 29 November 2007)

From these conversations, we can see that some laid-off workers have identified with the government's doctrine that they now must do domestic service because they do not have enough accumulated human capital. But added to this is the warning that if they do not work hard, their 'rice bowls' are in jeopardy because of competition from Filipino and well-trained women in the field. Nonetheless, the Chinese workers are used to the state's manipulation of their fates and future. For example, some workers I interviewed worriedly asked whether they would be allowed to keep their hard-earned jobs during the world Olympic Games in August 2008 in Beijing. Without formal Beijing residency, workers, especially rural migrants who do not have a temporary resident permit in Beijing, are routinely sent back to their hometown for government temporary population control during nationwide or worldwide events in Beijing.

While they may not have lost their work opportunities during the Olympic Games, their employment in domestic service sector was affected by the worldwide financial and economic crisis that began in 2008. This has been proved by a small group activity named 'how far is the financial crisis from you' organized by the Migrant Women's Club (see Chapter 6). In this activity, some domestic workers mentioned, 'people are cutting their spending, some employers who used two domestic workers before last year, now only hire one or hire nobody at all' (MWC 2009b: N.p.). In the summer of 2009, during another trip to Beijing, I also talked to some of the domestic workers I had previously interviewed. They told me that employers were reducing their demand for domestic service and that there were fewer job opportunities available than before, simply because some families were no longer able to afford to hire domestic workers.

Conclusion

Affected by economic globalization and neoliberal thinking, previous formulations of social and gender equality under the socialist planned economy have been quickly abandoned in the process of reform in China. The adopting of market mechanisms through a variety of means, such as rural industrialization, foreign investment and trade, the development of private enterprises, increased managerial autonomy for the state and collectively owned enterprises and the promotion of service industries has created a stable supply of domestic service workers in rural and urban China. While there has been an outward labour migration for women in rural areas, there has been an inverse migration of women from the public domain to the private sphere in urban areas (Woo 2002). The state of China, like other states in the world, plays a vital role in regulating the flow of labour and the conditions of employment and in facilitating or impeding accumulation processes, which frame the employment of domestic workers. In addition, from the history of the development of socialist China since 1949, we can see that women's labour is treated as a reserve pool – when labour supply was low in Mao's era, women were called from the home to the production domain, while, during the economic reform process, labour surpluses pushed women back into the private domain. The way socialist China dealt with women's labour power for economic purposes and the way Marx mentioned that capitalists dealt with the unemployed in a capitalist society are no different in nature. Therefore, it is safe to say that gender equality is subject to economic development, and the current extension of market relations in China make women's situation more unequal than it was under a planned socialist system.

4 Childcare crisis after economic reforms

> We found a nanny right after my child was born since there was nobody in my family who could help me. I had a late marriage, so I doubled my maternity leave to six months. After that, I went back to work and my child was left to the nanny during daytime.
> (Interview with a domestic worker employer, 25 October 2007)

> I feel that you Beijing people are really busy. The little girl's [the one she is looking after] mom often has to work overtime at her work unit. Sometimes she has meetings till midnight. She is too busy to take care of this child.
> (Interview with a domestic worker, 3 November 2007)

Neoliberalism-related economic reforms and restructuring have created not only the supply of domestic workers but also a great demand for domestic workers in cities in China. There are two main reasons for this. The most important reason is that government retreated from its social reproduction responsibilities as a result of the massive policy changes associated with economic restructuring. The government reduced expenditures on public services such as health care, education and childcare, and either privatized these services or introduced measures to expand and create new markets for them. These actions have inevitably caused a great care gap in city households, something that is akin to what is happening in Western society under neoliberal reforms. Western feminists have argued that the marketization and individualization of public social services create significant care gaps, particularly in childcare (Folbre 1994). Similarly, a recent study in China shows that private markets for childcare and early education are inadequate for working women, especially women from low-income families (Dong et al. 2009).

The second main reason for the increased demand in domestic labour is that the increasingly competitive labour market, after market-oriented reforms, has intensified the workload for workers. This also means that women have to spend more time at waged work, as is clear from the interviews quoted at the beginning of this chapter. This situation is further exacerbated by the demographic transition in China: while the fertility rate of women is declining with the 'one child policy', there is a rising ratio of the elderly (above 65) in the population (Dong *et al.* 2009). It is estimated that by 2050, the ratio of the elderly in the total population will reach 25 per cent (Hussain 2007). Increasing elder care also has an impact on women's labour force participation (Dong *et al.* 2009). To remain in the labour market and maintain family livelihoods, some women have to hire others to take care of their young, elderly and sick.

This chapter will examine the transition of China's welfare system, specifically, using childcare policy as an example to demonstrate how economic reform policies in China have created the demand for domestic service. The childcare policy is the most important element for women's equal participation in the labour market, and it once was a significant policy tool in China during the planned economic era to boost women's participation in the labour force. In this chapter, I will argue that the changed direction of childcare policies in recent years has not attempted to achieve an equal gender regime with both men and women acting as workers and caregivers. Rather, women still have to endure a double burden in order to participate in the paid labour market.

China's social welfare regime in the state-planned economy

In dealing with social welfare regime analysis in China, an awareness of welfare state typology in Western society would help with understanding the changes associated with the shift to the market mechanism. The theoretical modelling of Western welfare states by feminists can contribute to the understanding of complexities faced by the problems of Chinese social welfare provision.

In Western society, the development of welfare states is based on the emergence of workers as an organized class and the sharpened class conflicts (Therborn 2003). As Therborn argued, as a result of class conflicts, the welfare state in its early beginnings consolidated firmly on the male breadwinner and attempts to eliminate the risks, such as unemployment, ill health, industrial accidents and retirement that could jeopardize a man's capacity to support himself and his dependants. The welfare state also assumed the domestic presence of a housewife and her capacities in providing primary care for young children, the sick and injured, and the elderly. She concludes that welfare states were based on the twin principles of full-time male employment and stable heterosexual families. The analysis further classified the welfare state according to a typology that focuses on the strength of the male breadwinner model in terms of the traditional division of labour between the sexes and its implications for social entitlements. For example, in constructing their typology, Lewis and Ostner focus on how women are treated in the social security system, the level of social-service provision, particularly childcare, and the position of married women in the labour market. They argue for considering policy regimes in terms of their different levels of commitment to a male breadwinner–female housewife household form, which in ideal-typical form would 'find married women excluded from the labour market, firmly subordinated to their husbands for the purpose of social security entitlements and tax, and expected to undertake the work of caring (for children and other dependants) at home without public support' (Lewis 1992: 162). National social policies rest on underlying assumptions about who is the primary and who the secondary breadwinner or caregiver. The resulting typology is 'strong', 'moderate' or 'modified', and 'weak' male breadwinner states. Ireland, Britain and Germany are countries in which a strong male breadwinner model is in place since these countries tend to treat adult women as dependent wives for the purpose of social entitlement (Ostner and Lewis 1995: 186). In contrast, Belgium and France are countries that follow a 'moderate' male breadwinner model since each of the family's members is treated as a 'corporate individual' to be nurtured by social policy (Ostner and Lewis: 186). Sweden (Lewis 1992), and Denmark (Ostner and Lewis 1995) are seen to follow a 'weak' male breadwinner model because social policy has tended to define women primarily as workers instead of wives and mothers (Ostner and Lewis 1995: 186). For Sainsbury, a major shortcoming of the 'breadwinner model' is its concentration on the husband as the principal beneficiary and the main source of women's social entitlements (Sainsbury 1996). While clustering the Netherlands, the UK, and the USA together with respect to the breadwinner ideology and its effects on social provision, she suggests Sweden is a variant of the male breadwinner model – while not a complete individual model.

In contrast to the Western models, after the new China was founded in 1949 as a socialist country, the Chinese state promoted women's equal participation in the labour workforce, as I have shown in the first two chapters. Women were treated as equals to men as breadwinners. The state also made a great effort to provide care services for families, making the Chinese model during the socialist period a dual breadwinner/government carer model.

Under a central-planned socialist economy, public ownership of the means of production in industry and agriculture provided the basis for public social welfare support. In urban areas, welfare was tied to work. The work unit, or *danwei*, provided support to its workers from 'head to toe' and 'from cradle to grave' (Wong 2001: 38). In rural areas, people's communes and brigades provided work for the peasants as well as social and welfare programmes. As some scholars have argued, this organized dependence on both work and state support was celebrated as the victory of socialism (Wong 2001).

Welfare provision in the pre-reform period in urban areas

In urban areas, based on public ownership and direct government intervention, the Chinese welfare system has been historically based on a work-based welfare system since employment security and occupational welfare benefits were directly associated with occupational status during the socialist era (S. Y. Chen 1996). Chen argues that the state took a leading responsibility by making welfare policies, funding various programmes by profit or tax deductions, and monitoring their implementation by direct and indirect administrative interventions. The *danwei*, or work unit, usually acted on behalf of the state to implement these policies (Chen 1996). Urban welfare support provided workers with a lifetime of employment and work-based benefits, from pension to health care, housing, education and childcare. The most common type of urban work unit was the SOE, and it provided welfare benefits and services to which workers were entitled to receive from the state. There would be either no or very few needs that would not be included when a person was covered by the benefits associated with *danwei* (Chen 1996).

These comprehensive welfare benefits were guaranteed through labour insurance, labour protection and other occupational welfare regulations. The Regulations Governing Labour Insurance in the People's Republic of China was promulgated by the Central Government Administration Council in 1951, and first implemented in enterprises with 100 or more workers and staff.[1] The labour insurance covered employees' illness or injury, as well as employees' medical expenses, including those associated with childbirth and funerals of family members (Frazier 2002). It also distributed pensions to retirees based on earnings and years of service at the enterprise (Frazier 2002). In 1953, the Ministry of Labour revised the regulations to extend the coverage to a larger section of SOEs by issuing the Revised Draft of the Rules for the Implementation of the Regulations Governing Labour Insurance.[2] Later, in 1957, the Ministry of Public Health issued the Regulations Governing the Treatment of Occupational Diseases, accounting for the recognition and treatment of occupational diseases and associated insurance and welfare issues (Chen 1996).[3] These regulations provided every worker in a work unit with full welfare benefits. To female workers, besides the specific articles about women's maternity leave initiated in the 1951 labour insurance regulations, the State Council specifically issued the Notice on Female Worker and Staff's Maternity Leave to restate maternity leave and full wage payment for female workers in 1955.

According to these regulations, both male workers and female workers enjoyed full coverage of welfare benefits. The insurance programme operated through the enterprise, and enterprise-based unions served the welfare needs of workers (Frazier 2002). Welfare expenditures of the enterprise were directly counted into production costs (Chen 1996), and were collected from the enterprise budget or deducted from the total salary outlays (Frazier 2002; G. G. Liu *et al.* 2004). Workers themselves, as the beneficiaries, were not required to pay insurance premiums (Lin 2009). The benefits were not only provided for insured employees but were also extended to their lineal dependants (Lin 2009). Collectively owned and private sector enterprises also followed the labour insurance policy in providing welfare benefits for their employees (Liu *et al.* 2004). Financed through public budget, the state also established a social insurance programme for government institutions and other publicly owned organizations based on similar principles that served 'government employees, their dependents, veterans, educators, and college students' (Liu *et al.* 2004: 39).

The provision of pensions was mandatory for the enterprise and retirees were provided with not only pensions, but also medical benefits, housing and sometimes personal help (Chen 1996). Retirement ages were 60 for males, 55 for female cadres, and 50 for female workers (Chen 1996; Lin 2009; Frazier 2010). These guidelines were first established in the 1951 labour insurance regulations, and remained unchanged during the period of the economic reforms until today

(Frazier 2010). A 15-year contribution was required for a full pension payment (Lin 2009). In addition, the government provided support for the elderly who had no children and no relatives on whom they could depend, and for those who could not work and who had no other source of income with direct welfare support in urban areas (Chen 1996). There were two ways that the government provided support for these elderly: through institutional services that were free of charge and through home-based support (Chen 1996). The provision of this social welfare was the duty of Civil Affairs Administration (Chen 1996).

During the centrally planned socialist era, health care was provided through labour insurance. Workers were ensured access to basic health care needs, including both outpatient and inpatient services. Workers injured or disabled during work were entitled to free hospitalization and medical care as well as paid sick leave (Chen 1996). Work units also had their own clinics as well as hospitals to provide primary care and comprehensive medical services (Chen 1996). For example, before economic reforms, about 40 per cent of all general hospital beds were in the state-owned industrial system (Naughton 2007). Workers' lineal dependants, such as children or elderly relatives, could enjoy extended health care insurance as well (Liu, Zhang and Li 2010).

In terms of education, 70 per cent of state enterprises ran schools of some kind; therefore, workers' children could easily get access to primary and school education (Naughton 2007). Childcare facilities were also a popular feature of many work units.

Housing was regarded as a part of state welfare provisioning rather than as a commodity (Y.P. Wang 2003). Most large state enterprises and institutions built residential quarters adjacent to their workplace. Public housing was available to employees and rents were set extremely low. Both male workers and female workers had equal rights to housing. In the mid-1950s, the workers and staff in the industrial sector paid approximately 4.7 per cent of the standard wage for rent (Zhang and Zhang as cited in P. N. S. Lee 1995). The rental payments were reduced three times thereafter – during the Great Leap Forward, the early 1960s and during the mid-1970s (Lee 1995). The last reduction prior to the economic reform meant workers were paying ¥0.13 per square metre (Zhang and Zhang as cited in Lee 1995).

Through work units, the government provided not only welfare benefits, but also service facilities, such as hospitals and schools, as well as dining halls and sometimes even movie theatres. In addition to these facilities, workers and staff in the SOEs, which accounted for 78.3 per cent of all the working population in 1978, were also granted 'travel allowances, subsidies for bathing and haircuts and health care fees' that covered daily needs (Chen 1996: 66). During the pre-reform period, employment in cities provided workers with a certain level of comprehensive welfare that in some respects covered almost every aspect of human necessity.

Welfare provision in rural areas

The welfare needs of rural residents were taken care of by rural collectives. During the 1950s, a three-level administration system – the productive team, brigade and commune – was organized (Lin 2009). The system served a variety of functions, including social, economic and welfare functions (Waller 1981). Unlike the urban welfare system, which was guaranteed by the state through work units, the rural collectives funded the rural welfare system themselves and this funding was available only if the collectives generated a surplus from the sale of agricultural produce. As a result, the welfare for those working in rural areas was considerably below the standard of those working in urban centres. Nevertheless, this system provided basic services for rural residents, such as the 'five guarantees' scheme in addition to health care. The 'five guarantees' scheme was established in 1956 and provided the five basic needs of 'food, clothing, medical care, housing and funeral expenses for the elders without supporters, the widowed and the totally disabled' (Lin 2009: 249).

Primary health care was broadly available in rural areas during the planned economy period and peasants had access to basic health-care facilities. Rural residents were covered by Cooperative Medical Systems (CMSs), which were established during the collective movement after 1958 (Zhong and Gustafsson 2008). CMSs were jointly funded by government and rural collective organizations (Guo, Tan and Zhu 2009). In this period, new hospitals were opened at the rural county and township levels and new clinics at the village level in the three-level primary health-care network. Some villages were serviced by 'barefoot doctors' – who, after short medical training courses, spent roughly half their time doing medical work and the other half in agricultural work. This made it easier for rural residents to get access to health care (Zhong and Gustafsson 2008). At the end of the 1970s, CMSs covered 85 per cent of the rural population (Guo *et al.* 2009). This system ensured that rural residents had access to preventive health services, health education outreach and primary care at relatively low cost to the economy (Chen and Standing 2007).

The rural collectives also provided public service facilities. For example, childcare centres were opened for families and during the Great Leap Forward movement, communal dining halls were initiated.

Overall, through these measures in urban and rural areas, the state successfully established a social welfare regime that included care responsibilities supporting both males and females as breadwinners.

As childcare policy is particularly important for women to be fully involved in the labour force, I will use childcare policy as a specific example to demonstrate how Chinese state policy has changed from attempts to foster a dual breadwinner/ state carer model to dual breadwinner/family and market carer model.

Childcare policy in the socialist era

During the socialist era, childcare was a part of a near-universal public service. The government made a great effort to provide care for children from infants to pre-schoolers. In this public care model, the state took direct responsibility for the caring of children, an initiative that allowed women to work outside the home. The childcare policy in China was always connected with the liberation of women and the economy in ideological terms.

The CCP had a long history of using childcare as a tool to liberate women's labour power. Even as early as 1927 the leaders in the old revolutionary base, Jiangxi Province, suggested opening childcare and children's nurturing centres to improve children's social education and liberate women (Tang and Kou 2003: 23). During the Anti-Japanese War and the Liberation War in the 1930s and 1940s, opening nurseries to help women became widely popular in revolutionary strongholds such as Jiangxi and Shaanxi-Gansu-Ningxia.[4] On 29 June 1937, the *Xinhua Daily* published an article, 'The organization and construction of the border region government', in which the development of nurseries and canteens to promote women's full liberation was addressed. There were many other reports in newspapers at that time about the significance of opening childcare centres, and party leaders like Mao Zedong and Zhu De were very supportive of the development of childcare centres. They even made personal donations to the first childcare centre of the Shaanxi-Gansu-Ningxia border region (Tang and Kou 2003).

During this time childcare consisted of not only daycare but also boarding childcare centres. The experiences of the old revolutionary bases were widely publicized to other revolutionary bases where the CCP dominated. For example, from 1945 to 1949, when the new China was founded, a number of boarding childcare centres based on experiences in Yan'an were opened in the northeastern part of China (Tang and Kou 2003). In rural areas, public day nurseries also became available to women farmers. Because of the childcare centres in the old revolutionary bases, women's labour power was freed from a major responsibility and women were able, as a result, to plan an important role in the winning of the CCP-led Anti-Japanese War and the Liberation War. Women's labour was needed and clearly they could be available only if their children had care provided by the state.

In fact, during the period of the Republic of China, before the CCP won power, there had also been childcare centres. But those centres were mainly for early public education of children from wealthier families, namely, bourgeois families. In this case, children's education was the priority; liberating women had not yet become a political goal. Working-class families, which consisted of the majority of the population, could not afford to send their children to these childcare centres. It is not hard to imagine that there were very few childcare centres during this period. According to the statistics, there were only 1,301 childcare centres in all of China in 1949, and in total 130,213 children were enrolled in these centres, and the number of daycare teachers was 2,505 (China National Society of Early Childhood Education (CNSECE) 1999, 2003).

After the new China was founded in 1949, the Chinese government continued the tradition inherited from wartime to liberate women from domestic work and called on them to contribute to the socialist construction of the society equally with men. In 1952, the Ministry of Education enacted the Act of Tentative Specifications on Childcare, which specified that the childcare centres' task was to

> ... educate pre-schoolers and make their body and mind fully developed before entering elementary schools; at the same time, lighten mothers' duties

towards children in order for them to have time to participate in political life, production labour and cultural educational activities. . . .

(CNSECE 1999: 49)

To provide convenience to working parents, the policy stipulated that childcare centres should operate on a full-time basis and be open from 8 to 12 hours a day with no winter or summer holidays. Opening more boarding childcare centres was also encouraged.

Although pre-school education was considered an important task of childcare centres, their main function in the early period of socialist China was to solve problems for employed women. This is evident from the social welfare nature of nurseries and childcare centres. In the 1953 Revised Draft of the Rules for the Implementation of the Regulations Governing Labour Insurance, the State Council of the central government made it clear that enterprises should open collective labour insurance entities, such as nurseries and childcare centres, and other social amenities like baths, barbershops and so on. The Regulations stated that the goal of childcare centres and nurseries was to provide labour security and social welfare to workers. There also were specific measures to ensure children of working-class families could receive childcare. For example, a child whose parents both worked and had nobody to take care of him or her at home was given priority for a placement (He and Jiang 2007). Nursing and teaching fees were reduced or revoked for families with financial difficulties and childcare centres were opened in workers' residential districts (He and Jiang, 2007).

As both a public service and a welfare measure, childcare centres developed very rapidly in China. The state and municipal governments not only directly funded childcare facilities through educational departments but also encouraged work units – specifically party or government organizations, armies and state-owned enterprises and institutions – to open their own on-site childcare centres. These two types formed the majority of the childcare and nursery facilities in cities in China. In 1952, they accounted for 73.85 per cent of total childcare facilities.[5] In the following years, they continued to be the dominant types in cities.

There were more children per family at that time than during the recent three decades, but the availability of public childcare centres greatly relieved the double burden of women. Just as a mother, wife and full-time member of the staff of the Chinese Medical Association said in 1972, 'Chinese women need kindergartens to work for the socialist revolution' (Sidel 1972: 37). These centres provided high-quality service at very low prices. For example, the best-quality ones, which were run by educational departments, cost less than one sixth of a couple's monthly income on average at the end of the 1960s.[6] Work units' childcare facilities cost even less for workers due to their welfare nature. There was only a small charge for the child's care and the number of meals (daycare offered three meals a day) the child was to have at the care centres (Sidel 1972). To solve the conflict between infant care and work, nurseries accepted infants who were 56 days old and above since after 56 days of maternity leave, the mothers usually returned to work. From this time until the child could enter primary school at age seven, the mother could use the public child-care facilities that had been provided in work units, such as the nursing room, the nursery and the kindergarten (Sidel 1972). With an infant, the most usual thing for the mother was to take the infant to work with her and leave him or her in a nursing room. Since most mothers breast-fed their babies, this arrangement was the most convenient. Mothers of infants less than one year old were allowed to feed them twice a day and each time spend 30 minutes in the nursing room (Liu, Zhang and Li 2010). When the child was a year and a half old, the parents could bring him or her to a nursery. Even when a child was sick, the mother did not have to ask for leave since the nurseries had nurses to look after sick children (Liu, Zhang and Li 2008). The children attended kindergarten from age three until they entered primary school at seven. While parents often had the option to let the children be taken care of by a grandparent at home, over 80 per cent of the children in urban areas attended kindergarten (Sidel 1972). In Sidel's study, she told a story about a working mother with three children – thirteen, eight and three: the oldest one was in junior middle school and the eight-year-old was in primary school; they both ate in the dining halls near their home and were in schools six days a week; the three-year-old was in a 24-hour kindergarten. The mother's full-time work was never affected by child-care responsibilities during work hours and she only brought the kindergartener home for the day when she was free on Sundays. My own interview with a current domestic worker employer – Zhou – also proved the same point. Zhou told me that her mother worked for a big factory in Xi'an, Shaanxi province, and that Zhou was sent to the factory nursery when she was three months old. Her two siblings were also sent to the nursery at a few months of age. She said that her mother never complained that having three young children affected her ability to work (Interview, 8 October 2007).

Public-run childcare and nursery facilities were not the only types of childcare that existed. In 1955, the Chinese government proposed a 'walk on two legs (*liang tiao tui zou lu*)' policy, which was the development of both public and private childcare facilities (He and Jiang 2007: 5). The various childcare and nursery facilities included those collectively run by neighbourhood committees in cities, and by production teams and brigades in rural areas, and also by private daycare centres. In cities, childcare centres located in the neighbourhoods where people lived took either the children who lived in the district or children whose parents worked in the work units in the district. Collectively owned childcare facilities developed in massive numbers without precedent, primarily in rural areas, during the Great Leap Forward Movement from 1958 to 1960, when all the Chinese people were called to participate *en masse* in public socialist construction. During this period housewives were organized to work in neighbourhoods in cities, and peasants were organized to join communes and work collectively in the country-side. Communal dining halls and childcare centres were widely set up in rural areas at that time. Between 1956 and 1960, the number of childcare centres increased 42.4 times and the number of children in childcare centres increased 27.1 times (see Table 4.1), with the biggest increases occurring in the countryside (Tang 2005). From the period beginning in January 1961, under the state policy of adjustment (*tiaozheng*), consolidation (*gonggu*), enrichment (*chongshi*) and improvement (*tigao*), a change occurred that affected the number of children who would receive state-supported childcare. Those childcare centres running in good condition were kept and those in bad condition were closed (Hou 2004; Tang 2005). After this policy change, from 1961 to 1965 (before the Cultural Revolution), the number of childcare centres and the number of children in the centres dropped back down to 1956 levels. These changes can be seen in Table 4.1. Some statistics were not available in the several years during the Cultural Revolution in 1966–76. The Cultural Revolution has been called the 'ten-year of chaos' because of its brutal political and class struggles, and the significant losses it brought to the country and the Chinese people. But in this red era (*huohong de niandai*),[7] accompanied by Chairman Mao's slogan 'women can lift up half the sky', childcare centres and nurseries should have played an important role in liberating women's labour power. Childcare and pre-school education, as some Chinese scholars note, was reinvigorated (Hou 2004; Tang 2005). Sidel's study shows that during the Cultural Revolution, many nurseries and kindergartens opened to support women's production work. There were childcare facilities that ran from 6:00 a.m. to 6:00 p.m., and children could even stay until 9:00 p.m. if the parents had a meeting in the evening, and were able to spend the night if parents were on night shift. There were also 24-hour nurseries and kindergartens, and parents could bring in their child at any time around their work shift (Sidel 1972). Although childcare in rural areas seemed more casual and relaxed than childcare in the cities, in some communes, each production team had its own nursery and kindergarten and the nursery generally took children from one month to two years of age and the kindergarten from age two to six (Sidel 1972). Another pattern of childcare in the rural areas was for mothers to place their children in the nursery or kindergarten during the harvest or during other busy seasons when the women were needed to work in the field (Sidel 1972). Table 4.1 show the development of childcare facilities from 1949 to 1978, when the market-oriented economic reforms started.

It was clear that domestic work and care responsibilities was still hampering women from 'full, wholehearted participation in public service' and 'in any production labour', especially in rural areas, and the facilities in the planned economy era were not enough to meet the needs of all parents and children (Soong Ching Ling as cited in Sidel 1972: 184). However, with long hours of operation and flexible arrangements to meet different parents' needs, they did greatly ease the contradiction between paid work and care responsibilities (Liu, Zhang, and Li 2008). While childcare was mainly seen as a women's issue, work units' childcare centres were encouraged to take male workers' children as well. Therefore, childcare facilities served both male workers and female workers. Childcare as a gender equality issue was part of the government's motive behind childcare services mainly so that women had equal opportunity to participate in social production with men.

However, significant changes have been underway since the 1980s, especially in the mid-1990s, when market-oriented reforms started in state-owned enterprises

Table 4.1 Various childcare facilities in China from 1949 to 1978

Year	Childcare facilities (thousands)				Children in facilities (thousands)			
	Total	Run by Educational departments	Run by Work units	Other ownership*	Total	Run by Educational departments	Run by Work units	Other ownership
1949	1.3	0.8		0.5	130.0	93.0		37.0
1950	1.8				140.0			
1951	4.8				382.0			
1952	6.5	4.5	0.3	1.7	424.0	287.0	27.0	110.0
1953	5.5				430.0			
1954	6.3				484.0			
1955	7.1				562.0			
1956	18.5	4.5	2.5	11.5	1,081.0	392.0	185.0	504.0
1957	16.4				1,088.0			
1958	695.3	4.5	4.8	686.0	29,501.0	449.0	369.0	28,683.0
1959	532.0				21,722.0			
1960	785.0	11.0	282.0	492.0	29,331.0	811.0	14,459.0	14,061.0
1961	60.3				2,896.0			
1962	17.6				1,446.0			
1963	16.6				1,472.0			
1964	17.7				1,589.0			
1965	19.2	4.4	6.3	8.5	1,713.0	516.0	634.0	563.0
1973	45.5				2,450.0			
1974	40.3				2,638.0			
1975	171.7				6,200.0			
1976	442.7				13,955.0			
1977	261.9				8,968.0			
1978	164.0				7,878.0			

Source: Tang (2005: 39); China National Society of Early Childhood Education (CNSECE) (2003: 33).

Note: * Other ownership refers to collectively owned childcare centres in both cities and rural areas.

and institutions. Childcare services have gradually shifted from public provision of welfare under socialism to a free-market system of childcare financing, pricing, and delivery. These changes have caused childcare crises for some working parents.

Market economy and the childcare burden

Under the pressure of economic development, the Chinese government, like other governments worldwide, has been actively involved in promoting public sector restructuring, restructuring key social programmes and severe welfare reduction. In childcare service reforms, privatization is one of the most commonly advocated strategies in China. Changes to childcare services have involved two different types of privatization: the shift of services to the private sector, and the shift of government responsibilities to individual men and women and their families.

After economic reforms and after having opened China to the world, the Chinese government tried to shy away from its public childcare responsibility by reducing funding and other support in order to encourage the marketization of childcare. Overall government input in early childhood education is poor. For instance, from 1999 to 2001, public funding for early childhood education accounted for only 1.3 per cent of the total funding in education (CNSECE 2003). Also, work unit childcare centres, one of the major childcare arrangements for employed urban citizens, have been gradually eliminated since the mid-1990s. This led to the emergence of new childcare arrangements such as private childcare centres. In the early 1990s, the number of childcare centres was almost at the same level as in the 1980s, but from 1996 to 2003, both the number of centres and the number of children at the childcare centres decreased annually (Table 4.2). The declining numbers since 1995 have been closely associated with the rapid closing down of childcare centres along with the increase in state-owned enterprise reforms starting from the mid-1990s. The gradually increasing numbers of facilities and children in the facilities since 2002 does not mean that government input has increased. On the contrary, it reflects the steady increase of private childcare in the last few years as the old public childcare system has been gradually privatized. Table 4.2 shows the changes from 1979 to 2007.

Altogether, the changes have resulted in an insufficient public provision of childcare services and have further threatened gender equality and class equality in China.

The transformation of public childcare centres

Public childcare centres funded by the state and municipal governments, which are fewer in number compared with work unit centres, were the best-quality facilities under the planned economy era. These centres were the key schools for pre-school children. The facilities and teaching staff were so exemplary that they served as observation laboratories for the staff from other nurseries

Table 4.2 The statistics of childcare development in China, 1979–2007

Year	Childcare facilities (thousands)	Children in facilities (thousands)	Children age 0–6 (thousands)[a]	Children in childcare age 0–6(%)
1979	166.5	8,792.0		
1980	170.4	11,508.0		
1981	130.3	10,562.0		
1982	122.1	11,131.0		
1983	136.3	11,403.0		
1984	166.5	12,947.0		
1985	172.3	14,797.0		
1986	173.4	16,290.0		
1987	176.8	18,078.0		
1988	171.8	18,545.0		
1989	172.6	18,477.0		
1990	172.3	19,722.0		
1991	164.5	22,093.0		
1992	172.5	24,282.0		
1993	165.2	25,525.0		
1994	174.7	26,303.0	93,664.0	28.1
1995	180.4	27,112.0		
1996	187.3	26,663.0		
1997	182.5	25,190.0		
1998	181.4	24,030.3		
1999	181.1	23,263.0	104,983.0	22.2
2000	175.8	22,441.8		
2001	111.7	20,218.4	99,295.0	20.4
2002	111.8	20,360.2		
2003	116.4	20,039.0	93,420.0	21.5
2004	117.9	20,894.0	90,150.0	23.2
2005	124.4	21,790.3		
2006	130.5	22,638.5	88,215.0	25.7
2007	129.1	23,488.3		

Source: China Yearly Macro-Economics Statistics (National), China Data Online (accessed through Simon Fraser University Library Database).[b]

Notes:
a These data are calculated from a national 1 per cent sample survey on population changes for available years. To keep data comparability, this table does not mix-use available data from 10 per cent census and 1 per cent population change survey for some years. Since the figures include children in both urban and rural areas, the average rate looks much lower than the same rate in cities. I estimate the rate at is least doubled in cities.
b There are data absent from some cells because they were not being collected in some years.

(Robinson 1985). These public centres are still role models today, but they have experienced a big change in their funding arrangements.

During the childcare system reform of the early 1990s, childcare centres were subjected to government budget cuts and were gradually forced to be regulated by supply and demand conditions in the market. They are now called 'transformed childcare centres'. In Shanghai, the first transformed childcare centre appeared in

1993. In 2001, after almost ten years, there were 93 transformed childcare centres, accounting for 11.70 per cent of the total number of public-owned childcare centres in Shanghai (Huang 2005). An obvious characteristic of these transformed childcare centres is the result of the large-scale cut to government funding for the centres. For some transformed childcare centres, local governments not only stopped funding, but charged rental fees for the facilities. In addition, these childcare centres had to pay part of their income to the government. Although these transformed childcare centres are still publicly owned in name, their operation is private in nature. Because of tight budgets, childcare fees in these transformed centres have generally increased. Parents now are asked to pay not only nursing and teaching fees but also expensive sponsorship fees,[8] or they are forced to make donations that frequently exceed what most parents can afford. The majority of childcare centres now also offer various talent classes and interest classes such as piano and dancing to attract students and increase fees.

Rapidly disappearing work unit childcare centres

During the transition from a planned economy to a market economy, childcare centres related to state-owned enterprises and institutions faced unprecedented problems: some were closed down, some were merged with others and some are struggling to survive. The reason for these problems is that the reforms of the state-owned enterprises removed the welfare function of the enterprises. Since 1995, state-owned enterprises have been encouraged to hand over their elementary schools, hospitals and other welfare departments that were created during the planned economy to local municipal governments to improve their economic efficiency and lighten their welfare burdens. In the Opinions on SOEs Childcare Centres (CNSECE 1999) by several national ministries and committees,[9] the enterprises, especially those who had difficulties operating or managing, were encouraged to hand over nurseries and childcare centres to local governments. According to Du's study (2008), while the State-Owned Assets Supervision and Administration Commission of the State Council required state-owned enterprises to hand over the nurseries and childcare centres to local governments, there were no guaranteed subsidies for enterprises for doing this. Therefore, not all enterprise childcare centres have been handed over: those enterprises that performed poorly or went bankrupt shut down their childcare centres; some enterprises that are still making a profit have kept their childcare facilities, but tried outsourcing or other operational means in order to relieve the enterprises' financial burden; some state-owned enterprises, in the areas where the local municipal governments have higher fiscal incomes, have handed over their childcare centres together with their primary and middle schools (Du 2008).

This handing over process to the private sector is ongoing. In general, the trend is that the number of state-owned enterprise nurseries and childcare centres is declining. According to a report in the *City Morning Newspaper* (5 September 2001), the nurseries and childcare centres of state-owned enterprises and institutions are experiencing funding cuts and as a result are frequently closing down. This has caused the number of childcare centres to decrease from 3,300 in 1990 to 2,047 in 1995, a 30 per cent decrease. A study of the Chaoyang District in Beijing shows that, from 1995 to 2000, the number of nursery and childcare centres run by state-owned enterprises and institutions, armies and neighbourhood committees declined by 50.5 per cent (Zhang and Liu 2001). In 2004, the China Health and Nutrition Survey data showed that of the children at childcare centres, only 9.09 per cent were using work unit childcare centres, which, compared with the early 1990s, has dropped by two-thirds (Du 2008). In Heilongjiang Province, which was an old industrial base in northeast China during the planned economy era, available statistics show that in 1993, the childcare centres run by state-owned enterprises and institutions accounted for 87 per cent of the total number of centres in urban areas, and the children in these facilities accounted for 70 per cent of the children in childcare centres in the province. By 2003, the two percentages had both dropped to 30 per cent (Liu, Zhang and Li 2008).

Because work unit childcare centres could save not only money but also time for parents, they were very popular and many parents had to compete with each other to obtain a space in the surviving work unit centres. To accommodate more parents' needs, some centres had to expand their class sizes. For instance, in the few available large work unit childcare centres in Changsha in 1993, the average class size was 43.7 children per class, which was much bigger than the standard size of 25 children in the 3–4-year-old class, 30 in the 4–5-year-old class, and 35 in the 5-and-above class. This new average class size even exceeded the maximum of 40 students set by the Ministry of Education (Zhang 2005). Under this above-mentioned standard sized class for different age groups, a ratio of teacher to student numbers should be 1:6–1:7; however, compared to the increased class size, the teacher number did not increase accordingly. The consequences have been that the teachers were overburdened and the children could not get enough attention in the packed space.

Neighbourhood childcare centres

Created in the 1950s in urban areas, neighbourhood childcare centres were very convenient for women who lived in the community during the planned economy era. Neighbourhood childcare centres offered flexible childcare arrangements, for example, from boarding to full-time, part-time and holiday care to meet the different demands of parents (Liu, Zhang and Li 2008).

Neighbourhood childcare centres were collectively owned by local neighbourhood committees, which are the lowest-level government organ in cities. In the planned economy, these centres were the main choice for low-income families because the tuition was almost half that of public childcare centres. After the economic reforms, these centres also became the main choice of laid-off workers and rural migrant workers. It is estimated that currently one half to two-thirds of the children in these childcare centres are from low-income families (Zhang and Wu 2006). However, because of operational costs and other reasons, such as city rezoning (redivision of districts for development purposes), neighbourhood childcare centres have been decreasing every year over the last decade. For example, the number of neighbourhood childcare centres in the Xicheng District of Beijing has decreased from 50 in 1987 to 25 in 1998 and 17 in 2002, and it is still declining at present (Zhang and Wu 2006).

Private childcare centres

Compared to the situation of the three kinds of childcare centres mentioned above, private for-profit childcare facilities have developed rapidly in recent years. Since the economic reforms, government policy towards private childcare centres has been encouraging and supportive. Private childcare centres have surpassed other childcare centres in number, though the number of classes and students recruited still has not been able to catch up with public-owned centres. Table 4.3 shows the number of different types of childcare centres and their classes. Children at private centres accounted for about 31 per cent of the total number of children at childcare centres (Liu, Zhang and Li 2008).

Currently, there are two types of private childcare centres. One type targets urban residents and the other type targets rural migrants and basically has no credentials. The urban centres are usually formally registered with a local education department. Compared with the other types of childcare, formal private childcare centres are characterized by their high tuition fees since there is no uniform standard. In Beijing, each private centre can set its own fees. In fact, most private childcare centres are tailored to high-income families. Their high tuition fees include talent classes, such as piano, dancing, bilingual classes (English and

Table 4.3 Number of childcare centres and classes in 2006

Type*	Centres	Classes	Kindergarten
Total	130,495	788,701	294,204
Run by education department (public-owned)	26,877	386,053	235,479
Run by work units	5,512	39,295	4,906
Run by communities	22,680	77,607	8,359
Non-state/private	75,426	285,746	45,460

Source: 2006 Education Statistics, the Ministry of Education, as cited in Liu, Zhang and Li (2008: 64).

Note:
* The first three types are all state-owned childcare centres and during the planned-economy era, they were either directly or indirectly government-funded childcare centres. Only the last type are privately owned for-profit organizations. The childcare centres run by the education department are normally called public-owned since they were fully directly funded by government financial budget in the planned economy. Work unit childcare centres are run by work units; however, as these work units are all state-owned, the childcare centres are state-owned in nature. Neighbourhood childcare centres are collectively owned by neighbourhood committees. The neighbourhood committee is the lowest government organ in cities. Therefore, these first three types are all under public ownership. Since the advent of the market economy, these childcare centres have been pushed to market to make a living.

Chinese) and other classes that feed parents' hopes for their children's success. In 2007, private centres in Beijing charged ¥1,300–2,800 per month, excluding sponsorship fees (He and Jiang 2007). For comparison, the legal minimum salary rate in Beijing is only ¥730 per month. Feng Shiliang, a member of the Chinese People's Political Consultative Conference, noted[10] that the sky-high price (*tianjia*) of childcare is becoming a problem. Childcare centres that charge fees above ¥3,000 and ¥4,000 per month are everywhere in big cities, and childcare fees of ¥3,000, ¥4,000, ¥5,000, ¥6,000, even ¥10,000 and ¥20,000 per month, the highest record of childcare fees, are constantly being broken. Against this 'only higher, no highest (*zhiyou genggao, meiyou zuigao*)' phenomenon, some parents joke that the statement 'childcare fees are more expensive than university tuition' should be upgraded to 'childcare fees are higher than foreign university tuition'.[11] Feng Shiliang noted that this phenomenon has set a new threshold – parents with low income have no access to these kinds of childcare centres. He remarked that the over-marketization of early child education has called the sky-high priced childcare centres into place.

While the state has downloaded its responsibilities into both private and market solutions, the state does not even fulfil its supervision role. He argued that preschool education should not become a commercial good, but rather, that preschool care should be a public good; and it is the state's responsibility to provide these public goods. He suggested that a price limitation should be imposed upon childcare centres, and that the government should provide public childcare and guarantee funding for childcare service.

Feng Shiliang's blog has attracted considerable parents' responses. An anonymous parent replied that he or she lived in a remote suburban area in Beijing and the childcare fee had increased to ¥2,000 per month. This parent questioned whether people could survive this extraordinarily high cost. Many parents responded with the sentiment that early child education should be covered by public education. Even if the price is continually increasing, parents still have to compete with each other for the limited spaces in the current childcare centres. Another anonymous parent posted on the blog that they tried to put their child onto a waiting list one and half years before the actual entry time, but after asking for more than ten childcare centres, they found that all of the centres were full, and that childcare centres' waiting lists are already scheduled to the year 2013.

Although these private childcare centres charge high prices, they do not necessarily provide a high-quality service. Recently, newspapers have reported that some children in these private centres were abused either by the teachers or by other children. In one case reported in Shantou, in the Guangdong province, two childcare teachers allowed one little girl to physically abuse a little boy. These teachers not only taught the girl how to do it, but also videotaped the process with mobile phones. One of the two teachers received professional training in early child education and the other held a college diploma in English language. After the incident, both teachers were removed from the childcare centre, and the local education department also closed the centre for rectification. It was reported that similar cases have happened more than once, and three children have been beaten up like this in this childcare centre. This high-priced childcare centre has operated for six years and the headmaster was once elected in a nationwide competition as 'excellent headmaster'.[12]

The second major type of private childcare centres is the centre with no accreditation. As pointed out previously, the *tianjia*'s cost excludes its use by most members of the working class, and they – especially rural migrant workers – are driven to cheaper but illegally run childcare centres. These are centres that certainly are not on a par with *tianjia* private childcare centres. Compared to *tianjia* private childcare centres, these childcare centres charge low prices, but because of their lack of necessary facilities and qualified teachers they are not authorized to open by local education departments. They are therefore running illegally and the quality of this type of private childcare centre cannot be guaranteed. Recently, there were some newspaper reports that children were left in the childcare centres' commuter buses in the summer and died of heat exhaustion. For example, in a non-qualified childcare centre in Chaozhou, in the Guangdong Province, a four-year-old girl in the school bus was forgotten. She died on 19 May 2010.[13] There are other accidents in this type of childcare centre, for example, fire-related ones. On 3 September 2010, the *Beijing News* reported that the headmaster and a teacher of a non-qualified childcare centre were respectively sentenced to two or three years' prison because of a child's death in this centre.[14] The accident happened when the daycare teacher went out to buy vegetables during the children's naptime. Two children played with an electronic heater, the heater fell and it caused a fire. After the fire broke out, the teacher did not have much experience to save the children either, which led directly to a child burning to death. A parent, whose child went to the daycare centre before the accident, said that her child still goes to this kind of childcare, though a different centre. This type of childcare centre usually charge ¥200 each month – the only ones that migrant workers can afford. She said that it is not surprising these childcare centres are not comparable to formal childcare centres.

It was reported that in Beijing there were 1,298 childcare centres without qualification in 2009 (Zhou 2010), which was even higher than the number of total formal various types of childcare centres, which was 1,253. The existence of unqualified childcare centres is all due to two facts: people living at the bottom of society have no ability to pay for education, and the application procedure for permission to run a childcare centre is costly (Zhou 2010). The existence of such childcare centres therefore meets the current childcare demand and it is also supporting the people living at the lowest level of society (Zhou 2010).

Overall, the changes to the different types of childcare centres during the market-oriented reforms have led to the loss of the welfare function of childcare centres in liberating women under the planned economy. The government's downloading of its social reproduction responsibility to individual families and to the market has caused many problems that relate to a variety of accessibility issues. The most significant issues relate to costs.

High costs have prevented low-income families from gaining access to affordable childcare facilities (Dong *et al.* 2009). Sponsorship fees, teaching and nursing fees, and interest class fees have now become a financial burden for many families. In a survey of 14 provinces and cities in China, 36 per cent of the childcare centres charge sponsorship fees, ranging from ¥100 to ¥10,000 per year. In Beijing, some childcare centres charge ¥30,000 per year (Liu, Zhang and Li 2008). Sponsorship fees are the main funding source after the government cut funding. In addition to sponsorship fees, the current average monthly childcare fee in Beijing is as follows: public-owned centres charge ¥600–1,000; work unit facilities, ¥600–700; community centres, ¥500–600; private centres, ¥1,300–2,800. Only 14.4 per cent of parents feel that childcare fees are not burdensome (He and Jiang 2007).

The decreased publicly funded childcare programmes and also the lack of service mean that current childcare facilities cannot meet working mothers' needs. The lack of childcare centres in new communities has caused great inconveniences for some families in these areas. Because of the closure of work unit childcare centres, the development of new centres in residential communities should become a priority in early childhood education. However, it does not look optimistic. According to an investigation of 73 Beijing residential communities developed in the 10 years from 1986 to 1995, only 151 of the 179 planned childcare centres were built. Furthermore, of those 151 centres, 20 per cent were not used as childcare centres at all; the facilities were either just set aside or were used for other purposes (Lu and Liu 2001).

In addition, currently available childcare centres cannot really accommodate working parents' childcare needs, especially for children under three years old. Nurseries have now almost disappeared in state-owned, work unit and community childcare centres. Most of these childcare centres accept children only around two and a half years old and above. Without government policy support, these childcare centres show no intention of opening day nurseries for infants and toddlers. In Beijing, 24.8 per cent of 927 families surveyed by the Women's Studies Institute of China in 2007 had not been able to find a day nursery centre for their children under three; only 21.4 per cent of children under three years old (in both rural and urban areas) are at childcare centres (He and Jiang 2007). In the same survey, in Shanghai, 23.9 per cent of surveyed parents had also been unable to find a day nursery for their children under three (He and Jiang 2007). Among the 200,000 children under three, 79.7 per cent of them are not in professional childcare centres and are cared for by individual families (Liu, Zhang and Li 2008). However, it is not just a problem for infant care. Although the situation of children three years old and above is better in big cities such as Beijing where 90 per cent are in childcare centres (He and Jiang 2007), the overall rate of children in childcare centres in China, including children in rural areas, was only 41.5 per cent in 2006.[15]

The daycare centres' hours of operation are generally about 10 hours a day, from 7:30–8:00 a.m. in the morning until 16:00–17:00 p.m. Parents who both work and have no other helpers at home generally start work at 8:00 a.m. and finish at 17:00 p.m. – a normal workday in China. These hours are incompatible with the daycare hours. While some childcare centres charge for early drop-off and late pick-up, others do not provide such a service. According to a survey of parents of children in childcare, 28 per cent of them wished childcare centres would extend their operating hours; 41.6 per cent wished their children could stay overnight at childcare centres when there was a sick family member at home; and 22.8 per cent wished that childcare centres would help them take care of their sick children (Liu, Zhang and Li 2008).

Compared with the convenient service provided to parents – especially working mothers – under the state-planned economy, it is obvious that the current market-oriented childcare system reform has not met the market demand of parents.

In order to focus on generating profit, childcare has gradually lost its focus on care as most centres turn to providing mainly education-oriented services. Along with the one-child population policy in China, the childcare centres' function of education for young children has become a top priority. With only one child allowed per family after the family planning policy was put in place in 1979, children in China have become ever more precious. With a strong wish for a better life for their only child, parents now have high educational expectations for that child, regardless of the child's sex. It is therefore not surprising that the quality of child development and education has received excessive attention in Chinese society. To download its social reproduction responsibility, government policy has also emphasized the childcare centres' educational function by claiming that pre-school education is not the government's obligation and that parents have a responsibility to pay their share of their children's educational costs.[16] Therefore, there is now a trend for childcare centres to emphasize their increasing educational role while ignoring their care function.

Opening various ability-training classes not only makes it possible to charge higher fees, but can also shorten care time. To avoid the excessive burden associated with caring for younger children, some childcare centres now hold part-time parent–child classes for children under three years old, which requires an adult to be with a child to take different classes, such as language training and intellectual development games. These classes have nothing to do with childcare at all. Because of the requirement of parent participation, for education's sake, some working parents even have to hire domestic workers to take their children to these classes. In an interview with a domestic worker, I was told,

> I take the child to a parent-child class three times a week on Mondays, Wednesdays and Fridays. His mother has been looking for a day care centre for him, but no day care will take him because he is too young – less than 2 years old.
> (Interview, 7 November 2007)

With these changes, it has become very difficult for parents to find suitable childcare centres for their children. In situations where there are no facilities available, where the quality of available facilities is low, or where the cost is prohibitive, children have to remain at home to be cared for by mothers, grandparents or other relatives and domestic workers.

The impact on working mothers

As government and state-owned enterprises retreated from public childcare service and brought about the rise of private childcare service, mothers with young children have been seriously affected.

After the economic reforms, work pressure has increased more than ever before. Competition has been introduced into every industry. Even in government organizations and institutions, efficiency has become the standard against which to judge a person's work performance. Along with the downsizing of organizations, workload has increased accordingly. The intensiveness and competition at work has caused workers to work overtime. From the data published in the China Labour Statistics Yearbook,[17] we can see that the labourers' average working time in urban areas has passed the statutory working time of 40 hours per week; furthermore, since 2001, working time has been increasing almost year after year (Table 4.4). All of the domestic worker employers who participated in my study indicated that working overtime and having meetings during off-work hours was very normal for them. The work unit does not treat anyone differently even though some may have young children to take care of at home.

On the one hand, jobs now are more demanding than during the socialist era before the economic reforms. On the other hand, government childcare policies are much less supportive of women's employment than ever before. Since women are still considered the primary caregiver at home, less government support in social services has no doubt increased women's care responsibility. The government's assumption that women will pick up the slack has intensified their caring duties for children, in which they have to shoulder greater responsibilities with minimal resources. Compared with the socialist era before the economic reforms, women's double workload both in the home and outside it has intensified under such circumstances. Jin, one of my domestic worker-employer participants who works for a private company, told me:

> Only one child, whose child is not a treasure? I also want to spend more time with my daughter, but I have no time. Usually, in the morning when I get up

Table 4.4 The average weekly working time of urban employees (hours)

	October 2001	October 2002	November 2003	November 2004	November 2005	November 2006
Average (Male and Female)	44.9	45.2	45.4	45.5	47.8	47.26
Male	45.2	45.6	45.8	46.0	48.7	48.3
Female	44.5	44.7	44.9	44.9	46.7	45.9

Source: Department of Population, and Employment Statistics of National Bureau of Statistics, P.R.C. and Department of Planning and Finance, MOLSS, P.R.C 2005 (2006).

for work, she is still sleeping; at night when I'm off work, she has already gone to bed.

(Interview, 2 January 2008)

Women with high work demands or women whose work is incompatible with their childcare responsibilities can provide limited childcare time. Whenever needed, other caregivers have to take the place of the mothers. This is the reason why domestic service has become a growing industry in China.

While realizing the shortage of childcare centres, some local governments are taking measures to develop early child education. For example, in the next five years, the Beijing municipal government will enlarge its financial input in early child education, and pre-school education will be universal until 2015. In order to reach this goal, the Beijing municipal government is planning to build and transform 600 childcare centres into publicly owned institutions. The ratio of publicly owned childcare centres is set to reach 50 per cent. In the future, 80 per cent of new childcare centres in newly built residential areas will be publicly owned.[18]

Conclusion

Childcare policies have experienced big changes in the last two decades. The cutting of government budgets, the shutting down of work unit childcare facilities and the increasing privatization of childcare have created a heavy childcare burden for mothers who work. Compared to the state-planned economy era before the economic reforms, childcare policies have now changed their orientation from liberating women's labour power to getting women back to childcare and housework. This is in contradiction to the commitment to women's equal rights in the workplace as well as at home as women are responsible for most of the care work and household work. Just as studies of childcare policies in Western welfare states suggest, women's interests are always the last consideration in the justification of childcare policies (Marchbank 2000).

The childcare policy changes are just an example of the government's universal changes in social service, including health care and old age care. With the privatization of these services, the demand for paid domestic service has increased accordingly. Just as the globalization process is leading to the further widening of the gender, class and racial division of the role of childcare worldwide, opening the domestic service market in China has also led to an increase in the exploitation of migrant and laid-off women workers.

5 Domestic labour as precarious work in China

> I feel that they (employers) think they pay you money, and then they think you should do whatever they want. Just I can't bear the way they treat you.
> (Interview with a domestic worker, 27 November 2007).

> Such a 'have-no-choice-but-to-hire-domestic-help' consumer group leads to the fact that that they are extremely strict with domestic workers. It is 'hire a person and use her to death,' for fear of that the worker eats too much and doesn't work hard enough. This was the reason why we, the Beijing Home Service Association (BHSA), addressed an 8-hour sleeping time in regulating our Domestic Service Contract in 2004. However, this year when the Beijing Administration for Industry and Commerce issued the Contract, the concept of a specific 8-hour sleeping time was reduced to a 'secure basic sleeping time.'
> (BHSA 2007: N.p.)

Paid domestic workers in China, like everywhere in the world, suffer precarious working conditions and mistreatment from employers. In China, some workers are exploited by both the employers and through domestic service agencies that either hire workers directly or broker their work. The socialist ideology that people are equal and that all workers should be treated with respect has not been sustained in the domestic service employment relationship.

On the one hand, the market mechanism after the economic reforms has exerted stronger power in imposing market rules over socialist moral standards. The market economy has recreated not only the class division between domestic employers and workers, but also the unequal power relationship between domestic employers and workers through promotion of the conspicuous consumption of domestic service. As domestic service has become a consumer good that can be sold and purchased on the market, the rationale of work has changed. These changes have led to the fact that workers' working conditions and living status are far less important than the quality of service they can provide for their employers. In this market, the consumers – domestic employers – are gods, and market power teaches them to value their consumer satisfaction. Domestic workers, as providers of 'products', are required to adapt to the consumers' tastes and preferences.

On the other hand, the government still uses socialist rhetoric to educate domestic workers that they are equal to their employers in human dignity. The result of this contradiction is the lack of effective measures to protect domestic workers' rights. Since economic reforms have made paid domestic service a new employment arrangement in the informal economy, it officially has a different treatment from that of permanent, stable employment. The Labour Law which was enacted in 1995 does not cover domestic workers employed by individuals and households and little attention has been paid to the economic security and social security of the emergence of such a precarious type of work.[1] The Labour Law, chapter one article two, stipulates that this Law apply to enterprises, individually owned economic organizations (hereinafter referred to as the employer) and labourers who form a labour relationship with them within the boundary of the People's Republic of China. State departments, institutional organizations and social groups and labourers who form a labour relationship with them shall follow this Law.

In the Law, the household, as a private domain, is not included and the aspects of work covered are such as labour contracts, working hours, wages and labour safety. The Law relates to only workers in an employment relationship in the public sphere. To avoid misunderstanding, in the September 1994 Explanation of Certain Articles of the Labour Law[2] and the 4 August 1995 Opinion on Certain Questions during the Enforcement of the People's Republic China Labour Law,[3] the MOLSS made it clear that the Labour Law does not apply to domestic work. That is to say, the Labour Law stipulates that establishing a labour relationship and making a labour contract does not apply to individual domestic service workers and their private employers. Accordingly, the articles about mandatory social insurance also do not apply. Enacted on 1 January 2004, the Regulation on the Insurance of Workplace Injury also stipulated that it applies to the workers who have a labour relationship with work unit employers.[4] Domestic workers are again excluded from this Regulation because in China the household is not a work unit. This interpretation has been upheld by the Supreme Court. On 1 October 2006, The Supreme Court of the People's Republic of China Interpretation of Certain Issues on the Applicable Laws about Hearing of Cases of Labour Disputes ruled that disputes between individual or household and domestic service workers are not covered as labour disputes.[5] Unfortunately, the new Labour Contract Law, which was enacted on 1 January 2008, still does not take domestic workers into consideration.[6] Although the new law does cover some precarious employment arrangements, such as labour outsourcing and part-time work, the new law stipulates, as before, that employers are work units. Therefore, theoretically, the new law does not cover any domestic workers since private homes are not legally work units. But technically, courts do consider it as a labour relationship for domestic workers who are employed and sent to people's homes to work by agencies, as this form of employment resembles outsourcing, which is regulated by the current Labour Contract Law. However, since many domestic service agencies are intermediary companies who do not employ workers directly, the overwhelming majority of domestic workers, including those employed through the introduction by relatives and friends, are still excluded from the new law. Hence, it is clear that domestic workers whose employment relationship is confined to private homes do not enjoy the same labour rights that the Labour Law and regulations give other workers. This situation directly leads to the insecurity of domestic workers' conditions of work, including working hours, benefits, statutory holidays and social insurance. Consequently, it is not surprising to see that domestic service in contemporary China often resembles relations of servitude that prevailed in previous times. This stands in stark contradiction to China's ideas of equality in work and modern notions of employment protections.

In this chapter, I examine the employment of care workers, specifically nannies, and paid cleaners to reveal the precarious nature of paid domestic service. Two kinds of care workers – live-in and live-out – will be observed. The live-in care worker works for and lives with one family, and her responsibilities generally include caring for the children or the family's seniors and the household. The live-out care worker works five or six days a week for one family, tending to the children or the seniors and the household, but returns to her own place at night. Paid cleaners only clean houses, working for several different employers on a weekly or monthly basis. While many domestic workers are employed through agencies and cleaning services, a large portion of the labour market is employed through informal networks, such as acquaintance or kinship networks. This chapter will examine the different experiences among rural and urban, live-in and live-out, and agency and non-agency domestic workers.

Through this illustration of domestic workers' working and living conditions, I will argue that domestic workers in China lack basic economic and social security and that their rights as workers and humans are being violated. This is obviously not compatible with a harmonious socialist ideology.

Domestic workers' background information

There have been some significant changes to the domestic worker group since the first revival of domestic service in the early 1980s. To illustrate general trends with workers' experiences, it is necessary to provide details of domestic workers' characteristics.

Compared with the early 1980s when young, unmarried girls called '*xiao baomu*' dominated the domestic service market, there has been a gradual increase of the ages of domestic workers in the last few years, according to two surveys by the MWC (Han 2006). The findings indicate that the concentration of domestic workers fell into the age groups of 15–19-year-olds (22 per cent) and 30–34-year-olds (23.9 per cent), while the 2005 survey indicated that 20–39-year-old women accounted for 62.7 per cent (Han 2006). A survey from Xi'an city also shows that, in the past, *baomu* from rural areas were mostly young *xiao baomu*, but in the last few years the number of older *baomu* was on the rise, with 31–50-year-old *baomu* accounting for 62.5 per cent of the total (Y. L. Li 2006). Among my interviewees, young girls under 25 years old accounted for 23 per cent, while workers over 25 accounted for 77 per cent – the oldest was 50 and the youngest was 18. In an interview with the manager of SBFSC, he characterized the women as follows:

They are mostly married. Actually, in the past, it was not all young girls. The term '*xiao baomu*' is a derogatory term. Once *baomu* is said, a '*xiao*' is added. Even a 50-year-old or someone even older is called '*xiao baomu.*' From the usage of the language, it is an indication of discrimination. Just like in the Chinese culture, when people always say 'little wife, big husband (*xiao xifu, da zhangfu*),' it is actually discrimination in standard practice. In fact, in the past, it was not only young girls, but also many middle-aged women who were called this.

(Interview, 17 October 2007)

However, there is evidence in the last few years that domestic workers are older. This is because there are more work opportunities for young girls. Almost all older workers I interviewed told me that no young girls like to do domestic service and that young girls would rather work at factories and restaurants and make less money than serve people. Zhang is in her early 40s. She explained,

Sichuan young girls don't like to come here; they don't come to do this [domestic service]. Which young girl would like to do this? It's all because [we are] old and have no choice, that we come to do this!

(Interview, 27 November 2007)

Many older domestic workers are married and have children, but some have experienced unsatisfying marriages and divorced. Among my interviewees, 12.5 per cent of the domestic workers are divorced. Doing domestic service jobs can be a way for women to escape domestic violence and patriarchy and to enjoy a certain freedom. Zhang told me that at her domestic agency there are many women who have had unhappy marriages just like herself, and to them, the domestic service company is not only an agency but also their shelter. A worker from Hunan province in her mid-40s explained her experience:

My man did not take care of the family; he visited prostitutes, wasted all our money; he did not even care about our son and daughter, and he beat me. I divorced him, then I couldn't stay at home, so I went to our county town to work as a *baomu*. I got divorced in 1993; in 1995, I started to be a *baomu*.

(Interview, 30 October 2007)

Life is hard for single mothers, but the life of domestic workers who have children is not easy even if they are married. Many domestic workers have to leave their children with their parents or sisters in the countryside. Among my interviewees, the youngest child left behind by his mom was only five months old. Generally, both parents are working (*dagong*) in the city and leave the children with grandparents in the countryside. Compared to their older counterparts, young girl domestic workers relatively enjoy their personal freedom while they can avoid an early marriage in the countryside. Among my interviewees, Lan, a 21-year-old girl, said she came to Beijing because her family urged her to find a man and get married. Li, who was 22 years old, told me that she was upset when her mom wanted her to get engaged when she was 19. She was worried that if she got married at an early age, she would not have the chance to get out of the countryside, which she described as 'very feudal'. However, they also admitted that their moms wanted the best for them since marriage is necessary to secure a future for a rural girl. Given her rural identity and insecure, low-end domestic service job, there is almost no probability that she will marry a young man who is a city resident and has a city *hukou*.

In terms of educational background, the current domestic workers' educational level has improved to some degree compared with domestic workers who were illiterate or semi-literate in the socialist Mao era, but their basic education level is still junior high school or below. Among my interviewees, only 13.6 per cent have high school or college diplomas, and 43.2 per cent completed only junior high school. In total, 58 per cent completed junior high school or a higher level of education. The remaining 43.2 per cent did not finish junior high school, and among them, 6.8 per cent are illiterate and have never been to school. Tian is a 20-year-old interviewee from Li County, Gansu province, which is a big domestic worker export base. Her hometown is located in a mountainous area and there is no elementary school in her village. Children who want to go to school have to walk to the county town, which means that they have to leave home at 6:00 a.m. and come back home around 6:00 p.m. Because of the extremely harsh terrain that even bikes cannot cross, many children do not go to school, or they quit after or even before they finish elementary school. The farmers are very poor there, so they do not have enough money to support their children's education. In Tian's family, there are five girls, and only the youngest two have completed elementary school; the other three, including Tian herself, have not attended even one day of school. She said that boys generally get more education than girls. For example, all the children in her family were girls and her parents never encouraged any of them to go to school. A survey in 2003 by the MWC shows that 13 per cent of domestic workers are illiterate or semi-literate (Han 2006). Workers in my interviews who were from areas other than Gansu also addressed the illiteracy problem among some domestic workers. They said, '... they [illiterate young domestic workers] have no knowledge, do not know any Chinese characters, and some cannot even write their names – how can you expect them to protect themselves from harm?'[7] The illiterate workers' own words, 'What can I do without any education?', also expressed their having no choice but to do domestic service.

In Beijing, domestic workers are employed through two main channels. They may find employment through their kinship or native-place-based networks. A large number of domestic workers are recruited through organizational channels. For example, local women's federations and labour bureaus are responsible for recruiting workers in their local areas and then delivering these workers to companies such as SBFSC and Fu Ping Domestic Service Centre (FPDSC, a private shareholding company initiated by the famous Chinese economist, Mao Yushi), which have agreements with these local organizations. These companies supply domestic workers to urban households. The workers' attitudes towards these employment agencies are positive. Almost all the workers I interviewed who were employed by these agencies reported,

> It's much better to have a company. If any discrepancy happens between you and your employer, at least there is a company here to coordinate for you, though most of the time a domestic service company speaks on the employer's behalf.[8]

As this industry grows, increased specialization is emerging. For instance, besides the traditional *baomu* whose job is to take care of children and seniors, do the cooking, cleaning and laundry, new occupations, such as *yuesao* and *yuersao*, have arisen. *Yuesao* is a term that has appeared in recent years. It refers to domestic workers who specifically do neonatal care for newborns and moms. The domestic workers who specialize in looking after babies that are older than three months or 100 days are called *yuersao*. Generally, *yuesao* and *yuersao* are married women who have given birth to children themselves. After a brief training, their agencies send them to work for wealthier households since the pay is much better than that of an ordinary *baomu*. Currently, there is a trend to distinguish *yuesao* and *yuersao* from *baomu*. Some families now hire two domestic workers, with one taking care of the children and one doing the housekeeping.

Working and living conditions of care workers

Caring labour does not only involve physical labour. It also involves personal feelings and emotions, making it more vulnerable to exploitation. Some scholars who have studied the marginalization of care labour at the global level identify care labour as a type of 'emotional labour' (Hochschild 1983) or 'affective labour,' that is, 'labour that produces or manipulates affects such as a feeling of ease, well-being, satisfaction, excitement or passion' (Hardt and Negri 2004: 108). Caregivers have to control their emotions when they are working since they are expected to satisfy and please their employers. Their caring work also requires them to build up a trusting relationship with the cared for. Caregivers tend to be motivated by a genuine concern for their employers' well-being and caring becomes to some extent its own reward (Folbre and Weisskopf 1998). Because of this, and because of the intimate and trusting relationship between caregivers and those cared for, the wages of caregivers are sometimes set lower than those of workers with objectively comparable skills (Folbre and Weisskopf 1998). Caregivers may also do work that is beyond their original contract (Himmelweit 1999: 32). In addition, because they care about their clients, caregivers do not like to change clients to pursue their self-interest (Himmelweit 1999). Because of these emotional attachments, paid caregivers are easily subject to exploitation. Feminist economists have argued that caring labour has a 'care penalty', which means the work is paid less than is commensurate with workers' skills, working conditions are onerous and there is not always a union to look out for caregivers' interests (England and Folbre 1999: 41).

According to my research, most domestic workers in China are poorly paid, and their working conditions are far from satisfying. In many cases, they are treated very harshly by their employers, sometimes as less than human. Care workers from rural areas or other cities tend to live in their employers' homes; their Beijing counterparts are more likely to live out. Live-in workers are particularly susceptible to abuse since employers can control their entire lives – where they live, whom they know, how much they sleep and even what they eat. Workers from rural areas are particularly dependent on their employers because of their rural migrant identity. Their desperate need to earn money can cause them to be even more vulnerable than their laid-off urban-based counterparts.

Work responsibilities

According to my study, care workers' work responsibilities are not very clear and largely depend on individual employers' requirements. In most cases, even if the care worker is hired as a nanny, she still has to care for the whole family. In fact, she is a nanny for the whole family, including parents and sometimes grandparents. Besides their care responsibility, they also have to cook and do the housekeeping. They often work as housekeeper, cook and nanny all at once. Many interviewees told me that they do everything for the household. They are also asked to perform some humiliating tasks. Almost 90 per cent of the workers I interviewed have been required to hand wash adult underwear, and they felt quite humiliated by this type of work.

In the last two to three years, there have also been professional nannies whose specific duty is to look after children. The nanny takes care of everything related to the child (generally only one child in a family because of the one-child population policy in China) in an employer's home, just as a surrogate mother does. Because little children need attendance at night, these nannies sleep with the children as well. However, these professional nannies are few in number. Most nannies are the all-in-one type.

Pay

Although there has been a salary increase for care workers in the last two years because of the shortage in the number of care workers, compared with their workload and working conditions, most care workers are still underpaid. More than 90 per cent of my interviewees were not satisfied with their pay. According to my study, in Beijing, currently the lowest monthly wage rate for newcomers from rural areas is ¥800 a month, which is just above the minimum wage of ¥730 set by the Beijing municipal government.[9] Generally, taking care of children pays more than looking after the elderly because it is assumed that children need more attention and working with children is considered more professional. Nannies can usually get ¥1,500, but the assumption is that they will work 24 hours a day.

Care workers frequently get delays in the payment of their wages or even no payment for their work. One worker from Hunan province told me that she has been working for her current employers since April 2005 (and had worked for two and half years at that point), but has only been paid for the half year in 2005 at ¥500 a month. Even with half a year's salary, she had to ask for it numerous times because she had no money to buy herself stomach medicine. Her employer promised to increase her salary to ¥700 a month at the beginning of 2007, but she still did not receive any money until October 2007. She was recruited from her employer's hometown and did not sign any contract. She does not have any proof that her employer has not paid her either. I asked why she did not leave her employer, and she told me that she did not dare to leave because she was worried that she would not get any compensation if she left.

Another worker told me that her former employer fired her and she did not receive any pay for her last day of work. She asked her employer to pay her before she left the family, but the employer refused and threatened to call the police if she did not leave. She finally lost one day's wages.

Social insurance

It is a social reality that care workers lack various social benefits, such as pensions, medical plans and workplace injury insurance. According to a survey by Peking University, 60 per cent of the care workers in Beijing and Guangzhou do not have any social insurance (Z. Q. Wang 2007). For the people in my study, laid-off and unemployed city workers can contribute to pension plans and medical insurance in their household registration cities, but rural migrant workers are not covered by any government social benefit plans.

For migrant workers, the biggest problem comes from their lack of medical insurance coverage. Once they are ill, the huge medical expenditure is not what they can afford. In the 1980s, as the enforcement of the Household Responsibility System, in which the household became the basic management unit of agricultural production, took place, the Cooperative Medical Systems that were relying on the collectivization of agriculture collapsed (Guo, Tan and Zhu 2009). The coverage of rural health insurance decreased from about 80 per cent of the rural population in 1980 to only 6.6 per cent in 1998 (Zhong and Gustafsson 2008). Consequently, rural residents had to carry all costs for health care (Zhong and Gustafsson 2008). During this transition process, rural women were particularly affected. For example, the impact of health-care reform on the provision of basic services, such as reproductive health care, affected women in particular. The changes in health financing, which have driven up costs, resulted in disparities in health-care access and outcomes by gender (Chen and Standing 2007).[10] The lack of health security in rural areas has come to the Chinese government's attention. In 2002, the Decision of Further Enforcing Health Care in Rural Areas by the Central government and State Council agreed 'to gradually establish new rural CMSs that cover main illnesses ... till 2010, [when] new CMSs should basically cover all rural residents' (Guo, Tan and Zhu 2009: 247). Since 2008, this nationwide cooperative medical plan that was enforced by the Chinese government has tried to cover almost any person in a rural area with an agricultural household registration.[11] However, in reality, because this plan is voluntary instead of mandatory, and because farmers are required to pay their share, some economically disadvantaged people are still not covered. Some studies have examined the gendered implication of the new rural cooperative medical service, which has excluded some disadvantaged women such as widowed elder women or other women from poor households (Guo, Tan and Zhu 2009). Rural migrant workers are included in the new CMSs since they have rural *hukou* registration. In my interviews with rural domestic workers, they told me that they joined the CMSs in their hometown, but it barely meets their medical needs. This is because, under this new plan, rural residents are reimbursed for the medical expenditure in their hometown hospitals only. Migrant workers who live and work in cities have few opportunities to receive treatment at their hometown hospitals, where the medical facilities as well as doctors' skills fall behind hospitals in the cities, and thus would never get any reimbursement in reality. My interviewees told me that this plan was good to their frail parents rather than to them. Once they get sick in cities, they still have to pay fully for their treatment; however, they do use the medical plan in their hometown to buy some medicines to bring to the cities in case of minor illnesses since the medication fees in rural areas are lower than in cities.

Because there is no universal medical plan, medical treatment for care workers is an urgent problem that needs to be solved. The workers told me that employers usually give them free medicine for minor diseases and injuries, such as a cold and a small cut on a hand. But for serious illnesses, employers are reluctant to pay if it is expensive because, in reality, employers are not responsible for workers' medical fees. Many workers told me that they can generally bear minor diseases, but if they are seriously sick, they have to quit their job and move back to where they are from.

Workplace safety is unregulated for domestic workers because it is not covered in current government regulations. If domestic workers are injured during work, the question of who should pay for all the medical treatment has become a big issue. Trouble arises if the medical fees are beyond the means of the workers and the employers. A well-known case reflects the precarious situation of domestic workers.[12] Zhou Dailan was a 42-year-old migrant care worker who worked in Shanghai. On 24 December 2003, while she was cleaning the windows for her employer, she fell from the fourth floor to the pavement below and was seriously injured. The huge medical fee stopped her from getting immediate treatment because her own family could not afford it, and it was difficult even for her employer to help pay part of it. In the end, her treatment was paid for with the help of donations from individuals and organizations as well as the small compensation her employer was compelled by the court to give. However, the issue should not be a matter of determining whether the employer or the worker should pay for treatment of domestic workers' workplace injuries. It should be the responsibility of social insurance. If domestic workers' workplace safety were covered by social insurance, medical treatment would no longer be an issue.

After the Zhou Dailan accident, the Shanghai municipal labour and social security bureau and two commercial insurance companies, Ping'an and Taiping, implemented a commercial domestic service insurance in July 2004 (Wang, Si and Chen 2010). This insurance covers as much as ¥100,000 for domestic workers who are injured, disabled or die at work, when the employers pay ¥30 per year to purchase the insurance. The benefit levels of this insurance include death and accidental injury medical expenditure compensation of ¥100,000; disability and accidental injury medical expenditure compensation of ¥100,000; and non-disability accidental injury medical expenditure compensation of ¥10,000; in total, the highest compensation is ¥100,000 (Wang, Si and Chen 2010). The statistics data from Shanghai labour and social security department showed that until the end of 2006, 72,000 households purchased this insurance for their domestic workers (Wang, Si and Chen 2010). However, this is only a local experience in Shanghai and it is not nationally promoted yet.

In recent years, to prevent and reduce workplace injuries, some domestic agencies in Beijing have educated their workers about not performing dangerous tasks that certainly do not belong to their care responsibilities, including mopping the outside of windows. Some workers said that their agencies told them clearly which tasks are considered dangerous and should never be done by them even if the employers insist. Some bigger domestic agencies have been looking for ways to deal with emergency medical treatment. For example, SBFSC stipulates on the contract that employers should pay 20 per cent of workers' medical fees (Interview, 29 November 2007). FPDSC is trying to raise an emergency relief fund to help workers in need (Interview, 27 October 2007). One former FPDSC worker told me that in 2006, when her leg got inflamed, the company paid 70 per cent of her medical fees. In Shanghai, some domestic agencies are also experimenting with buying commercial insurance, such as accident insurance and serious illness insurance, for domestic workers (Zhou 2006).

Working hours

Long working hours are very normal for care workers, especially the live-ins. More than 60 per cent of my interviewees reported that they work more than 10 hours a day. A nanny told me:

> 'I get up at 6:00 a.m. and go to sleep after 10:00 p.m. You calculate how many hours this is! 16 hours! No break! My employer almost owns me!'
> (Interview, 7 November 2007).

Some nannies are required to be available almost 24 hours a day, such as the nannies whose sole duty is to look after a child. Yang said: 'I work 24 hours. Even at night, she [the one and a half-year-old she is looking after] sleeps with me' (Interview, 7 November 2007). These nannies unanimously told me that with a child sleeping beside you it is impossible to sleep well because you have to feed them or may have to change diapers in the middle of the night.

For live-out workers, although their working time is supposed to be fixed, for example, from 7:00 a.m. to 6:00 p.m., it is very rare that they can get off work on time. One worker gave me an example about how her employer wisely took advantage of her. She is off at 6:00 p.m., but her employer likes to call her around 5:00 p.m. and tell her what to cook for dinner, but usually not all the ingredients are available and she has to wait for the employer to bring things home. When the employer gets home, it is already 5:30 p.m. Since it takes more than half an hour to finish the cooking, she usually does not leave work until 6:30 p.m. When the family hosts a party on the weekend, she has to prepare food for all the guests, which takes her an even longer time. She has never been paid for those extra working hours.

Weekends, statutory holidays and paid sick leave

In Beijing, many agency workers are now allowed to have one day off each week, but it still depends on employers' decisions. Some employers would rather pay overtime than give their workers just one day off. According to my study, non-agency workers still work seven days a week and do not get any extra pay.

During three-day statutory holidays, such as Labour Day on 1 May and National Day on 1 October, agency workers can normally take one day off. Most non-agency workers do not yet enjoy the same treatment. Unlike workers in other industries, who are legally entitled to double pay for working during statutory holidays, domestic workers who work during these statutory holidays only get paid the usual wage. Chinese New Year is a special holiday. Usually workers take a few days to visit their own families. This is the only time during the year when they are allowed to visit their own families. Some employers may give their workers a cash gift before the New Year; however, domestic workers are generally not paid while they are away for their family reunions.

Domestic workers have to work even when they are sick because there is no paid sick leave. If they are too sick to work, it is time for them to leave. One worker told me that she tripped and fell while grocery shopping for her employer. She got a slight concussion, but her employer did not show any consideration; instead, she was blamed for running too fast. She said: 'I felt so sad; she didn't even ask me if I was o.k. After I fell, there was a big bruise here, and this arm could not lift' (Interview, 27 November 2007). She had already been working with this family for five months, and the employer had wanted to renew her contract for another year before she had the injury. But after that, the employer did not want to keep her anymore. She could not cook the next day, but no one in the family invited her to have meals with them. She was forced to quit right away.

Training

Many domestic workers do not receive any job-related training. According to a survey in Beijing, Guangzhou and Chengdu, 26 per cent to 47 per cent of domestic workers were not trained (Wang 2007). From my interviews, I found that many domestic service companies in Beijing provide certain kinds of training for domestic workers before sending them to employers' homes. This usually focuses on training for *yuesao* and *yuersao*, who are hired especially to take care of children. However, because of the cost, most small private agencies do not provide any training for their workers. I discovered the reason during an interview with a labour authority officer:

> Should domestic workers be trained? Sure they should! It was to train them that our department worked out National Occupation Standards! Why do domestic service companies not provide training to workers? Because the companies have to pay a part of the training fees! Do you know how much one month's training costs? Room and board and training for one worker cost about ¥800! The common way of providing training is that the company pays the ¥800 to train the worker; once the worker is hired, this training fee will be deducted from the worker's first two months' salary. However, if the worker quits in less than a month, the company will have to swallow the loss. Domestic companies do not want to take any risk.
>
> (Interview, 7 November 2007)

As is evident from the above interview, no free training is provided by domestic service agencies in the cities; workers have to pay back the fees once they are hired. However, there is free training provided by the government for labourers who want to become domestic workers. To solve the problem of re-employing laid-off workers, the Chinese government is giving laid-off workers free skills training in many areas, including domestic service. Since 2003, the Chinese government has also allocated a special budget to improve rural migrant workers' skills. However, the fund has not been properly used for migrant workers. In Beijing and Chengdu, about 35 per cent of domestic workers were trained by government funding while in Guangzhou, the rate was only about 17 per cent (Wang 2007).

Without any training, domestic workers' work could be dangerous. They lack not only the skills to fulfil work tasks but also the knowledge to be able to protect themselves against any potential abuse and possible workplace injury.

Contracts

In a market economy, contracts should be an efficient tool for protecting both domestic workers and employers' interests. However, overall in China, domestic workers have low rates of signing service contracts. It is reported that, while 72.13 per cent of domestic workers in Beijing have signed contracts, there are more workers with no contracts than those with contracts in Guangzhou and Chengdu (Wang 2007). Agency workers normally sign contracts, but non-agency workers do not have any contracts.

In some cases, even with contracts, care workers' interests cannot be secured. To attract employers and make more profit, many agencies' contracts are unambiguously partial to both the employer and the agency. For example, I saw the articles in an intermediary agency's contract: If a domestic worker wants to quit, she must give the employer 14 days' notice; on the contrary, if the employer wants to terminate service, she or he needs to inform the domestic worker only seven days in advance. Another article on the same contract states,

Without asking for permission from the agency company in advance, any discrepancy that arises between the employee and the employer is the domestic worker's responsibility.

A nanny told me:

> The agency's contract? [It is useful only if] you don't have an accident, if you do, the responsibility is on you; the agency does not take any responsibility. It is very unfair.
> (Interview, 7 November 2007).

To safeguard the fairness of the domestic service contract, on 1 January 2007, the Beijing Administration for Industry and Commerce issued a uniform contract for domestic service agencies, in which the domestic workers are employed by the company to work for the clients. But the uniform contract does not apply to intermediary agencies that introduce workers to employers and charge commissions to both sides for every successful introduction. Even in this contract, there are ambiguous words that may leave domestic workers vulnerable to exploitation. For instance, in the article outlining the responsibilities of the domestic service companies' clients, the contract states that clients should grant domestic workers 'daily basic sleeping time' and 'give appropriate overwork pay' if they need their workers to work on statutory holidays. However, as the director of the BHSA said at the beginning of this chapter, the contract should specify an 8-hour sleeping time since 'basic' does not indicate an amount of time. A former laid-off worker who is doing domestic service and knew the Labour Law of China, pointed out another ambiguous term referring to 'appropriate pay' in the contract: '¥2 a day? ¥5 a day? How much is 'appropriate'? 'The contract does not set a standard. So these areas are still not fair for us workers' (Interview, 27 November 2007). She said that the Labour Law entitles workers to three times their daily wage rate for working on statutory holidays and questioned, 'Aren't domestic workers workers?' (Interview, 27 November 2007).

Accommodation and meals

In China, employers are supposed to provide live-in domestic workers with free meals and accommodation. However, in this respect, domestic workers are still treated like servants in the old society. They are usually not allowed to have the same food as their employers and sometimes they cannot even have the better leftovers.

> If a meat dish is left the first day and you are home alone the next day, you still cannot eat it. She (the employer) will ask when she comes home from work, 'Hey, where is yesterday's leftovers, that meat dish?' After she says this once, you will not eat it next time, right? Some rules are invisible. She does not clearly speak out, but she has some expectations of you!
> (Interview, 12 October 2007)

A worker told me that, once she ate a boiled egg left from the previous meal, and the employer's mother, an elderly lady, said, 'A maid is allowed to eat eggs?' (Interview, 27 November 2007). Generally, without permission, workers are not allowed to touch fruit, eggs, milk and other good foods. It is common for workers to be under-fed. Since workers perform manual labour, they need more food to get enough energy, but the employers do not allow them to cook or eat enough. One of my interviewees told me that she lost four kilos in one month, and a young girl who had worked for the same employer lost seven kilos in just one month.

It is quite common for domestic workers not to have their own bedroom because the apartments in big cities are small. Most nannies share a room with the child they look after. Care workers who take care of elders sometimes have to sleep in the same room as their charges of the opposite sex. Compared with those conditions, nannies' living conditions are much better. Due to lack of rooms, it is not rare that some domestic workers have to sleep either in a living room or on a closed balcony, where there is no privacy. Two domestic workers whom I interviewed even had to live with their employers' dogs. One of the workers quit the very next day because she was scared of the huge dog at night and she could not bear the humiliation of sleeping with a dog.

Many workers are allowed to shower only once a week, even in the summer. To control the workers' shower time, some employers turn off the gas while the workers are still showering simply because they do not want to pay the high costs for the hot water. Among my interviewees, 10 per cent encountered this problem, and they said they caught a cold as a result. A worker told me her former employer was even a doctor.

> I went into the bathroom to shower, and then she (the employer) turned off the gas; it was all cold water. I had to put on my clothes and come out. After I came out, I asked, 'What's the matter?' She told me 'Aiya, the gas was off.' I know the gas could not be off unless somebody turned it off. I can't be fooled. I used gas for many years at home. It is impossible that the gas went off if nobody shut the valve. Then I caught a cold that day. I phoned the friend who had introduced me to that employer, and I told her I could not work for this family anymore. How can I survive if I keep working (for them)!
>
> (Interview, 27 November 2007)

All workers are seen as potential thieves because of their inferior rural background and poor economic situation. As the only outsider in the employers' homes, if the employers lose anything, they suspect the domestic workers first. One 20-year-old girl told me that her employer searched not only her personal belongings but also her body twice. She said that to prove her innocence, she let the employer search her; she did not know that the employer had no right to do that. A worker who was suspected of stealing a painting by her employer's mother felt very insulted: 'That (painting) is not a small thing. It is so big! Assuming I stole it, where could I hide it? I live in their house' (Interview, 7 November 2007).

Some workers' personal freedom is restricted; they cannot freely go outside and contact families and friends. Because some employers do not trust the workers, not all the workers get keys to the home. This greatly restricts the workers' personal mobility. To some workers, their employers' homes are no less than prisons. They have to wait until their employers are home before they can do anything that involves leaving the house, even for job-related duties, such as taking out the garbage, if it requires them to go outside. I heard this story during an interview: one worker went to take out the garbage, and she met some other workers and chatted for a few minutes, but when she tried to get back inside, she found that she was locked out. No matter how loudly she knocked on the door, the employers pretended not to hear. She had to crouch down in the hallway and wait for the employers finally to acknowledge that she needed to get inside. She knew that her employers were angry with her for taking too much time to perform her duties and with her making friends with other workers. Generally, employers are very concerned that their workers might talk about what goes on in the home behind the employers' backs. Some employers see their privacy as more important than their workers' personal freedom.

Verbal and physical abuse

Living in employers' homes makes the employers' abuse of domestic workers harder to detect. Domestic workers in China, as elsewhere, can suffer physical mistreatment by employers, such as verbal abuse, assault and battery, and sexual harassment. Since verbal abuse happens all the time, workers get almost inured to it. 'Sometimes I just think that I'm not capable enough and that's why they always rebuke me' (Interview, 30 November 2007). These words represent part of some workers' feelings towards the verbal abuse they have to endure. A 20-year-old girl from Anhui Province told me her story: in 2004, when she was seventeen, she found her first job in Beijing. Her employers were both teachers, and they hired her as a nanny at first and told her that she did not need to do any chores that were not related to the care of the child. But later they required her to do the housework as well. The employer couple and their parents always rebuked her for not properly cleaning the dishes and the floor. She imitated their tone: 'Look at the state of the floor! And the dishes! Why bother cleaning them at all? Are you stupid? Our previous nannies were never as stupid as you! Are you a pig? You're so pigheaded!' (Interview, 30 November 2007).

She said that the employers even asked her if she was a human being. After she answered 'Yes', they would tease her, saying, 'So stupid! You don't even have a brain! Your brain is flooded with water [meaning it does not work properly]!' She told me: 'Those words were so offensive, and others were even more so! I can't even say them out loud! I had to continuously say, 'Sorry! Sorry! I will be careful next time!' (Interview, 30 November 2007).

Under such circumstances, she cried almost every day at that home. She hid under her blanket and cried quietly at night. She could not let them see; otherwise, they would criticize her again. After having worked for the family for one month, she asked her employers if she could quit when they did not pay her on time. Realizing that she had no intention of sticking to her three-month contract, the employers impatiently let her go, saying: 'Okay, okay, let her go, she is as stupid as a pig anyway!' She worked there for one month and seven days but only got paid for half a month (¥200); the other half of her salary was deducted for her mistakes. The girl said that she felt lucky that her employers did not beat her because she was afraid they might beat her.

Her worry was not uncalled for. Verbal abuse and physical abuse sometimes occur hand in hand. Although few cases of physical abuse have been revealed to the public so far, that does not mean physical abuse is rare. Some domestic workers simply lack the knowledge of their own rights; others choose to bear it for fear of losing their jobs. During my interviews, one worker reported that her male employer sometimes pinched her neck. The worker, in her late 40s, said that her employer almost choked her once when she asked for her salary. The employer not only physically abused her but also liked to tease her. The worker had divorced her ex-husband due to domestic violence at home, but her employer would often ask her for details of how her ex-husband used to beat her. Although the other participants in my study were not physically abused, some nannies did tell me that they have seen workers who were beaten and returned to the agency companies. The Anhui girl I cited earlier said that she once saw an older domestic worke, who had been severely beaten and had a bloody imprint on her face when she returned to the agent company. The agency helped to deal with this case. Unfortunately, for the purpose of my study, she could not recall where that worker came from, but she did remember that the worker went back to her hometown and she has not seen her since.

Agency workers are in a better situation than those workers who come into this industry through informal networks since the abuse may be reported to the agency and dealt with right away. For workers hired through informal networks, their employers' abusive behaviour may be hidden until obvious signs on the workers make concealment impossible. In 1999, a few mainstream newspapers, including *China Youth Daily*, and *China Women's News*, reported the case of a 14-year-old nanny in Guangxi who was beaten many times by her employer. When she was finally sent to a local hospital, the doctor found wounds all over her body, and she was on the verge of death. However, this was not a unique case. Cai Minmin was introduced by a fellow villager to domestic work in Zhuhai, Guangdong Province, far from her hometown in Henan Province. Minmin started to work for her employer, a university graduate in her 30s, when she was 15 years old. She worked for her employer for five years, until January 2006, when her case was exposed in the mass media.[13] In fact, her employer had abused her since the fourth or fifth month after she had started working there. During the five years, the employer frequently beat her with fists, a hammer, chopsticks, and a stick . . . anything she might have on hand. This physical abuse caused Minmin to be seriously disabled. Her face, ears and nose were disfigured, her lips were asymmetric, and her mouth could no longer close; she lost 12 teeth, and her left arm was broken and deformed. The doctors anticipated that Minmin needed at least 20 surgical operations to recover fully.[14] The employer was finally sentenced and the case caused a great sensation.

In addition to battery, sexual harassment happens very often in the closed work environment of domestic workers. Sometimes, the harassment even develops into rape. Because of threats from the employer or the fear of losing face under the traditional ideology that girls should stay chaste, the majority of victims endure it silently. This makes sexual harassment even harder to detect. On 8 August 2003, *Beijing Legal Daily* reported that, in two months, a single man over 50 years old raped four domestic workers he hired through a small agency. The youngest worker was only 14 years old, and the oldest was only 18. After the rapes happened, not one of the four girls reported the case to the police. The last worker who was raped told her sister, and it was the sister – also a domestic worker in Beijing – who reported the case. The man was sentenced to life in prison.

However, even when the case is reported, lack of proof sometimes prevents victims from receiving justice. I was told a story of what happened to a young girl from Gansu Province who was raped by her employer. After the employer had already confessed to the police, the employer's family members provided medical proof that the employer did not have sexual capability. Because the young girl did not have enough proof the employer was set free. In the end, the girl left the city very upset and vowed she would never come to work again!

In 2005, the MWC surveyed 206 domestic workers in Beijing and found that 6.3 per cent of these workers had been sexually harassed.

Because there is no protection or well-known channels for redress in the issue of sexual harassment, particularly for under-age workers, it is impossible to paint an accurate picture of sexual harassment in the domestic service industry in China, but it undoubtedly happens everywhere. In many other provinces and in cities other than Beijing the situation may be even worse.

Some domestic workers have even become the targets of criminals. On 19 September 2010, a news item titled 'Baomu Killer Self Confessed to have Murdered 8 People' appeared in a local Northeast newspaper, *City Evening News*.[15] It was reported that a 51-year-old disabled man living in Jilin city, Jilin Province, had serially murdered eight people in his home since May 2009, and seven of his victims were female rural migrant domestic workers. These domestic workers were mostly divorced and widowed. The four identified victim domestic workers' ages were 42, 49, 53 and 55 respectively. Some of the victims were sexually abused before they were murdered. The man said that he had murdered these victims just for money. He specifically looked for rural women domestic workers who were single in this city and he hired these victims through a roadside labour market because nobody would have noticed them. In this market, except for a few service agencies, most rural migrants just come here to market themselves as domestic workers (female) and truck drivers (male). The hiring process is based on both parties, employer and worker's consent, with no third party involved and there is no way to verify both sides' real identification either. The killer had also hired domestic workers through agencies, but none of the agency workers was murdered. This is because the agencies usually keep both domestic workers and employers' information and some of the agencies do follow up. Therefore, for domestic workers who lack resources and no money to pay agencies, the informal labour markets increase potential dangers. This case has called the attention of Jilin police to strengthening the supervision of the floating population in the city.

Leaving

Because of the low-end nature of domestic service work, there is almost no opportunity for advancement. Rural migrants do not even have any chance of staying in cities, although changing jobs is part of the domestic worker's daily life. The job can be for one day, one week or two to three years, which is almost the longest time they might work for one employer. Job stability is extremely low.

It is very easy for an employer to fire a worker. If an employer is not satisfied with a worker, she or he might return the worker to the agency the very same day. Therefore, every new job might be risky for the workers. Some agencies give a seven-day trial period to both workers and employers, which means that a worker might have to change jobs after the seven days. If an employer does not want a worker anymore, the worker has to leave immediately. A Sichuan worker told me that her former employer asked her to leave on the fifth day. It was already 5:00 p.m. when her employer told her to leave. Being wintertime, it was dark and cold outside, so she asked if she could stay till the next morning, but her employer said no, and she had to leave that night.

If a worker wants to leave her employer, it may not be easy. The employer would think, 'Why do you want to leave? Didn't I treat you well enough?' The employers may not want to pay the worker's full salary for their last period of work. The employers may also use other approaches to punish the disloyalty of their workers or slander the worker's reputation in a public space. On 5 September 2009, because of the unbearable leaving of her *xiao baomu*, a famous disabled athlete Sang Lan who became paraplegic because of an unexpected injury in training before a competition, wrote a blog article 'What is Domestic Service?' and posted it on the internet.[16] In the blog, Sang Lan posted more than 35 photos, taken from bedroom to bathroom, kitchen and doors, to display how her *xiao baomu* did not work hard and how disappointed she was. She also videotaped the scene when the *baomu* was leaving and uploaded this to the internet. The *baomu*'s father was sick and sent into hospital, and the *baomu*'s family members called her to go back; after the *baomu* received her wage, she asked the employer for leave. The blog was posted after she left. The *baomu*'s note for permission to leave and her wage receipt were posted on the internet as well. At first, this blog not only exposed the *baomu*'s name, but also her image and personal identification number. Later, the name and ID number were erased, but the *baomu*'s personal information was still disclosed. On 7 September, once again Sang Lan posted an article to criticize the domestic service sector and called for a true domestic service.[17] She insisted on a blacklist for domestic workers with a bad service record. These blogs attracted many readers and some readers openly criticized her way of dealing with the *baomu*'s leaving. *Beijing Youth Daily*, *Legal Daily*, and Beijing Television channel 8 followed up on this story. CCTV-12, a China Central TV channel that focuses on law and society, developed a programme to discuss how to regulate China's domestic service sector ('Everybody Talks about the Law', *dajia shuofa*). In the show, both Sang Lan and her *baomu* were invited, and both sides shook hands and made peace. When they hugged each other, everybody in the show applauded. Although this incident has finally come to an end, it has only just started the exploration of how to secure both domestic workers' and employers' rights through law and regulation.

Generally, if the working environment is bearable and the employers are not too difficult to work for, care workers would like to stay as long as they can. For example, nannies will stay until the children get older (about two to three years) and the family does not need them anymore. The workers told me that if they are lucky enough to meet a good employer, they would keep working for the employer because they are not sure what kind of employer they may encounter the next time. Most of my interviewees just thought that their current jobs were acceptable (*cou he*), but not satisfying. However, they are afraid to look for new jobs. Many of them said they wanted to leave the domestic service industry but, because of their lack of education, they did not have any other choices.

Precarious working conditions of cleaners

Cleaners are the second most numerous category of domestic workers in China, after care workers. Cleaners work for a wide variety of people, from singles to stressed working families to the elderly. They are generally hired to do the laundry and the house-cleaning. Depending on the employers' demands, they may have to cook for the families or drop off and pick up school-aged children as well. Some cleaners have regular employers, but most of them have to work for casual employers, which means they do not know who they are going to work for. They may be employed for anywhere from two hours to all day long for a single family, but the minimum is two hours. Since they are paid on an hourly basis, they are called '*xiao shi gong*', which means hourly worker.

The general employment model for cleaners is that they sign contracts with an agency, and the agency sends them to work for different households. According to my study, there are two types of agencies in Beijing. One is the employer-type agency – the agency is the employer who hires cleaners as employees on a contract basis, normally for half a year. The cleaners retain the right to renew new contracts, but if they break a contract, they have to pay a ¥200–300 fine (Interview, 31 October 2007). During the contract period, the company provides free lodging, work uniforms and pays the cleaners' salaries each month. Cleaners have to obey the rules of the company. Another type of agency is the intermediary company, where cleaners pay a ¥100–160 registration fee per year to register with the company. Within the registration year, the cleaners are able to come to the company hiring hall to wait for work (Interview, 26 November 2007). For each posting they get, the cleaners pay back a percentage of their wages to the company. The company does not manage the cleaners.

Cleaners have more autonomy than other domestic workers do. They may choose when to work and which family they want to work with. In addition, after finishing their tasks at one place, they leave for the next employer – they do not have to face the same employer every day, like care workers do. Whether they live with their own families, or live in lodging provided by their agencies, in both circumstances they have their own space, whereas nannies do not.

Unlike caring and housekeeping jobs, which involve both rural migrant workers and laid-off workers, cleaning jobs are taken on solely by rural migrant workers. The reason is that cleaning is considered purely menial labour, while caring for others requires more skill.

The following section gives examples of cleaners' working conditions, which are considerably different from those of nannies and other domestic workers.

Daily working hours

The cleaners I interviewed normally work more than eight hours a day; the average is 10 hours. For convenience, agent companies are set up in residential areas and so are cleaners' dormitories. The agencies' clients live either in the same neighbourhood as the agency or very close to the neighbourhood. The cleaners' hours at the employer-type companies are regulated from 8:00 a.m. to 8:00 p.m. But in reality, there is no fixed time when the cleaners can get off work since they may be hired to work in the evening, at 7:00 p.m. or 8:00 p.m., after their employers come home from work. In such cases, they may get off work around 9:00 p.m. or 10:00 p.m.

The intermediary companies do not regulate the cleaners' work hours. The cleaners can choose when they want to go to their companies and wait for phone calls from employers. Since the cleaners live with their own families, they have to choose the work hours that allow them time to fulfil their responsibilities at home. However, to make more money to pay rent and to support their families, most of them have to get up very early in the morning and come home very late in the evening. These cleaners usually juggle family duties and wage work as best they can.

Cleaners work for different employers and none of the cleaners know how much time they will need to spend at one house; therefore, in order to finish their work for one family and switch to the next scheduled family, most of the time they have to skip lunch, or eat as simply as possible. One sweet potato or a piece of pancake would be all they could have as a meal. All of my interviewees reported that they did not have time to eat until they got off work.

Income

The cleaners I interviewed earned more than most nannies. Cleaners can each make more than ¥1,000 a month in Beijing. Their income is calculated by the hour so that the more hours they work, the more income they can make. Since their work is continual menial labour from family to family, the work intensity is heavier than that of care workers.

In my interviews, cleaners indicated that they usually are paid in one of two ways. One way is that the agent company pays them once a month according to a minimum salary (*baodi*) – ¥300 or ¥400 per month – plus a percentage of the hourly wage rate of ¥8 per hour (*ticheng*), which is ¥3 or ¥2.5 per hour of work. Everyone can get her minimum salary by perfect attendance according to the companies' rules. If workers ask for sick leave or personal leave, the minimum wage will be deducted by the number of days they are absent. It is worth mentioning that employers pay the agencies ¥8 per hour for the referral of the cleaner. The other way is that workers get paid directly by the families they serve. Employers pay them ¥8 per hour, out of which workers have to pay their intermediary agencies ¥1.5 per hour for the work they get from the agencies.

Unlike care workers who may not be paid for their work, cleaners get their salaries on time. However, according to my interviewees, a frequent problem for cleaners is that employers sometimes miscalculate their working hours in order to pay them less. For example, cleaners may have worked for two hours and twenty minutes, but most employers bargain to pay for only two hours, even though the rule in this industry is that for any work less than half an hour, employers should pay for half an hour. Sometimes, the employers may ask the cleaners to do a little extra work, such as washing a few pairs of slippers or cleaning a kettle, after the cleaners have already signed out. Therefore, workers frequently are underpaid.

Training

Generally agent companies provide cleaners with basic skills training before they start work. When a new worker first goes to work, her agent sends an experienced older worker to work with her. Through the older worker's guidance, the new cleaner gradually becomes familiar with the working procedures, including where to mop first and which areas should be left till the end, how to use the vacuum, and so on. Thus, the new workers' efficiency quickly increases.

In addition to work skills, some agent companies also teach the new workers communication skills for transactions with employers so they can try to avoid trouble. Personal safety is also covered by the training. Most workers have been told not to try to do dangerous tasks, such as cleaning the outside of the windows for employers, even if they are asked to do so.

Training is only one side of the work; since workers have to face different people every day, it is unlikely that no new problems will arise. Some formal agent companies, such as Manager Liu's company, have a 15-minute daily meeting in the morning to summarize the previous day's work and restate points of attention for the new day (Interview, 30 October 2007).

Weekend and statutory holidays

Cleaners do not get weekends and holidays off, although theoretically some of those who register with intermediary companies have the autonomy of choosing to take a break on weekends and public holidays. However, the policy is 'no work, no pay', so earning an income translates into no breaks.

The rule of the employer-type agent company I interviewed is that workers can have one day off per month, and during statutory holidays, such as Labour Day and National Day, workers can take two of the three-day holidays off. However, the workers told me: 'Nobody takes any days off, [we are] afraid of making less money. Only if we really have something to do we take one day off; if there is nothing we must do, none of us rests.' (Interview, 31 October 2007)

> It is not easy to make money. We only get 2.5 *yuan* an hour. Taking one day off means we make no money for that day. If we don't take a break, even if we only work for 8 hours a day, we can at least have 20 *yuan*, on top of a day's *baodi* – 10 *yuan* for that day, right? So nobody takes a break.
>
> (Interview, 21 November 2007)

Because there is no economic security, cleaners try to work as much as possible while the condition of their bodies allow them to and while there is enough work available. The intermediary agent workers, who can choose work hours and workdays, told me, 'All of us have to raise a family. Where is [the choice] of working or not working? We don't have a choice; we have to work' (Interview, 3 December 2007).

Xiao An, who is a 33-year-old from Anhui province living in a rented place with her husband and their fifth-grade son, said that she had counted the days she took off work, from the (Chinese) New Year till now (3 December 2007) – the number of days she did not work was fewer than 10.

Occupational hazards

According to the cleaners I interviewed, habitual repetitive physical labour made many old workers who have been in this industry for two or three years get arthritis and back and shoulder aches. Cleaners have to work with cold water all the time when they clean peoples' homes, even in the winter. Many cleaners told me that because employers have to pay for hot water, some of them simply turn off the hot water when cleaners come to work. The icy frozen water has caused arthritis in many workers' hands. In addition, many interviewees said that the skin on their hands cracks in the winter and causes a lot of pain while they work.

Another occupational hazard is shoulder and back aches. In China, people usually have hard floors, either wooden or laminated; to take good care of the floors, cleaners are required to use a piece of towel to hand-wash the floors, which means they have to either kneel down or squat to clean off the dirt. Working over a long period of time, cleaners' shoulders and backs gradually become injured. When they bend down to wash the floor, they feel pain in all of those body parts. In addition, since cleaning a client's floor takes about one hour or even longer, most of the time they have to kneel down on the floor, which often bruises their knees. Especially in the summer, when they wear very thin clothes, kneeling down on the hard floor is painful. At the employee-type company I interviewed, Manager Liu bought kneepads for the cleaners. However, most cleaners do not get any protection against occupational hazards from their agent companies.

Social insurance

Like other rural migrant workers, cleaners do not have any pension plan or unemployment insurance. Because of their rural peasant identity, the only social insurance they enjoy is the overall medical plan for peasants in their hometown, as explained in the care worker section.

However, the cleaners I interviewed were optimistic. They said at least they could make more than ¥1,000 per month, which was a much higher income compared with staying in the countryside. They told me that they were generally in good health, and as long as they were not sick in bed and had the ability to work every day, they would not worry about their life. They did not even entertain hopes of things that only city residents have, which were beyond their ability to reach. The land of which they own a users' right in their hometown is their final source of insurance.

Abuse and mistreatment

Because of the difference of social standing between rural migrant workers and city residents and the degrading image of domestic service work, it is not surprising to find that cleaners are treated harshly by some employers.

Information from my interviews revealed that one common abusive situation is the monitoring of the cleaners' labour. Some people who hire cleaners think that these rural cleaners might be lazy and try to steal stuff; to get their money's worth, the employers make efforts to monitor the work process. However, many cleaners indicate that they feel very nervous under surveillance, and even more, they feel wronged. A worker who has been doing cleaning work for more than two years told me:

> Wherever you work, some people always like to watch you! I feel very uncomfortable! I work hard even if they do not follow me! I do this job, but I am not a thief who is trying to steal something! Whatever, I feel very aggrieved in my heart!
>
> (Interview, 31 October 2007)

Manager Liu told me that there have even been several times when his workers were suspected of having stolen USB keys, MP3 players and watches. But after a few days the employers found these items in their homes and phoned the company back and apologized. Manager Liu said her workers did not even know what USB keys or MP3 players were, and those suspicions hurt the workers' feelings considerably. Some workers once wanted to quit because of these kinds of charges.

If the cleaners break something, they may get into trouble since some employers demand that the workers pay unreasonable high prices to replace the item. I was told that on one occasion an English teacher from a famous key high school in Beijing tried to charge a cleaner ¥2,000 for a broken decoration, which is seven times higher than the original value of ¥300. In the end, the worker's agent company took the broken piece for evaluation in the Ministry of Public Security in China. With the evaluation certificate, the employer had to accept a ¥300 compensation paid by the cleaner. The agency's manager frowned upon the way that the highly educated teacher treated the rural migrant worker:

> Some employers extort workers. They think, 'Ha, rural migrant workers in cities! No way out and nowhere to turn to! No matter how much I ask, you have to pay it.' They are totally extorting migrant workers' hard-earned money.
>
> (Interview, 30 October 2007)

It is ordinary practice for cleaners to pay back employers for the items they damage. Agent companies do not take any responsibility, but they generally try to make sure that the compensation is reasonable. To avoid possible trouble, agent companies also teach workers strategies of asking their employers to move seemingly expensive items instead of trying to move those items by themselves.

Verbal abuse is not uncommon and quite often clients/employers rebuke the cleaners until they cry. Although physical beating is rare, I did hear a story about a 19-year-old cleaner who was beaten and chased to the elevator by an older male client. Although she got wounds all over her breasts and had to pay for the medical treatment by herself, the employer did not receive any punishment. It had been more than one year after the incident when I interviewed the cleaners, but everyone who knew about the beating case was still pained by it. A young girl worker did not want to say anything about her work environment by directly telling me: 'The human beating case hasn't been solved yet! What do you want me to say? What can I say?' (Interview, 31 November 2007). When she said this, her face turned red because of anger and helplessness. The cleaners all felt vulnerable to clients' power. A worker in her early 30s also told me about her sense of helplessness towards the incident: 'Whatever he [the employer] said, he was in the right since he had a lot of power, right? But no matter how useless we are, we are at least human beings!' (Interview, 31 November 2007).

The cause of the beating was actually very simple: the beaten cleaner forgot to bring the service card[18] for the client to sign; therefore, she asked if the client could sign out next time when cleaners came to work again. The client first refused, using very coarse language and then began to beat the worker's breasts with his fists. He even arrogantly claimed, 'I am a retired director-level official. You go report me at any police station! They [police officers] are under my leadership!' (Interview, 30 October 2007). The police officer who came to deal with the dispute obviously favoured the client. Even the manager of the agent company was not allowed to witness the investigation. There was nothing the company could do to protect its worker. At last, the girl was believed by the police officer to deserve the beating since the client claimed that the girl cursed him first and he was forced to hit her. After this happened, the girl quit her job the next day. For a very long time, other cleaners in the same company were scared and on edge when working in people's homes.

Cleaners sometimes also encounter sexual harassment from male employers, but it is generally verbal or 'light' harassment, such as touching the cleaners' hands. No rape has been reported among my interviewees or through the mass media. One reason is that cleaners do not live in their employers' homes, and they are often sent to work in pairs by their companies; another reason is that cleaners have close relationships with their companies, and the companies also tactfully refuse to send any worker to some employers with bad reputations.

Job stability

There is a high turnover rate for cleaners. Some workers work for only two or three months before they quit. It is very hard to keep workers.

Just as there is an increased demand for domestic workers, the demand of cleaners is also on the rise. Cleaners' job responsibilities have been widening as the market demand goes up. Their job has been transformed from traditional cleaning into diversified work tasks, including cooking and picking up children from school. However, increased work tasks have not brought an increase in their income accordingly. A low hourly wage rate (¥2.5 per hour), heavy physical labour and a degrading work environment stop many cleaners from working for a long period of time. Two years on the job – even just one year – is considered a long time. Although domestic agencies try to keep their workers by signing a one-year contract, most workers accept only a half-year contract. They would rather renew the contract more frequently than give up their personal freedom of quitting without being charged a fine.

Conclusion

This chapter shows the 'Chinese characteristics' of paid domestic work and how paid domestic work differs from precarious paid domestic work in other parts of the world, as well as the variations in the conditions of different types of paid domestic work.

I have demonstrated that while the rise of domestic employment has helped solve the increasing needs of city residents for care and other domestic services, it has also created a new inequality between domestic workers and their employers. The marketization of domestic labour has not only legitimated male privilege in private homes, but also allows privileged groups of women to take advantage of disadvantaged women – rural migrant women and laid-off city workers who can be exploited because of their need for income and the lack of available alternative jobs. Hiring domestic labour not only reaffirms the image that women are responsible for domestic work, but also involves direct exploitation by paying domestic workers as little as possible while asking them to work as long as possible. Whether from the jobs' long and unregulated hours, low pay and lack of social benefits or from maltreatment of domestic workers by their employers, paid domestic work can be seen as exploitive and abusive. Despite government assurances to the contrary, domestic service is still painfully associated with the servitude in ancient Chinese history and has retained images of inferior and laborious service.

The current domestic workers' precarious working and living conditions have proved that the economic and social circumstances in China have favoured employers' interests in the failure to grant labour protection to domestic workers. This is a big contradiction to the socialist ideology that asserts that everybody is equal and all work is to be equally valued. When socialist moral standards begin to erode in the market economy era, it is time for the government to create concrete strategies to make certain that every labourer enjoys worker's rights. Domestic workers, like workers in the industrial domain, should be covered by protections and benefits granted by any government regulations.

6 From individual resistance to unionized negotiation

There is no doubt that domestic workers are exploited, marginalized and socially disadvantaged in contemporary China. Their plight is reflected in their precarious working conditions and a lack of protective laws and regulations. However, they are not passive victims in the unequal power relationships with their employers. Just as there have been different forms of resistance or refusal against power in economic exploitation, domestic workers have struggled for their rights as workers and human beings.

Foucault has analysed the correlation of power/resistance and conduct/counter-conduct. He stressed that resistance is 'coextensive and absolutely contemporaneous'[1] to power, but resistance and counter-conduct go beyond the reverse image of power or purely negative acts of disobedience; in order to resist, one must activate something 'as inventive, as mobile, as productive'[2] as power itself; and even apparently personal or individual forms of counter-conduct have a political dimension, which can modify power relations between individuals and have an effect on the potential for action.[3] He recognized women's rebellious conduct in history as 'linked up with the problem of women and their status in society, in civil society or in religious society' (Foucault 2007: 196–7). Foucault's philosophical analysis can certainly be used to explain domestic workers' resistance in China. Feminist literature on women's resistance and activism has also indicated that women are agents and activists in their own rights (Basu 1995; Rowbotham 1992). Feminists argue that, 'in inequality, injustice and human subordination, the individuals are accountable for change and improvement in society' (Rowbotham 1992: 315). In addition, to achieve social equality and justice, 'the self-action of sizable groups of people', which means collective action is necessary (Rowbotham 1992: xiv). In China, domestic workers' resistance to injustice and exploitation involves both direct action against oppression by individual women and collective action for social change. In recent years, non-government organizations (NGOs) which work on behalf of women migrant workers have been developed to undertake the work of protecting migrant domestic workers. Since 2003, domestic workers have also begun the process of unionization. Although organized resistance is still in an embryonic stage, it has begun to exert power in negotiating for domestic workers' rights.

In this chapter, I will examine the concrete approaches that domestic workers use in their everyday resistance and explore different organizations and their roles in protecting domestic workers' interests. I will argue that domestic workers' resistance comprises a range of struggles by poor women against gender inequality. Shared experiences of oppression during the collective action taken by women's NGOs and the process of unionization have contributed to feminist consciousness among domestic workers and domestic workers clearly have been empowered through collective action. At the same time, their resistance is about not only gender-specific grievances and concerns, but also basic worker's rights and human rights. The unionization of domestic workers has indicated that domestic workers' resistance is part of new working-class struggles in the reformed China. Domestic workers' class-consciousness is gradually fostered during this resistance as these workers relate to workers in other industries. As throughout the world, precarious workers are extremely hard to unionize,[4] but there is no reason to think that the domestic workers' movement could not be part of the working-class movement in China. As workers, domestic workers should be considered as part of the mass working class because only if their struggle for job and economic security is combined with the struggle of the mass labour movement will their rights and interests be secured.

From individual resistance to collective action, domestic workers' resistance in China is a great example of a force that 'resembles aspects of the feminist movement' worldwide and of how human beings could act to improve their lives and societies (Rowbotham 1992: 310). This chapter will start with personal, individual experiences of domestic workers' resistance.

Everyday forms of resistance

One distinctive feature of domestic service is that workers are isolated from one another. The privacy of the workplace dictates that, most of the time, domestic workers have to make individual negotiations with their employers. Since their strategies are fragmented and individualized, the agency of individuals may be limited. However, domestic workers still have the potential to resist oppressive employers by being picky about employers, refusing to do certain jobs, arguing, walking out on the job and getting better legal protection through collective action. Personal resistance strategies are immediate but not sufficient, which is why legal protection and collective action are needed. This part of the chapter deals with personal strategies; I will discuss legal protection and collective actions in the following parts.

Looking for a good employer

Seeking a good employer has become a strategy that domestic workers use to avoid potential oppression. Although laid-off workers and rural migrants do not have much choice but to find work as domestic workers, they do choose their own employer. According to my interviews, domestic workers' choices are largely based on the employers' age groups, with a preference for young over senior employers. They believe that young people are more generous and offer better conditions. In their own words, older employers are too '*koumen*' and '*shebude*' (both words mean stingy). A domestic worker in her early 20s from Gansu province told me about her former employer, who was an elderly lady:

> ... that old lady was so miserly that she thought paying me 700 hundred *yuan* (a month) was high. I told her that there is nothing lower than 700, and 700 is the lowest pay. She also calculated that you take 4 days off each month, then how many days you actually work! ... She didn't like it when I showered because she was worried that the water and gas would cost her too much ...
> (Interview, 3 November 2007)

One *yuersao* in her 30s from Anhui province, generalized:

> Never work for old ladies in Beijing. They are too stingy. When you turn on the light, they would say 'Turn it off!' When you turn on the tap, 'You [always?] leave the water running; do you know how much water costs?' Just like that! They would rather you didn't eat, didn't drink, worked well and asked to be paid less!
> (Interview, 7 November 2007)

Some workers do not like the fact that the older generation still treats them like the old *baomu* in a feudal society. They told me, 'Old people's notions have not changed much. They wonder why *baomu* need to take breaks.' They ask, 'Don't I pay money for you to work?'[5] One informal essay published in the *Migrant Women's Club Domestic Workers' Brief* by the Zuo Ling Domestic Service Company (ZLDSC) also reported that the workers in this company complained they were more discriminated against by elderly people than by younger ones (ZLDSC 2007).

This stereotype of people's age reflects not only domestic workers' expectations of being paid better and having better living conditions, but also an implicit analysis of experience. Some domestic workers told me that the older generations value thriftiness because, in the past, nobody had a high income, and many of these employers were originally peasants; however, these should not become excuses for why they would rather pay domestic workers less.

Aside from the employer's age, gender is also a factor in employees' perceptions of their employers. If the employer is male, workers generally ask if there is a landlady in the family (a tactful way that domestic workers use to ask if the man has a wife at home). If the answer is yes, they may agree to work for him; if the answer is no, they would not work in his home for fear for their personal safety. Most workers also choose not to take care of old men since sexual harassment could happen.

Other factors that affect domestic workers' choices include how big the employer's house is,[6] how many people live in the family, or whether the elderly person they will be taking care of can move by her- or himself. Some workers also express their right to rest. They will ask to take one day off every week and ask for breaks during statutory holidays. After gathering this information, they bargain for an acceptable salary or tell employers they cannot take the job.

The fact that domestic workers dare to ask about their employers' situation and bargain with them shows that huge progress has been made. This change has happened only in the past two years and is related to the growing market demand for domestic workers. Before that, only employers could choose the domestic workers. It is quite common for employers to feel offended by domestic workers' questions since their absolute authority is challenged during the bargaining process. They feel that domestic workers are being fussier. Some employers lose their temper when workers ask about their situation; some even fool workers by concealing their real circumstance. For instance, in order to pay workers less, they may deliberately claim that their house is only 100 square metres instead of the actual 400 square metres. However, when the workers find out that they have been fooled, they have to find an excuse to quit for their workload is far heavier to clean a big house than a smaller one where they may still have a separate room.

Resisting control and exploitation at work

In general, the employer has the authority to set the workplace rules and the tasks that domestic workers are supposed to follow; however, for many workers the situation can be changed through strategic resistance such as: agree, but do things their own way anyway; refuse certain jobs; negotiate and reason with employers; argue and threaten to quit to exert pressure on employers. To avoid trouble, some workers choose to overtly agree with but covertly oppose their employers. A laid-off worker in her early 40s said that her employer was very picky and always tried to teach her how to do things properly; however, the employer's requirements were not always reasonable. The worker reported,

> When she [the employer] assigns me some new tasks and tells me to do my work her way, I would say 'o.k.,' I don't say anything that may offend her. I agree with her first, and then after she is gone, I still do things my way.
> (Interview, 3 November 2007).

I think her attitude reflects most domestic workers' attitudes towards their employers. I have sometimes heard employers complaining about how their workers do not listen to them. An employer described her *baomu*, who had been working for her for three years: 'Sometimes [the worker] listens to you, sometimes not. But she does not always do things according to your requirements. When you mention that she has done something wrong, she does not admit her mistakes' (Interview, 25 October 2007).

The employer gave me an example of how her *baomu* refuses to listen to her. She asked the *baomu* to clean the floors, especially rarely reached corners and the ceramic walls of two bathrooms before the weather turned cold, but after waiting for one week, the *baomu* still had not done the job. She said that she had to remind the *baomu* again. But she did not want to hire someone else since she had hired five different ones already, and the current one was considered the most suitable. Another important reason was that it was too time-consuming to look for a new *baomu*. Domestic workers who have worked for a long time in this industry know how to take advantage of employers' reluctance to spend more time and energy to find another worker.

There are various examples of workers' refusal to do certain jobs or defending their rights to be treated justly. The most common task that workers will no longer perform is washing underwear by hand. A live-in worker in her early 40s defended her resistance in terms of rights: 'It was not an issue of whether or not I should wash her underwear but, rather, of human dignity! (Interview, 27 November 2007). She said that she had never done such work for any family. Her attitude was, 'No matter how long you [the employer] put it there, I'm not going to wash it for you!' (Interview, 27 November 2007). Although the cleaners I interviewed did not address the issues of human dignity, they shared their experience of resistance. A 30-year-old cleaner said that she would put the underwear aside when she did the laundry, and the employers would have to wash it themselves. In a cleaners' focus group, all four participants talked about an employer who was over 40 years old and well known to them. The cleaners described her as extremely dirty because she always asked the cleaners to wash her bloody underwear. One of the cleaners said she had only worked for the employer once and she would never go back a second time. Seeing the employer's soiled underwear, the cleaner suspected that the employer had some kind of gynaecological inflammation. She told the employer that she would not wash 'this thing' and that she was leaving, then she washed her hands and got ready to leave. The employer phoned her agent company and complained about her, but as there were no other cleaners available at the company at that moment, the employer's attitude softened, and she told the cleaner, 'I will wash this myself! I didn't say that you had to wash it! I will wash it!' The employer took out the underwear and asked the cleaner to finish doing the laundry.

In their struggle for their rights to eat properly and to have reasonable living conditions, some workers choose openly to discuss these matters with their employers. A laid-off worker from Sichuan province recounted the full story of how she changed her former boss's rules, which said that she was not to shower or eat the same food as they did. She said that the employers (an elderly couple) only allowed her to shower when the female employer showered, which was once a week; when the female employer was not showering, the employers just took away the hot water valve. She said that, even though she could have showered in secret since she knew how to turn on the hot water, she did not. 'To be frank, they would not even find out if I showered 10 times behind their backs. But I had to strive for my rights! I had to do it openly and aboveboard' (Interview, 27 November 2007). She then explained to the employers that she felt very uncomfortable not showering, and besides, she had to cook three meals every day with her hands. No showering meant her hands could not be that clean either; making buns with dirty hands would not bring health to anybody. She suggested that she would give up a meal in exchange for a shower. The employers were finally persuaded to let her shower freely. She also broke the rules that said she was not to eat eggs and fruit from her employers' house. She told the employers that her bodily health was the most important thing while making money was the second, so she wanted to be equal with them in life – that is, whatever the employers ate, she could eat; anything the employers did not want, she did not want either. She told me that she said this to every employer she had worked with.

The refusal to eat leftovers has been a big issue for many domestic workers. Many workers said that if it was something left in a dish, they would be willing to eat it since every family eats leftovers, but if it was leftovers from their employers' bowls, they would rather not eat it. A worker told me that her former employer tried to offer her some rice or other food in the employer's bowl, but she refused by saying she was full and could not eat anymore. After that had happened two more times, the employer never treated her that way. The worker said, 'You could give me some before you eat, but after you've already had half, then you ask me to have some? I don't want that!' (Interview, 27 November 2007).

For live-in workers, defending their right to rest has become important. A few agency workers told me how they wanted the right to take a day off every week. Twenty-two-year-old Xiao Luo would rather have a day off once a week than make extra money by working overtime. She asked the employer to let her quit if the employer did not want to grant her the right to take a day off. She won the battle, although her employer was very reluctant to give in. She said, 'Now I can take a day off; I don't work overtime. I never wanted to' (Interview, 3 November 2007). It is more difficult for workers hired through informal channels to fight for their right to rest since they do not have any organizational network. However, some workers enjoy the freedom to rest to a certain extent. Forty-three-year-old Xiao Tang said she was freer than most other domestic workers in her neighbourhood were because she strived for it. Many workers admired her.

Face-to-face arguments happen when workers do not want to bear the humiliation employers cause them to suffer. A 44-year-old live-in worker said that her employer, who was in her late 30s, once suspected she stole some peaches. The worker had actually served the peaches to the employers' guests, but the employer had forgotten about this. The worker felt that this was not only about peaches, but also about self-respect. She spoke up to let the employer know that she felt that she had been unjustly treated. A 22-year-old worker told me about an elderly lady she used to take care of. The elderly lady always lost her temper and picked on the worker until she could not take it anymore. She said, 'I respected her, but that was not the case' (Interview, 3 November 2007). She finally told the employer that nobody could do this job unless that person really did not care about self-respect or her own life but only cared about the money. The employer did not even respond. Domestic workers agree that it is normal to argue with employers: 'I sometimes felt that arguing was not a bad thing. The employers can get to know us better and we can get to know them more and find out what they are thinking. Mutual understanding deepens!' (Interview, 3 November 2007).

Resist with feet

'At worst I quit!' 'If you are not nice to me, I will not work for you!' If they are not satisfied with their employers or feel that they are being mistreated, domestic workers will leave to seek employment elsewhere. They may either fabricate an excuse to leave or directly tell their employers that they cannot work there anymore. An employer gave me an example of how one of her former workers, a married migrant worker, left her:

> She said that something had happened at her home and she had to go back to her hometown. Her husband recently contracted some more land and needed her help to do agricultural work. Her mother was not in good health. So she could not do this work anymore. She had to leave. But later I found out that it was because she thought I did not pay her well.
> (Interview, 25 October 2007)

Rong is a 43-year-old laid-off worker. When I interviewed her, she had just broken her contract and left the last employer. Because she was continuously not getting enough food at that employer's home, her stomach aches made it very hard for her to sleep at night. In addition to this, she could not stand being suspected of stealing things. But the most important reason she left was that her employer had a rule that when the employer yelled at her, whether it was her fault or not, she was not allowed to explain, and the only word she could say was 'Yes'. After working there for one month, she left:

> Who could work longer in her home? I lost eight jin^7 in weight and could not sleep! But I didn't tell her why I left. I just said that my daughter was getting married and I had to go back home. I told this lie. Generally I don't lie, but there was no way I was going to keep working there!
> (Interview, 27 November 2007)

To avoid any trouble, domestic workers normally leave that way. However, some workers openly inform the employers and ask the employers to send them back to their agent companies. This usually happens after disagreements or conflicts. Workers admit that this way does not do them any good because they might get a bad record in the agent companies for conflicts with employers and breach of contracts.

At the end of 2007, a Beijing TV station specifically made a show exploring this new phenomenon of domestic workers dumping their employers, something that has happened only in the last few years. Experts in the show considered it a positive change and confirmed that, by doing so, the employment condition of domestic workers has made much progress. They also noted that it is normal for everybody to seek better pay and a better working environment. While for some domestic workers leaving employment may indicate a desire for higher income and better working conditions, the high turnover may equally indicate the opposite – that is, that this occupation is not worth the struggle. Some workers simply leave the domestic service industry permanently because they do not want to remain in an industry with such degrading employment conditions.

Domestic workers' individual voices are clear in the demand for human dignity and mutual respect. These voices from the bottom of the social ladder represent the awakening of domestic workers' rights consciousness and class-consciousness. A laid-off worker said that she had demanded no conditions from employers other than equality in human dignity. 'You [employer] contribute to society; I contribute to your family. We are equal in human dignity. Nowadays, people need domestic service, and it is accepted as an occupation in our society' (Interview, 27 November 2007). Not only laid-off workers but also migrant workers, especially young people, have begun to seek respect and dignity from employers. As another young migrant worker said,

> If you respect me, I'm sure I can work for you. If you criticize me for this and condemn me for that every day and I have to keep my anger in check, how can I do a good job? Respect is mutual! To be frank, if we respect you [employer], you also need to respect us! We also have dignity – you cannot say whatever you want to say!
>
> (Interview, 3 November 2007)

Legal resistance

In the fight for equality and human dignity, domestic workers are not only limited to everyday resistance, which is quiet, disguised and individualized. Their 'weapons of resistance' also include resistance that protects their 'lawful rights and interests' (*hefa quanyi*). Lawful rights and interests mean the rights and interests that they have already been granted by government through policies, laws, principles and legitimating ideology. Scholars, such as O'Brien and Li, use the term 'rightful resistance' to describe the type of resistance that was used by farmers in rural China to contest the unfair treatment they received at the hands of the political and economic elite (O'Brien and Li, 2006). This concept of *hefa quanyi* is similarly used to defend the right of the new underclass of domestic workers.

Although the free market does not always ensure the protection of rights, in recent years, China's legal reforms have improved both the enactment of primarily substantive legislation and the legal process itself (Woo 2002). There has also been an effort to professionalize the legal profession, which has included increased training of lawyers and judges to consolidate their legal knowledge (Woo 2002). Terms like 'rights and interests', 'rights and obligations' are 'making inroads into Chinese law and jurisprudence' (Woo 2002: 317). The legal system changes have not only 'created opportunities for the assertion of legal rights, but have increasingly placed responsibility for the assertion of those rights on individuals, and thus fostered a sense of "rights consciousness"' (Woo 2002: 309). These changes have made it possible for domestic workers to assert their legal rights that are guaranteed by the Constitution and the civil code in China. Currently, the violation of domestic workers' labour rights is still covered under civil law cases instead of labour disputes; and workers have a chance of winning rights issues if they appeal through the proper channels. Domestic workers have been getting more opportunities to win law suits after the central government enacted policies to guarantee more equal treatment for migrant workers. A 2003 document on labour migration, The Notice on Improving Rural Migrant Labour's Employment Management and Service issued by the State Council, states that improving legal procedures (contracts, on-time payment of wages) and the working and living conditions of migrant labourers (health care and social security benefits) were to be a focus for government action.[8] While the policy initiatives' concern is migrant workers in the production domain, it has also affected domestic workers because rural migrant domestic workers have learned to use these government policies to protect themselves. A 41-year-old migrant domestic worker who had a junior high school education told me the story of how she took her employer, who owed her ¥200 in salary, to the local labour bureau. At first, the employer not only refused to pay, but also called the police to take the domestic worker away. In front of the police officer, the worker insisted that she did not do anything wrong and said, 'I'm not going with you [police officer]. I will only go to the labour bureau. There are government departments who should take care of this case, but not you!' (Interview, 26 November 2007). The police officer finally drove the worker and the employer to the labour bureau, but the employer refused to go in and walked away. Although the worker did not get her salary back, her behaviour signals a growing rights consciousness and awareness of where to go to for help.

Some domestic workers have also learned to use the law to defend their rights in the case of serious labour rights violations. I have read a case in which a domestic worker sued her employer and her agent company for not paying her one-month's salary. According to the contract, the worker was sent to the employer from 10 November 2006 to 9 December 2006. Her monthly salary was ¥1,200. To make sure the employer paid on time, it was agreed that the employer would pay the ¥1,200 in advance to the company and then the company would pay the worker after one month. If either the worker or the employer wanted to terminate the contract, they would have to give the agent company a seven-day notice; otherwise, 5 per cent of ¥1,200 would be charged to the party who failed to give notice before breaking the contract. However, the employer did not pre-pay the ¥1,200 to the agent company and on 8 December 2006 the employer asked for an exchange of domestic workers because the family was not satisfied with the worker's work. Neither the employer nor the agent company paid the worker. Therefore, the worker took them to court and sued them. Even though the agent company should bear joint responsibility with the employer, the employer was ordered to pay the worker ¥1,154 within seven days of the judge's ruling. The employer appealed. After mediation in the second hearing, the employer agreed to pay the worker ¥1,000 and that the worker would take care of the first hearing fee of ¥70, while the employer would pay the second hearing fee of ¥120.[9]

Due to time, cost and an unequal power relationship with employers, there are still some limitations for domestic workers who formally seek redress through

From individual resistance to unionized negotiation 115

courts as well as through the local labour bureaus. If possible, they try not to go through these procedures.

However, domestic workers have begun to see the laws as a useful weapon in China's transition to govern the country by laws rather than by administrative orders. They now have some enthusiasm for learning about laws. Once, I saw a worker with a Labour Law brochure in her hand at an agent company. After she saw the interest on my face, she said: 'I just want to know more about it. Then I will know how to protect myself' (Interview, 27 November 2007). Another time, when I did an interview with a worker in a different agent company, the 41-year-old rural migrant worker told me, 'I think the best way is to become more familiar with the law. If we know the law, we will know how to protect ourselves, right?' (Interview, 26 November 2007).

Some workers have attempted to use the Labour Law to ensure their right to rest and to triple or double pay for work performed during statutory holidays including the 2010 Mid-Autumn Day on 22 September (the holiday was 22–24 September); and the National Day was 1 October (the holiday was 1–7 October). According to the Labour Law, workers should be paid triple on the statutory days, 22 September and 1 October, and be paid double on the other rest days, 23–24 September and 2–7 October. A newspaper reported that an employer in Nanjing posted on the internet that her domestic worker insisted the employer should pay her triple for the statutory holidays and double for break and if not, the employer should then accordingly give her some days off (Xiang 2010).[10] According to the contract, the employer pays her worker ¥1,800 per month, including two days off, to take care of the employer's disabled mother. The contract did not address any overtime work pay during statutory holidays. The employer was distressed because, according to the Labour Law, the worker's request was reasonable, but in reality the Labour Law is not really applicable to the employer/employee relationship in domestic service and both sides did not mention the overtime pay during statutory holidays in the contract; therefore, the employer did not want to pay the extra ¥1,000 and she was reluctant to give the worker alternative days off either because it would mean a lack of care of the disabled mother at home, as the employer would be back at work. The poster immediately attracted more than ten employers following the appearance of posters in the residential district. The employers found that their domestic workers' requirements were almost the same: they wanted to be paid double if they could not rest during statutory holidays. Early before the National Day holiday, some domestic workers living in this residential community who knew each other talked about how to ask the employers to increase their holiday pay. Some domestic workers wrote down the statutory holiday pay calculation method from newspapers to study it. Although the employment relationship between domestic workers and employers does not fit the current Labour Law, this case posed a challenge to domestic workers' legal rights and it has indicated that domestic workers are not only learning how to protect their legitimate rights, but are also expressing these rights.

Besides the individualized resistance, domestic workers use various networks to protect themselves. The personalized nature of the domestic service employment has not totally set domestic workers apart from each other. Living in the same community, domestic workers have opportunities to meet and provide each other with some sort of emotional support, as I have mentioned in the last story. In addition, the development of domestic service agencies in recent years also allows them to share strategies about handling employers, finding new jobs and dealing with disputes. Although solidarity in the workplace is very rare, domestic workers' rights and interests have drawn the attention of women's NGOs, trade unions and international organizations.

Organizing domestic workers

Since domestic work involves privacy in private homes and highly personal relations between employer and employee, the public has long ignored domestic workers' rights and interests. It was not until the mid-1990s that domestic workers' problems gradually started to draw some attention and since then organization of domestic workers has begun. Through the organization process, domestic workers have been empowered, and their rights' consciousness has been nurtured and raised.

NGOs in China

Domestic workers' problems in China first attracted the attention of women's NGOs in the 1990s. Using NGO here, I refer to organizations that are not government-related which basically receive funding and support from international organizations and foundations such as Oxfam Hong Kong, the United Nations Development Fund for Women (UNIFEM) and the United Nations Thematic Group on Gender (UNTGG). There is also some funding from personal donations. So far, two types of NGOs are involved in protecting domestic workers in China. One of these is the social service type, which provides direct services and immediate help to domestic workers. The Migrant Women's Club (MWC) in Beijing is a good example of this category. The other type of NGO involved is the research type. These focus on research and study, and try to promote domestic workers' rights and legal protection. The Centre for Women's Law Studies and Legal Services (CWLSLS) of Peking University in Beijing and the Research Centre for Women's Development and Rights (RCWDR) of Northwestern Polytechnic University in Xi'an are the best representatives of this type. In this section, I will introduce these NGOs and their major activities in promoting the protection of domestic workers.

The Migrant Women's Club (MWC)

Among domestic workers, migrant women are the most vulnerable. On 7 April 1996, the Migrant Women's Club, which is affiliated to the Cultural Development Centre for Rural Women, was founded in Beijing. Its founder Xie Lihua is vice editor-in-chief of the *China Women's News* (newspaper of the ACWF). This was the first non-government organization in China to provide services for migrant women who come from the countryside to the city to find jobs, mainly as domestic workers. The Club's objectives are to uphold migrant women's legal rights, improve their lives, build their capability and acquire space for the group's development in cities (MWC 2006). Since the day it was founded, the Club has provided urgent service and support to domestic workers though various programmes, including an emergency fund, legal aid and support network.

Because migrant women lack basic medical insurance and have no money for medical fees, in December 1999 the MWC set up an emergency fund. This fund provides emergency aid to migrant women who undergo sudden illness or injury at work, infringement of personal safety, such as rape and physical abuse, or ungrounded dismissal from work. Up to now, 26 migrant women have received aid from the emergency fund (MWC 2006).[11]

The Club also provides free legal aid to migrant workers. Through the Law Maintenance Group for Migrant Women, which was set up at the Club in April 2002, the Club offers effective legal aid to migrant women. The group now has two full-time paid lawyers and dozens of volunteer lawyers and law students who work on migrant workers' behalf free of charge (Interview, 12 October 2007). Many domestic workers actually get to know this organization through its legal aid. A teacher, Xiao Wang (*anonymous name*), at FPDSC who was a domestic worker back in 2000, was one of them. Xiao Wang came to Beijing when she was 17 years old. During the 13 months she spent in her employer's home, she never took a day off and was often beaten until she was lacerated and bruised all over. The Club helped her win her case in court (MWC 2006). Furthermore, with the help and training the Club provided, she became a teacher at FPDSC. I attended one of the training classes for domestic workers that she organized on 27 October 2007 and was impressed by her confidence and enthusiasm in serving domestic workers.

During the process of providing legal aid, the Club felt the urgency of initiating legal recommendations to safeguard domestic workers' rights and interests in Beijing (MWC 2009b). In April 2006, at the Fourth National Conference for Migrant Women's Rights and Interests, the Club publicized the Regulations on Safeguarding Domestic Workers' Rights and Interests in Beijing (Recommendation) (MWC 2009a).

To build a supportive environment for domestic workers, under the sponsorship of Oxfam Hong Kong, the MWC established a programme called the Domestic Workers Support Network, in July 2003. This network forms a linkage between sending agencies, which are mostly local women's federations in rural areas, with receiving domestic service agencies in Beijing. This opens communication between the sending and receiving agencies in order to share knowledge on legal rights, citizenship and skills training (MWC 2009a). The network has its own bi-monthly publication, the *Domestic Workers Support Network Brief*,[12] which shares knowledge and information on domestic service, creates a communication space for domestic workers, employers and agencies, and provides some basic information on cooking and caring. In addition, through organizing different activities in this network, domestic workers can meet, talk, relax and learn together, and build a strong support network for each other.

The most prominent feature of this Club is that it empowers migrant women to protect and manage themselves. One of its staff members I interviewed, Xiao Fang, said she had worked in the domestic service industry for about ten years before she got involved in the Club office's work. She had attended a lot of the free training offered by the Club, such as gender training and citizenship awareness training. She said:

> I was deeply touched by the gender training I received here. It opened a door for me! Really, the 35 years of education in my life were not as useful as the education I received at the Migrant Women's Club. The education [I received here] will definitely affect the rest of my life!
>
> (Interview, 12 October 2007)

The free training and other activities such as debating, reading and field trips, not only enriches migrant women workers' leisure lives, but it also enhances their ability to protect themselves and adapt to city life. However, most domestic employers did not like their employees attending the club's activities, Fang told me. She said that many employers were reluctant to let their domestic workers have any contact with the outside world for fear of the workers' self-growth because they considered such self-growth a threat to themselves (Interview, 12 October 2007). Despite the employers' displeasure, the strength and ability of domestic workers as a group are gradually increasing. Fang and Wang's examples have reflected these changes.

This service type of NGO has greatly made up for the deficiency of government policies. It has played an important role in supporting and organizing domestic workers. The research type of NGOs that are involved in domestic workers' rights and legal protection are located at universities. However, their research is not limited to academia alone; they often enable the relevant social forces to make a concerted effort for change.

The Centre for Women's Law Studies and Legal Services of Peking University (CWLSLS)

The Centre – also named Beijing University Women's Law Study and Services Center (BUWLSSC) – was established in December 1995 in Beijing. It was the first NGO of its kind in China to provide legal aid and women's rights education. Its staff members consist of law professors and graduate students from Beijing University and other institutes of higher education as well as some part-time lawyers (CWLSLS 2006). Since 2006, the Centre has carried out the Domestic Workers' Rights Project, sponsored by the UNIFEM and the UNTGG, in Beijing, Guangzhou, Chengdu and some other cities. In each of these cities, the project members of the Centre organized training workshops for female domestic workers about the domestic laws and international conventions protecting female workers' rights. These rights refer to items from the Constitution of the People's Republic of China, the Labour Law, the Law of the People's Republic of China on the Protection of Women's Rights and Interests, the International Covenant on Economic, Social and Cultural Rights and the Convention on the Elimination of All Forms of Discrimination against Women (CWLSLS 2007). From the feedback of the participants, these workshops benefited them greatly by improving their knowledge of the relevant laws and raising their awareness of safeguarding their own rights (CWLSLS 2007). Through meetings with domestic workers, employers, domestic service agencies and representatives from relevant government departments and non-government organizations, the members of the Centre learned about their perspectives on the protection of domestic workers' rights. They drafted the Regulations on Protection of Domestic Workers Labour Rights and Interests to regulate the working conditions, social security and training of domestic workers in dispute settlement in the workplace and so on. The Centre has hosted workshops and discussions to obtain suggestions and constructive criticism of the draft. I attended a workshop on 8 December 2007. The participants from government organizations, academia and domestic service companies had an in-depth discussion about the draft and provided positive feedback for improving their proposed policy.

The Research Centre for Women's Development and Rights of Northwestern Polytechnic University (RCWDR)

In Xi'an, the capital city of a northwest province Shanxi, the Centre for Women's Development and Rights at Northwestern Polytechnic University has been actively promoting domestic workers' legal rights and interests. Established in 1993, the Centre has been doing research and intervention projects in collaboration with universities and organizations such as trade unions and women's federations. Its members consist of faculty, lawyers, judges, staff from trade unions, women's federations and labour associations, and other volunteers (RCWDR 2008).

The Centre launched its Domestic Workers Network Support Group project jointly with Xi'an Municipal ACFTU, Xi'an Women's Federation Re-employment Service Centre and Xizhen Domestic Service Company in 2002 (ACWF and ILO 2009). This project, originally sponsored by Oxfam Hong Kong, targeted domestic workers. The objectives of the project were 'to train marginalized women workers, establish a grass-roots network among women who have been marginalized in employment, promote women workers' rights to form an association, seek social resources, and improve employability, vocational skills, and negotiation skills' (ACWF and ILO 2009: 14)

During the process of organizing grass roots domestic workers peer-to-peer groups and empowering them through various training, such as training related to organizing and unionizing, the Centre has successfully raised domestic workers' collective awareness (Li and Feng 2005). Under the Centre's assistance, some domestic workers started the Xi'an Domestic Workers' Union in September 2004. It was the first private union of its kind in China organized from the bottom by marginalized groups (Li and He 2004) (see next section).

The participation of Xi'an Municipal ACFTU, Xi'an Women's Federation and other government agencies provided political support and other resources (ACWF and ILO 2009). In order to urge the local government of Xi'an to pay attention to domestic workers' rights and interests, this Centre also attempted to initiate local regulations for protecting domestic workers in Xi'an (Li and He 2004).

From the above, we can see that the work done by the NGOs to improve the domestic worker situation in China has had a positive impact. Through their funding and support, international organizations, such as Oxfam Hong Kong, UNIFEM and UNTGG, have made significant efforts in organizing domestic workers and promoting domestic workers' rights and interests. Their work has not only directly benefited domestic workers in protecting domestic workers' *hefa quanyi*, but also called attention to domestic worker issues in China.

Unionization

In addition to the international organizations' support of these NGOs, the official workers' organization in China, the ACFTU, also began an experiment in organizing domestic workers through embracing private domestic workers trade unions. Some successful examples have already sprung up in the last few years. I will use two examples I found in my research to illustrate the current unionization of domestic workers and indicate that, although there is still much work to be done to explore better collective forms of resistance, this process has already started and will be a significant new direction for the Chinese workers' movement.

Unlike Western countries, where most workers' unions are organized autonomously and independently, the Chinese trade union system is semi-official. Institutionally, trade unions are the bridge and bond that the Communist Party uses to unite the working class in China. It allows party organizations at each level to be responsible for setting up new unions, the nomination of trade union leaders, as well as the transmission of party policies to workers (Lee 2009). The organization at the highest level is the ACFTU: both local trade unions and industry trade unions belong to it. The Trade Union Law (adopted in 1950, revised twice in 1992 and in 2001) empowers ACFTU as the leader of all trade unions. Accordingly, Article 11 of the Trade Union Law (1992) stipulates that 'the establishment of basic-level trade union organizations, local trade union federations, and national or local industrial trade union organizations shall be submitted to the trade union organization at the next higher level for approval'.[13] In other words, only trade unions that are organized according to the Trade Union Law and belong to the ACFTU are legal. It is forbidden to organize independent private trade unions. According to the law, any enterprise with 25 employees or more should establish a grass-roots union under the auspices of the ACFTU. Under the central planned economy era, because of the state-owned nature of the economy, the union's dual role as representative of worker interests and promoter of the national, common interests worked well and the government-controlled form of union organization had never been challenged, as the working class, employers and government shared a consistent interest.

Under market reform, the union's role is to bridge the Party and the working class and legally represent workers' interests through collective bargaining and signing contracts with employers. However, the economic reforms mean unions face a huge challenge of membership crisis. On the one hand, unemployed and laid-off workers have lost their union membership during the restructuring process of state-owned enterprises. On the other hand, the increasing number of rural migrant workers, along with the rise of domestic private enterprises and foreign-owned enterprises, has long been kept outside the union system both because of their peasant identity and the private and foreign sectors' imperviousness to union organizations. In 10 years, union membership in the public sector decreased by about 15 million between 1990 and 2000 (Lee 2009). In private and foreign enterprises, the union membership rates were 9.6 per cent and 31.1 per cent respectively in 1998 (Lee 2009).

Confronted by these new circumstances, ACFTU has been trying to adapt its system to represent the diversification of workers according to the guiding ideology that 'where there are workers, there should be trade unions established' (W. Q. Chen 2008: 36). Therefore, while endeavouring to get those precariously employed laid-off urban workers from SOEs unionized, the ACFTU issued in August 2003, a Notification on Effectively Safeguarding Rural Migrant Workers' Legal Rights and Interests, which granted rural migrant workers the right to organize and join trade unions (Ran 2009). Migrant workers from rural areas have been officially recognized as part of the working class in cities since then.

Two domestic workers' trade unions were organized during the adjustment of the trade union system in China and they both belong to the official trade union system. The one in Beijing was set up under the assistance and guidance of its higher-level trade union organization, and the one in Xi'an was grass-roots organized by domestic workers themselves and approved by its higher-level trade union. Although legally unions are entitled to sign collective agreements and engage in collective bargaining with employers by the Trade Union Law (2001), neither of these two domestic workers' organizations has been involved in these processes yet. The biggest reason is that the Labour Law does not regulate the employer–employee relationship in domestic service. Therefore, there is no legal basis for unions to bargain wage and working conditions for domestic workers. Another reason is that unlike workers in the production domain, domestic workers are scattered throughout individual homes. Normally one worker faces one employer, and the employers' situation varies in terms of financial situation and family construction, making it very difficult to bargain in a collective contract. Another reason, also a very serious reason, is that domestic workers' employers are not considered an opposite class to domestic workers, given the fact that many employers are also working-class families. The socialist ideology believes that all people are masters of the country. As a result of these complexities for domestic workers, so far, these domestic worker unions act more like mediators than defenders of workers' interests. However, if workers experience any intimidation by employers, the unions do represent workers to solve grievances through mediation by exerting power that resides in the union's semi-official organizational nature.

From my study, the two unions each have a specific focus. Because of the top-down formation procedure, the Beijing union focuses on recreation and education and this continues the traditional union function under a socialist planned-economy era. The one in Xi'an focuses on legal protection and problem solving. This is more directly involved with the workers because domestic workers from the bottom voluntarily organized it.

Tai Ji Chang Community Domestic Workers' Union

The domestic workers' union in Beijing was the first domestic workers' organization in China. On 24 March 2004, Tai Ji Chang Community Domestic Workers' Union in Dong Hua Men Sub-district, Dong Cheng District was founded (Zhang and Wang 2004; Zhu 2004; Ji and Bai 2006). The first members were 26 workers from six different provinces (Zhang and Wang 2004; Zhu 2004; Ji and Bai 2006). Among them, the oldest was 51 years old and the youngest was 20 (Zhang and Wang 2004; Zhu 2004). The workers were excited to have their own 'home' in Beijing. According to the union's youngest member, He Hongmei:

> In the past, I felt very scared when I saw the reports of abuse and bullying of domestic workers from newspapers and television, and the only thing I could do was to pray I would not encounter such families. Although I feel very good now, I don't know what's going to happen later. When I thought of this, I felt hopeless. Now, with the domestic worker's union, I don't worry anymore. I feel support in my heart and no anxiety anymore.
> (He Hongmei as cited in Zhang and Wang 2004: N.p.)

All the progress that has been made so far – from organizing domestic workers to setting up the union to develop activities for domestic workers – was no easy task. The organizer of Tai Ji Chang Community Domestic Workers' Union and former chair of the community's Federation of Trade Unions, Zhang Zhiping, said that she started to organize this union at the end of 2003, and after that,

> ... it was very easy to do domestic workers' work. After they knew the trade union would protect their legal rights and interests, they were happy from the bottom of their hearts, and they got very actively involved. But because of the nature of the work in the domestic service industry, some employers did not really support the unions.
> (Zhang, as cited in Ji and Bai 2006: N.p.)

She then had to go from door to door to persuade employers that the domestic workers' union was not actually organized to resist employers but to serve and safeguard both parties' legal rights and interests (Zhang and Wang 2004; Ji and Bai 2006).[14] Even after the union was set up, organizing for these members to take part in activities was challenging since the employers did not want their domestic workers to go outside very often because it would affect their work for their employers (Ji and Bai 2006). So far the trade union's activities have mainly focused on knowledge training – regarding laws and regulations, service skills, popular-science knowledge and health care in daily life – and various cultural activities in the community library and the chess and board games room to enrich cultural needs (Zhang and Wang 2004; Zhu 2004; Ji and Bai 2006).

Few domestic workers have sought redress through this union since it was founded. This is mainly because the domestic workers who have joined this union are very few in number and some new domestic workers do not even know there is such an organization in the community. In addition, the union does not have an office, funds or place for activities; however, the establishment of this union has been a good experiment in organizing domestic workers (Zhu 2004; Ji and Bai 2006).

Xi'an Domestic Worker's Trade Union

Xi'an Domestic Worker's Trade Union was founded on 23 September 2004. It was the first domestic workers' union in China that was actually organized by domestic workers themselves. While attending the Domestic Workers Network Support Group at the Research Centre for Women's Development and Rights of Northwestern Polytechnic University, some domestic workers began to realize that, as individuals, they had no power or resources to improve their status and situation, and that organization is a better way to pursue their legal rights (W. Wang 2006). Upon their request and under the assistance of the Research Centre and the Laid-off Workers' Employment Centre, the Xi'an Federation of Trade Unions, this Domestic Worker's Trade Union was organized. There were 162 domestic workers who became the first union members. Their average age was 40 and upwards and 60 per cent were single mothers. The union members were almost all laid-off workers from state-owned enterprises and 30 per cent of them had spouses who were laid-off as well (Y. L. Li 2006). To date, the number of union members has reached more than 700, and female workers accounted for 98 per cent of the membership (ACWF and ILO 2009).

The high percentage of unemployed workers was because the main body of domestic workers in Xi'an city consists of laid-off workers from SOEs. It was estimated that there were about 10 thousand domestic workers in Xi'an, and they were mainly from some large-scale state-owned enterprises in western and eastern suburbs (Su 2004). Compared with their former SOE worker identity, these former laid-off workers who are current domestic workers feel that they have experienced discrimination and lost their rights and interests in domestic service.

The union's aim is that if domestic workers have disputes with or feel discriminated against by the employers, the union can help them to solve problems; and the union can help domestic workers go to the trade union arbitration committee in the city's federation of trade unions (Su 2004). The union will try its best to protect domestic workers rights and interests, such as getting paid the full amount on time and workplace safety, even though there are still no explicit laws and regulations to protect domestic workers (Su 2004). In the one year since the union was founded, through mediation and negotiation with the employers, it has helped 77 workers with financial difficulties and 15 workers by protecting their labour rights regarding wages and workplace injuries (Y. L. Li 2006: 210). For example, under the union's assistance, a worker got back her ¥58 salary for 10 days' work that the employer had owed her for seven months. The worker, Fu Hongli, said excitedly, 'Although it is not much money, I did the work and I deserved it. Thanks to the union for helping me get justice back' (Fu Hongli as cited in Y. L. Li 2006: 210). The union also successfully asked an employer to pay a ¥200 medical fee for an injured worker who broke her ankle on the way to work (Y. L. Li 2006).

According to ACWF and ILO's report (2009), under the support of Xi'an Municipal Trade Union, the domestic workers' union arranged for free medical examinations for its female members, and the union also worked closely with the Women's Federation, the community and other institutions to mobilize resources for assisting poor domestic workers.

Although this union has done some work in protecting domestic workers' rights and interests, the chair of this union felt it was still a difficult task to negotiate with employers because no labour laws and regulations could protect domestic workers' employment (Y. L. Li 2006). In addition, there is a lot of work to do for the union to develop and grow in strength.

In the overall discussion of the collective actions in this section, one problem that particularly needs attention is the lack of freedom for some domestic workers to leave their employers' homes. This is a particular obstacle in the effective organization of these workers.

Conclusion

This chapter explored three levels of resistance: personal resistance to or negotiation with employers, seeking legal protection from the government through the work of NGOs and organizing collectively through trade unions. From this development trajectory, we can see that domestic workers' awareness of rights has improved; they have gradually been empowered and their struggle for better working conditions has gained public attention.

Personal struggles may be weak and fragmented; however, the development of a consciousness of individual rights could be identified through the resistance in specific cases. This consciousness is especially evident in the cases that looked for legal resolutions for their rights as both workers and human beings. Individual rights consciousness is the basis for this type of organized resistance.

In China, NGOs have played a crucial role in organizing domestic workers, raising their rights consciousness and empowering them. Even the unionization of domestic workers relies on a close relationship with NGO activities. NGOs' work is indispensable in China, given the current situation that laws and regulations in protecting domestic workers' rights are almost non-existent. NGOs will keep playing an important role in organizing domestic workers. However, to save domestic workers from dehumanized working and living conditions, their workers' identity should be recognized first, which means that they should be seen as members of the mass working class in China.

The unionization of domestic workers can obviously allow them to address class struggle and build solidarity, although domestic workers' class position is sometimes contradictory. For example, while some workers are employed to facilitate the participation of other workers, such as some domestic workers who work in agencies, the workers hired through kinship or community connections are almost an example of pre-capitalist social relations propping up emerging capitalist ones. Different unionization strategies need to be explored to show the solidarity of domestic workers and to enlarge union coverage.[15] Unionization of domestic workers should become a trend in the long term as the domestic service industry grows in China.

In order for this to happen, the role of domestic workers' unions needs to be secured by relevant labour laws and regulations in the future. It is difficult to protect domestic workers if the employer-employee relationship in domestic service is not recognized as a labour relationship under the current labour law and regulations. Basic system changes need to occur to secure domestic workers' human and labour rights. This system change needs the concerted effort of the Chinese government, trade unions, other NGOs and institutions.

7 Establishing domestic workers' rights

> Social development is closely related to the people's well-being. More importance must therefore be attached to social development on the basis of economic growth to ensure and improve people's livelihood, carry out social restructuring, expand public services, improve social management and promote social equity and justice. We must do our best to ensure that all our people enjoy their rights to education, employment, medical and old-age care, and housing, to build a harmonious society.
>
> (Hu Jintao 2007: N.p)

As the new market-oriented economy has created a new paid domestic labour force in China and it is unlikely to disappear in a short time, in order for domestic workers to seek adequate address and redress of their exploitation and oppression, it is necessary for the government to realize that, as a form of economic activity, domestic service deserves the same labour protection and support that apply to the production sector. Domestic workers should enjoy the same workers' rights and human rights as other workers. The demand for domestic workers' rights not only complies with the ideology of gender and class equality in a socialist society, but also conforms to the international call for labour rights in a global economy. It is the government's responsibility to save domestic workers from inhumane working conditions, exploitation and abusive situations. This complies with the Party's goal to build a 'harmonious society' to 'promote social equality and justice' and ensures all people's employment rights and other basic rights.[1]

This chapter explores the possibilities of the government's efforts for domestic workers whose experiences of exploitation and oppression cut across the current focus of the laws and regulations in China. It aims to seek solutions in global as well as national frameworks. This chapter considers both legal and practical solutions to achieve recognition of domestic worker's employment rights. It will first look at International Labour Standards and other international conventions to provide an overview of the internationally recognized rights and protections to which domestic workers should be entitled. Then this chapter will consider some particularly legislative measures that have been adopted in some countries. In the last part, by making occasional reference to some creative measure of certain other countries, it will explore possible initiatives that the Chinese government should take to regulate working and living conditions of domestic workers, and ultimately to empower the workers to actively claim and enhance their rights.

International frameworks

At the international level, the creating of normative action for domestic workers dates back as far as the mid-1930s (ILO 2010). In 1965, the International Labour Conference (ILC) adopted the Resolution concerning the Conditions of Employment of Domestic Workers (Blackett 2010). The Resolution recognized that the 'urgent need' to establish minimum living standards was 'compatible with the self-respect and human dignity which are essential to social justice', for domestic workers in both developed and developing countries; and urged member states to introduce 'protective measures' and worker training programmes, in accordance with International Labour Standards (Blackett 2010: N.p.). It has been more than forty years since the ILC Resolution was adopted.

Since the 1990s, the concept of a human-rights-based approach to economic development has gained importance. The Declaration on Fundamental Principles and Rights at Work and its Follow-up, adopted by the International Labour Conference in 1998, sets out the core labour standards that all International Labour Office (ILO) member states have an obligation to respect and promote:

(a) Freedom of association and the effective recognition of the right to collective bargaining;
(b) The elimination of all forms of forced or compulsory labour;
(c) The abolition of child labour;
(d) The elimination of discrimination in respect of employment and occupation.

(ILO 2007: 7)

In addition to these fundamental rights and principles, decent work, which promotes decent and productive work in conditions of freedom, equity, security and human dignity, is a primary objective of the ILO. The term 'decent work' was first introduced by the ILO Director-General, Juan Somavia, as the title of his report for the 87th session of the International Labour Conference in 1999 (ILO 2007: 47). On International Women's Day, 8 March 2006, the Director-General reiterated, 'Decent work is built on respect for fundamental principles and rights at work – including freedom from discrimination' (ILO 2007: 47). Decent work has four strategic objectives: labour standards and human rights compliance (fundamental rights and principles at work); employment and income opportunities; social protection and social security; and representation (social dialogue and tripartism) (ILO, UNIFEM and (BUWLSSC 2009: 2). According to the decent work agenda, all workers have the right to decent work, not only those working in the formal economy, but also the self-employed, casual and informal economy workers, as well as those, predominantly women, working in the care economy and private households. As more women workers are involved in domestic service worldwide in recent years, their decent work has become a focus of ILO agenda. ILO promotes the Agenda on Decent Work for Domestic Workers: Rights, Productive Jobs, Social Protection and Representation in Domestic Services 2006–15. In June 2010, the International Labour Conference at Geneva adopted a resolution calling for the drafting of an International Convention and Supplementary Recommendation to extend labour standards and social protection to the world's domestic workers.[2]

ILO also undertook specific studies to make domestic work visible and extend labour protection to domestic workers (Blackett 1998; Ramirez-Machado 2003). For example, from 2006–2008, ILO carried out a project to promote decent work for women in Asia, Combating Forced Labour and Trafficking in Domestic Workers in South East Asia and Hong Kong. From March 2009 to April 2010, ILO undertook a project, Promotion of Equality and Decent Work for Women: Prevention of Human Trafficking, Protection of Domestic Workers and Capacity Building for Gender Equality, in China and seven other countries in Asia. Also, in late 2009, ILO sent a questionnaire to member states regarding the possibility of a new instrument to provide better social protection for domestic workers. These efforts are initiatives to achieve recognition of domestic workers' employment rights.

ILO labour conventions cover all workers, including domestic workers. In addition to ILO labour standards, some other international instruments also protect and promote domestic workers' rights. These instruments include: the Universal Declaration of Human Rights (UN 1948); the International Covenant on Civil and Political Rights (ICCPR) and the International Covenant on Economic, Social and Cultural Rights (ICESCR) (UN 1966b); the Convention on the Elimination of all Forms of Discrimination against Women (CEDAW) (UN 1979) and its Optional Protocol of 1999; the International Convention on the Protection of the Rights of all Migrant Workers and Members of their Families (UN 1990); the UN Declaration on the Elimination of Violence against Women (UN 1993); the Beijing Declaration and Platform for Action (UN 1995) and its follow-up; and the Millennium Development Goals (UN 2000). Although few instruments address the particular aspects of domestic service work, they are universal in nature and should apply to all workers.

National experiences of labour legislation/regulation on domestic workers

Some national states have already taken action by granting domestic workers equal rights as other workers. In a study of domestic work from a legal perspective by the ILO in 2003, of more than 60 studied, only 17 countries, including China, have set no specific regulations on domestic work in their basic labour legislation, while 19 countries have enacted specific laws or regulations dealing with domestic work. Two examples of such countries are Sweden and Demark. Another 19 countries, such as Canada (Ontario) and the Philippines have devoted specific chapters, titles or sections in their labour codes, employment acts or acts regarding contracts of employment (Ramirez-Machado 2003).

In addition to the above-mentioned actions of extension of general labour legislation/regulation to domestic workers, and specific national and/or local labour legislation/regulation for domestic workers, the third type of strategy that national states take is that of national or regional collective agreements, combining elements of existing contract law with specific regulations extending coverage of contract rules to domestic workers (Blackett 2010). For instance, in France, domestic workers are covered by not only the Labour Code, but also a National Collective Agreement (CCN). The CCN is considered to be one of the most innovative devices in the French law on collective agreements. CCN both clarifies rights available under the Labour Code and provides standards that are more favourable for domestic workers (Blackett 2010).

There are specific examples that some nation-states and regions take in regulating working conditions, such as wages, hours of work and rest, safety at work, health or social security insurance. I will discuss these resolutions in detail as they pertain to China's situation.

What the Chinese government can do

China has experienced significant changes in its socioeconomic, legal and international context since the economic reforms and opening the door to the global world. China's legal reform that promotes 'ruling the country by law' has opened a new legitimate arena for individuals to pursue their legal rights with greater autonomy, as I have analysed in Chapter 6. In addition, 'rising rights consciousness in Chinese society provides a social milieu within which invocations of rights are more likely to gain broad-based support' (Pei 2010: 31). From the analysis of Chapter 6, we can see that domestic workers' rights consciousness is also on the rise. Under the influence of transnational advocacy groups, Chinese labour NGOs, such as the Migrant Women's Club, also contribute to promoting a culture of rights (Lee 2010). Finally, 'China's extensive and deepening integration into the international community in general, and its various commitments to international laws and institutions in particular' (Pei 2010: 31) have provided a new source of support for domestic workers' rights. All these factors realistically contribute to achieve recognition of domestic workers' employment rights and social justice.

As a member of the global international society, China has signed a series of international conventions, which commit to labour rights and gender equality since the late 1970s. China has ratified the following ILO core conventions, which are relevant to the protection of domestic worker and migrant worker rights: C100 Equal remuneration Convention, 1951; C111 Discrimination (Employment and Occupation) Convention, 1958; C138 Minimum Age Convention, 1973; C182 Worst Forms of Child Labour Convention, 1999 (ACWF and ILO 2009).

China signed the International Covenant on Economic, Social and Cultural Rights (ICESCR) in 1997 and the International Covenant on Civil and Political Rights (ICCPR) in 1998. China also signed the Convention on the Elimination of all Forms of Discrimination against Women (CEDAW) and the Beijing Declaration and Platform for Action (1995). According to the stipulations of the covenants, China would be required to report to the UN on its fulfilment of the covenant obligations within two years of their ratification. These stipulations and other formal obligations under these covenants may exert pressure on the Chinese government to fulfil its international commitments. Furthermore, as a socialist country, China has a responsibility to uphold workers' rights and interests.

There is no doubt that China should prioritize decent work conditions for domestic workers. The Chinese government has a responsibility to ensure that domestic workers are protected by labour standards and it also has an obligation to hold both employers and employment agents accountable for minimum standards of working and employment conditions. Without legal employment status, domestic workers cannot be guaranteed their wages, welfare, working hours and labour protection. The most urgent rights domestic workers want to have are concrete and tangible: to be paid regularly and on time and to be paid a living wage that could support their families; to be covered by social insurance; to have some time to rest; to be free from fear of being abused; and to retain their human dignity. Therefore, the main goals the government should achieve are to recognize, to protect, and to reach out and organize domestic workers (Haspels 2010). Borrowing from advanced experiences of other countries and regions such as Canada, the United States, Singapore and Hong Kong, the immediate strategies the government should take are as follows.

In order to recognize domestic workers, the government can take action in legal and statistical areas. First, it should extend the coverage of already-existing domestic laws that protect other workers in China, such as the Labour Law, the Regulation on the Insurance of Workplace Injury and the Labour Contract Law, to fully cover the rights of domestic workers. The exclusion of domestic workers from these laws takes away domestic workers' rights as workers and reinforces their disadvantaged position in employment that historically has been assigned a diminished value. Some national and regional examples have shown how national law and legislation can recognize domestic work as employment, worthy of regulation and labour law protection. For example, 'Employment of Househelpers', chapter three in the Labour Code of the Philippines, details employment standards including minimum wage, opportunity for education, treatment of househelpers, board, lodging and medical attendance.[3] In Hong Kong, domestic workers are covered by the Employment Ordinance.[4] In Canada, for example, the provincial Employment Standards Act (ESA) in British Columbia[5] and Ontario[6] covers all domestic workers, including immigrant workers that come to Canada through the Live-in Caregiver Program. The ESA sets minimum standards for wages, hours of work, holidays and other working conditions. Domestic workers have the same rights as other employees in workplaces under the ESA. In addition, domestic workers in British Columbia, Manitoba and Ontario are covered by health-and-safety regulations and workers' compensation. It is important to recognize that domestic workers face many risks in their daily tasks, such as illness, infection, exposure to chemicals, awkward and repetitive tasks, heavy lifting, fatigue and stress. In Latin American countries such as Bolivia, domestic workers were guaranteed an eight-hour day and the right to social security in legislation in 2003. In the same year, Peruvian domestic workers won the right to a two-week paid holiday (Fox 2005).

Without law coverage on domestic service, some local governments have attempted to make local regulations in China. In 2001, Shenzhen People's Congress issued a regulation, which addresses the responsibilities of domestic service agencies, employers and domestic workers. Zhengzhou city also passed similar regulations on domestic service (ACWF and ILO 2009).

If domestic workers are covered under the purview of the current labour laws and other national laws and regulations, their minimum pay, workplace safety, social insurance and other labour rights will have to follow national standards, and their equal labour rights as other workers would be addressed. However, coverage under the law is only part of the solution. To prevent domestic workers from maltreatment, effective enforcement is necessary.[7]

Second, current laws should be enforced in order to provide actual protection in practice. Strong and effective legal labour standards offer no protection if they are not enforced. Therefore, current laws that can protect domestic workers from delayed payment or abuse should be made more accessible to domestic workers since not every domestic worker knows how to assert their lawful rights. Domestic workers need not only the protection of improved employment standards but also greater access to laws and regulations to assert their rights. Currently, in China, when workers have complaints, they can go to a local arbitration committee of labour disputes, which is a government institution, to ask for arbitration free of charge. If workers are not satisfied with their adjudication, they may institute a lawsuit. These official mechanisms for dealing with labour disputes should cover domestic workers.

Third, make domestic work and domestic workers visible through regular systematic data collection (Haspels 2010). Currently, there are no national statistics for domestic work and domestic workers. The scale and number of this employment category totally rely on estimation. For such a big and growing domestic service industry, this situation is unbearable. Domestic workers' contribution to economic development in China needs recognition. National and provincial statistics should collect these data annually.

To protect domestic workers, the government should take measures to ensure that paid domestic workers, like all wage earners, have fair terms of employment and decent working and living conditions. In order to protect caring labour, cleaners and other forms of paid domestic labour, it would be useful to study the roles that state regulation plays in defending standards and working conditions of all forms of paid domestic labour.

First, standardize the work tasks of domestic service. The national occupation standards should try to specify what domestic workers are responsible for and what kind of work they should not be required to do (such as cleaning the exterior of the windows in a high-rise building). Once these standards are set, domestic workers can have legitimate grounds for refusing to do certain dangerous and/or demeaning work tasks that some employers may ask them to do.

Second, the state should formulate a standard national employment contract that specifies wages and working conditions by the Ministry of Human Resources and Social Security of the People's Republic of China (MOHRSS). Different levels of local government can make modifications according to actual social and economic situation. At the international level, some countries and regions have already made standard contracts. In Hong Kong, domestic workers' basic rights and responsibilities are specified in a standard employment contract (ID407), the Standard Employment Contract for Foreign Domestic Helpers,[8] which is the only document recognized by the Government of the Hong Kong Special Administrative Region. Under the Contract, workers are entitled to a minimum allowable wage, free medical treatment (including medical consultation, hospital stays and emergency dental treatment), at least one rest day in every period of 7 days, 12 statutory holidays, paid sick leave and sickness allowance, etc. In Canada, the Live-in Caregiver Program Sample Contract[9] stipulates the wage and working conditions as well as terms of separation. In general, the contract should specify that domestic workers enjoy minimum wage coverage, and the minimum wage standard for live-in domestic workers should be the net wage income after the dining, accommodation expenses and relevant insurances are deducted. The contract should also specify living conditions when the employer provides accommodation and food. The French CCN provides detailed regulations of accommodation, which is used as an accessory to the employment contract (Blackett 2010). For instance, it stipulates that each domestic worker must have an individual room that can be locked from the inside and be closed with a key (Blackett 2010). It specifies in particular that domestic workers who care for children must have a space that is separate from the child's room (Blackett 2010). In China, the living conditions should also specify safety and respect for the worker's privacy. In addition, the contract in China should specify that the food provided for domestic workers must be the same as the employers. Other aspects, such as domestic workers' annual leave, occupational safety and social security should also be covered. Employment protection in China is the responsibility of the MOHRSS and therefore the MOHRSS should take measures to make standard employment contracts. It is worth stressing that a written contract which specifies working and live-in conditions between domestic workers and their employers can secure both parties' rights and interests.

Third, mechanisms need to be in place to ensure domestic employers realize and are accountable for domestic workers' rights and interests. In China, no formal mechanisms exist to ensure that employers are accountable for their misdeeds. When they pay someone to clean their home and care for their children or elderly, they tend to approach these arrangements not as employers with a particular set of obligations and responsibilities but as consumers. This consumerism under the market economy has caused employers to assume that they are superior to their workers and are entitled to treat them in any way they choose. Without mandatory action by the government, employers can and will probably continue to abuse domestic workers with impunity. Hence, it is the government's responsibility to provide employers with a basic understanding of their role and responsibilities as employers. We can learn from experiences from other countries, such as Singapore, where all employers who employ domestic workers for the first time, except for those seriously disabled or sick, are required to attend the Employers' Orientation Programme (EOP) – a three-hour programme held by the Ministry of Manpower (MOM). The employment guidelines for employers of foreign domestic workers are also available at MOM's website.[10] A page of the guidelines is devoted to spelling out penalties for abuse and ill-treatment. For employers who deliberately cause hurt, wrongfully confine domestic workers, use words or gestures intended to insult the modesty of a woman, or criminal intimidation, penalties can include up to seven years' imprisonment and/or a fine and caning, depending on the severity of the abuse. For rape, the penalty is 8–20 years imprisonment and caning with not less than 12 strokes. In addition, an employer who fails to pay salary, and/or fails to provide adequate food and rest or requires workers to perform dangerous tasks will be barred from hiring domestic workers. Convicted employers and their spouses will not be allowed to employ another foreign domestic worker for the rest of their lives. Since 1997, the Singapore government has been actively barring abusive employers from hiring foreign domestic workers. The number of employers barred rose from 4 in 1997 to 33 in 2001 for just 10 months of this year from January to October (Yeoh, Huang and Devasahayam 2004).

Fourth, the behaviour of domestic service agencies needs regulation. In China, the State Administration for Industry and Commerce of the People's Republic of China (SAIC) and its local bureaus are the government institutions that regulate domestic service agencies. Currently, many agencies only charge domestic workers intermediary fees, and beyond this, they generally do not provide any protection or guarantees for the workers they recruit. The Labour Contract Law, which was effected on 1 January 2008, stipulates: 'No labour dispatch agencies or working units may charge any fee against any dispatched workers' (ILO, UNIFEM and BUWLSSC 2009: 14–15).[11] In Article 60, chapter five; however, according to the research of ILO, UNIFEM and Beijing University Women's Law Study and Service Center, some domestic service agencies still collect deposits from domestic workers and charge management fees to employers, which usually account for 15–25 per cent of the total payment by employers. And some maternity care agencies charge a management fee of up to 30 per cent of the total payment by employers (ILO, UNIFEM and BUWLSSC 2009). In addition, some agencies violate government regulations by keeping domestic workers' identification papers. The SAIC and its local branches should not only entrust and make sure domestic worker companies screen both potential employers and domestic workers but also require domestic agencies to call back the worker if an employer conceals information or abuses workers. Since 1 January 2007, the Beijing Administration for Industry and Commerce has been trying to implement a sample standard service contract between domestic employers and agencies that employ domestic workers and send them to work at households.[12] Under this contract, domestic employers as consumers are required to provide true information to agencies, provide a safe working environment and safe living conditions to agency workers, guarantee workers four days off a month and enough time to sleep every day. Agencies have the right to stop providing service to those employers who register false information or exploit or abuse domestic workers.

This sample contract would provide some protection to workers if it is mandatory. However, so far the sample contract is not a requirement for domestic agencies, which means that domestic agencies keep the right to use the contract or not. In addition, the sample contract applies to only the agencies that hire domestic workers as employees, and it is not related to intermediary agencies. Therefore, in reality, the protection of workers is still very limited. However, this practice is a good example of how domestic service agencies' market activities could be regulated. Domestic agencies should be informed that they have responsibilities to protect the workers they recruit. If complaints are received about the behaviour of an agency, the SAIC and its local branches should adopt punishments either through fines or through banning the agency from the domestic service industry.

Fifth, the national fiscal budget for the training of domestic workers needs to be increased. Since the majority of domestic workers are poor women from rural areas, they desperately need working skills, information about city life, as well as knowledge about how to protect themselves in an abusive situation. Pre-work training is therefore very important. However, as Chapter 5 has shown, many of them have not received any form of training. Lack of the skills for urban domestic work, information about their rights and support to assert their rights can not only harm them but may also cause unnecessary damage to employers' homes. Therefore, the government should increase the financial budget for domestic workers' training and ensure that workers attend free training before they go to work.

Currently, the national fiscal budget for training rural migrant workers is allocated to labour-export areas, namely rural areas. The local governments in rural areas, therefore, are in charge of training labourers before they migrate to cities. However, it seems that the funding has not been effectively used given that many rural migrant workers are not really trained. Some local labour-export governments, such as Quzhou, Zhejiang Province, are trying to authorize and pay relevant institutions to provide domestic service employment training for migrant workers and laid-off workers while governments pay for these training initiatives (H. F. Wang 2006). While this may become an effective way of providing free government training, another approach is to allocate a certain amount of fiscal funding to labour-import places – cities – since having the training in cities may be more practical. Some domestic service agencies in cities, such as Beijing, Shanghai and Tianjin, place great importance on training and have developed a highly effective training system. For example, the Fu Ping Domestic Service Company in Beijing has its own training school that can train domestic workers from the beginner to the intermediate level. Using its own training materials, this company trains the trainees it recruits from less economically developed provinces and areas in China. The courses are designed to teach basic skills in cooking, nursing and taking care of the elderly, and to qualify trainees for domestic service in cities. The beginner-level training focuses on cooking and housekeeping, in which trainees learn how to use appliances properly, such as the gas stove, microwave and vacuum cleaner, and they also learn how to cook some dishes. It is a way to get new trainees used to the modern applications of city life. Intermediate-level training places emphasis on nurturing and care-giving skills, which are considered higher-level training. In each level, a certificate is issued for the trainees who successfully finish the courses. The company is responsible for looking for employers for trainees once they complete their training. The government can try to use these resources in cities to train domestic workers.

After the global financial and economic crisis in 2009, 40 million people, 60 per cent of whom are rural migrants and urban laid-off workers between the ages of 40 and 50, have lost their jobs in China (ACWF and ILO 2009; ILO, UNIFEM and BUWLSSC 2009). The Chinese government is increasing its effort to promote employment in the domestic service sector. Several government departments, the Ministry of Commerce (MOFCOM), Ministry of Finance (MOF), and the ACFTU, launched a Joint Project on Domestic Work, which aims at providing free vocational skills training to both rural migrants and urban laid-off workers (ACWF and ILO 2009; ILO, UNIFEM and BUWLSSC 2009). The Project aimed to train 200,000 domestic workers in 2009 (ACWF and ILO 2009; ILO, UNIFEM and BUWLSSC 2009). Specific training institutions, trade unions or qualified domestic service companies may get involved in these workers' training (ILO, UNIFEM and BUWLSSC 2009). One point that is worth mentioning is that, while the training seems to be necessary, it should not be implemented in ways which reinforce the view that women's employment in domestic service is 'natural' as the government has done before. Gender mainstreaming the training sessions is important.

Sixth, special emphasis needs to be placed on improving migrant workers' employment conditions in cities. Although the Chinese government has been actively reducing employment barriers for rural migrant workers in the last thirty years, because of their rural *hukou*, they still do not enjoy the same employment rights, such as pension plans and medical plans, as urban residents do. Some specific *hukou* reforms in last few years, such as the 'selling' of *hukou*, benefited only a very small elite of eligible migrants. The 'blue-seal' *hukou* benefited more urban migrants than rural migrant workers (Sun 2009a: 7). Since the late 1980s, many city governments began charging migrants high fees in exchange for *hukou* in towns and cities (Fan 2008). The fees were ranging from several thousands to tens of thousands of yuan and were often higher in large cities than in small cities and higher in the city proper of large cities than in the outskirts (Cao 2001; Fan 2008). Beginning in the mid-1990s, some large cities, such as Shanghai, Tianjin and Shenzhen, began to offer 'blue-stamp' *hukou* to migrants who met high-skill requirements and were able to make sizable investments (Wong and Huen 1998; Fan 2008). The blue-stamp *hukou* could be converted into a formal urban *hukou* after a certain period of time (Fan 2008). However, these practices, especially the blue-stamp *hukou*, was tailored for those wealthy migrants, including urban industrialists, rich merchants and top salary earners who can afford to purchase commercial housing in designated areas at locally set prices in big cities like Beijing and Shanghai (F. L. Wang 2005). It was obvious that no rural migrant domestic workers have the economic ability to buy a city *hukou* (Sun 2009a). Domestic workers' 'full' workers' rights depend on full workers' rights for migrant workers since the majority of domestic workers are from rural areas. On 4 November 2005, the Chinese state council published the Notice on Further Strengthening Employment and Re-employment, in which the following guiding principles were addressed:

> Develop employment in rural and urban areas simultaneously . . . and improve the urban employment environment for migrant workers and lift the barriers to entry into city and trans-regional employment for the rural labour force, and perfect the policies and measures on the protection of migration and trans-regional employment for rural labourers.
> (Central People's Government, China, 2005)[13]

From this notice, we can see that the Chinese government intends to improve rural migrant workers' employment. However, there should be specific measures to address the needs of the migrant working class.

Seventh, educate and raise awareness of the general public towards decent work for domestic workers. While facilitating more and more workers to join domestic service industry, the government should improve domestic workers' image and social status in the society. The government should use various mass media, such as television and newspapers, and the internet to educate the public about why domestic workers should enjoy full workers' rights and how domestic service contributes to overall economic development in China.

Eighth, strengthen the cooperation and coordination of different government departments on the protection of domestic workers. Currently, besides MOHRSS and SAIC, MOFCOM is also involved in the domestic service sector. This is because domestic service is regarded as a commodity in China and all commodity-related issues are regulated by MOFCOM. MOFCOM and its bureaus at different levels are in charge of monitoring domestic service associations (ACWF and ILO 2009). The China Domestic Service Association, under the administration of MOFCOM, is the only national-level association for domestic service agencies in China (ACWF and ILO 2009). The association acts as a bridge between government and domestic service agencies, regulates domestic services, shares information, and monitors and puts forward recommendations (ACWF and ILO 2009). The Beijing Administration for Industry and Commerce is responsible for the activities of BHSA. Although commerce departments and the domestic service associations mainly concern the quality of domestic service offered by domestic service agency workers, their work does provide certain protection to agency workers in reality, for instance, through the sample contract introduced by BAIC, and the work of BHSA, which I have analysed in the last few chapters. Recently, MOFCOM has been interested in establishing a nationwide domestic service network and is planning to promote standards on domestic services and a system for occupational training, pricing and dispute resolution for domestic service agencies in the domestic service sector (ACWF and ILO 2009). For rural migrant workers, the public security office also has responsibility for their protection since it is responsible for issuing temporary resident permit to them (ILO, UNIFEM and BUWLSSC 2009). Since these above-mentioned government departments all have played a role in promoting domestic service in China, they should strengthen cooperation and integrate their advantages to protect domestic workers' rights in the future. If possible, a competent authority may be defined (ILO, UNIFEM and BUWLSSC 2009).

To organize domestic workers

Domestic workers need to break the isolation of the workplace and claim their rights collectively. They need to organize in order to get their voices heard and their situation improved. In reaching out and organizing domestic workers, trade unions, women's federations and other NGOs can all take measures and use their resources.

ACFTU has a responsibility to organize domestic workers. In Chapter 6, I discussed two domestic workers' unions and their significance as a beginning for the official trade union system to get domestic workers organized. Trade unions at all level can help domestic workers organize by extending membership to them.

ACWF and its women's federations at different levels have been actively organizing rural migrant workers and laid-off workers to join the domestic service industry. ACWF is a mass women's organization supported by the CCP. Its basic functions are to represent and safeguard the rights and interests of women and promote gender equality in China to give domestic workers a sense of security.

Other NGOs, such as the Migrant Women's Club in Beijing, can empower domestic workers and promote their rights and interests through a series of activities, for example by organizing training workshops for domestic workers. As I have analysed in Chapter 6, under the influence of transnational advocacy groups and international organizations, these NGOs have been successful in organizing domestic workers in China. On 28 October 2009, for example, the first domestic workers' mutual help organization in China – the Beijing Migrant Women Domestic Workers' Cooperative – promoted by the MWC, was opened (MWC 2009a). This is a new attempt to organize domestic workers.

The government can use these NGOs' resources to reach out to and organize domestic workers in order to improve the domestic workers' situation in China.

On 1 September 2010, Premier Wen Jiabao chaired a State Council executive meeting, to study and plan the development of policies and measures for domestic service.[14] While the meeting vigorously promoted marketization, industrialization and socialization of domestic service to gradually establish a variety of household service systems to meet families' demands in both urban and rural areas, it also addressed the need for that development of the domestic service market to be combined with government guidance; policy support combined with regulating management, and employment promotion combined with protection of rights and interests. The meeting identified policies and measures to protect both domestic employers and workers. As consumers, domestic employers' legal rights and interests were addressed in the following points.

- Regulate the market order, improve the industry's self-regulatory mechanism and regulate service activities.
- Strengthen market supervision, govern domestic agencies' practice according to the law, severely punish illegal business operation and safeguard the legal rights of domestic service consumers.

Domestic workers' rights and interests were addressed as a policy effectively to safeguard the legitimate rights and interests of domestic service employees, to regulate the relationship of rights and obligations between domestic service agencies, households and domestic service workers, and to safeguard domestic service workers' labour remuneration and rights to rest.

In addition to these rights, the meeting also specifically mentioned the free training of domestic workers to strengthen employment service and vocational skills training; improve the public employment service system, and provide free vocational guidance and placement services to domestic service employees; make domestic service employees the focus of vocational skills training, and implement training programmes and training subsidies.

Undoubtedly, this meeting showed not only that the government has realized a healthy development of the domestic service market is inseparable from the protection of domestic workers' rights, but it is also taking measures to promote domestic workers' legitimate rights.

Conclusion

Domestic workers provide important care and domestic services for households, which enable male and female workers to be able to participate in the labour market; therefore, domestic workers and the work they perform are inseparable to the economic development in a country and the world (Blackett 2010). There should be a decent work agenda to recognize domestic workers and value the importance of domestic work, as ILO has promoted. In China, establishing domestic workers' rights is accommodated in the goals addressed by President Hu Jintao at the CCP's 17th Congress. The Chinese government should recognize domestic workers' rights and interests and take pragmatic solutions to protect them and make domestic work a gainful employment. From legal framework to multiple mechanisms to ensure implementation and enforcement, and mobilization of domestic workers into trade unions or other NGOs, these are all essential ways to meet domestic workers' needs. Whether or not domestic workers' precarious employment will be improved depends on the government's effort. I believe that, under pressure from the international community and by learning from the good experiences of other countries and regions, the domestic workers' circumstances in China will gradually improve.

While establishing domestic workers' rights is urgent, we should never overlook the 'inherently exploitative nature' of hiring an economically less favoured woman who is from a disadvantaged group, either rural migrant women or laid-off women workers, to do 'work that remains socially undervalued' (Blackett

2010: N.p.). Although much hope is pinned on the government's effort to restore some respect and dignity to domestic work and domestic workers, it is still a question of how domestic workers' rights can be achieved in the face of 'a relentless informalization of the economy and of employment, in China as well as the rest of the world' (Lee 2010: 76). In addition, whether the improvement in working conditions and labour rights of domestic workers under the situation of state channelling and facilitation of some disadvantaged women to serve more privileged women and their families contribute to a 'harmonious society' is also under challenge. Therefore, while establishing domestic worker's rights is an expedient strategy, to build a 'harmonious society' as it means in the long run, the Chinese government needs to think about what a 'harmonious society' with gender equality and social justice really looks like and what actions may achieve it.

8   Conclusion

The preceding chapters have examined the causes and nature of the rise of private domestic labour in China, an occupation that had been all but abolished under the earlier socialist regime. The underlying basis for the rise and nature of private domestic work has its roots in the economic transition of China from a centrally planned economy to a market-driven economy. The marketization of labour and the retreat of the state from social provisioning typifies an economic direction that China is pursuing, one 'that will earn China a rightful position on the playing field of global capitalism' (Yan 2008: 52). Under the notions such as economic growth and globalization, a new social inequality and gender inequality has been naturalized in the Chinese society. As a new underclass, paid domestic workers have inevitably become a new social reality.

One objective of this book is to place the new underclass of domestic labour that is taking shape and their precarious working and living conditions in a socialist feminist perspective. It traces the development of private domestic labour as a consequence of the development of capitalist markets within a socialist state, and its implications for the state's policy on the nature of women's labour. As has been noted throughout, there is a shift in state policy towards what constitutes acceptable work for females built on an entrenched family patriarchy and ideology about the gendered distinctions with regard to care work.

To achieve this goal of showing the interrelationship of patriarchy and capitalist labour markets at work in contemporary China, this book has analysed the different domestic employment regimes that have existed historically in China. My aim has been to show the root of the devaluation of women's domestic labour and demonstrate how the low social status of private domestic labour in contemporary China can be traced, in some respects, to the continuity of gender inequalities represented in different historical periods. I have identified the unequal gender relationship and the gendered division of labour in Chinese society as evident in the pre-reform economic era, a time when women were called upon in an unprecedented way (in the name of egalitarian socialism) to participate in the waged labour force. Even in this period, gender inequality was not eradicated and served as a basis for shaping women's greater vulnerability in the current period of restructuring.

Specifically in Chapters 3 and 4, from analysis of both the workers and their employers, I have demonstrated how state policy and the rise of a capitalist labour market have alienated women who perform care work into two confronting classes – domestic workers and their employers. Through the legitimization of private domestic service, hidden gender inequalities that existed during the pre-reform socialist era have become enlarged, more visible and directly related to class distinctions. The household registration system (*hukou*) has further divided the domestic worker class into two hierarchical categories – rural migrant workers and laid-off workers, with rural migrant women at the bottom of a worker's hierarchy based on place of origin.

In arguing that new class inequalities are most evident in the domestic service industry, I have used the words and stories of care workers and cleaners to illustrate women domestic labourers' alienated work. I have analysed domestic workers' resistance to employers at both the individual and organized levels. By comparing rural migrant workers' and laid-off workers' working conditions, I have displayed the three layers of social strata among women, with employers at the top who exert power on both laid-off workers and rural migrant workers, showing clearly that migrant workers are at the bottom. This class and gender division, as evidenced through the marketization of domestic work, shows the extent that social reproduction is still being seen as entirely women's responsibility. It is through the connections between state patriarchy and family patriarchy that women as a gendered class have been marginalized and disadvantaged in a restructured China.

Overall, this book has focused on what happened to gender equality and class equality in the wake of private domestic service during the economic reform and opening up to global capitalism in China. Using socialist feminist theories, it has contributed to the understanding of private domestic labour-related social problems, including workers' rights and the shifts of gender order in contemporary China. This book has not only analysed the current situation, but also explored policy solutions as the Chinese government works towards its goal of developing a 'harmonious society'. From a future-oriented perspective, this study hopes to pose a challenge to policymakers as well as scholars about how to solve private domestic labour problems in China.

Further reflections

The lack of economic and social security for domestic workers is not a phenomenon that is unique to China. Rather, it is a worldwide phenomenon; there is mass migration of domestic workers from less developed countries to developed countries and areas during economic globalization and neoliberal welfare state restructuring. Domestic workers throughout the world are subject to exploitation and a lack of basic labour rights and human rights. Although paid domestic workers' precarious situation has received an ever-increasing amount of attention throughout the world since the 1980s, and many national states and international organizations, including the International Labour Organization, have taken measures to extend labour protection to domestic workers, paid domestic workers' labour and human rights have not substantially improved. It is still an issue that is almost invisible and is certainly not considered a problem with regard to economic development agendas. Yet, as long as domestic work is still an undervalued woman's work, and as long as domestic workers are still economically underprivileged, the exploitative nature of domestic work remains unchallenged. Under such circumstances, establishing domestic workers' rights cannot actually change the nature of gender inequality and social injustice in a society. Therefore, it must be complemented by some other remedies, such as public provision of various care needs and the gradual abolishment of the gendered division of labour in order to reconcile 'social reproduction' with market production.

To contribute a further understanding of domestic labour issues in China, I will use China as an example to explore how a more equitable society can be achieved.

Public provision of social reproduction

Public provision of social reproduction did liberate Chinese women from domestic burden in the socialist era, as I have analysed in the first few chapters. China has a record of providing services, particularly for children. It is the neoliberal restructuring that led to market-driven services and a serious decline of state-provided social care services. The rapid decline of public social care services that used to back up women's labour market participation in the socialist era has resulted in women's participation in the labour market only being possible if other women take over care work and domestic work at home. I have demonstrated in the preceding chapters that the government's withdrawal from its social reproduction responsibilities has increased not only gender inequality, because women are expected to assume household responsibilities, but also inequality and class divisions between women. In order to live up to its commitment to gender equality and the cause of workers, the Chinese government should try to keep or develop public care service facilities to provide workplace supports for employees with caring responsibilities, rather than shrinking them. The government should have the financial ability to input more funding into the social reproduction area because thirty years of economic reform and transition to a market-oriented economy have led to huge economic development and continuous national financial income increase; and these economic gains have created the material basis of providing public support for social reproduction. According to the national statistics, in 2005, the GDP reached ¥183,085 hundred million and jumped to fourth place globally (Liu, Zhang and Li 2010). Compared with 2000, the GDP increased by 57.3 per cent and the average annual increase rate is 9.5 per cent. The stable and continuous economic development has brought financial income gains. In 2005, the national financial income is ¥31,649 hundred million, which was increased 1.36 times compared with 2000, and the annual increase amount was ¥3,651 hundred million (Liu, Zhang and Li 2010). It is time for the government to rethink its role in social reproduction and support workers with caring responsibilities under a socialist market economy.

Furthermore, since care work in Chinese society is still perceived as a woman's job, gender equality cannot be achieved to maintain male privilege in the home.

Therefore, battling the shifts in the 'gender order' associated with market-socialism needs a long-term strategy.

Abolish the gendered division of labour

If the social importance of domestic work cannot be recognized and both men and women having a responsibility to share in the domestic work cannot be seen as a matter of common sense, the gendered division of labour will continue to be reinforced by the growth of the domestic service industry. Given women's unequal status in comparison with men in economic, cultural and political life, society should, ideally, recognize and value the importance of different forms of care without reinforcing the misconception that care work is something that only women can or should do. To change the gendered division of labour, women and men should be able to take equal responsibility for care work and household work while they both enjoy equal participation in the public domain. Everybody should be both carer and worker. As Fraser (1997) suggested, according to the universal caregiver welfare state model in Western society, states should promote gender equity by effectively dismantling the gendered opposition between breadwinning and care giving and encourage men to perform care giving too. Therefore, in the long term, the government should make an effort to eliminate the gendered division of labour in Chinese society by transforming the dual-breadwinner/market carer or informal carer model under the market economy into a dual-breadwinner/dual-carer regime. Men and women from all social strata should equally participate in the labour force and share domestic responsibilities. There would be no class inequality in domestic labour under a dual-breadwinner/dual-carer regime.

It is my hope that this study might help to establish understanding of what is happening in the changes in gender order and class division in China as China increasingly is influenced by global restructuring. A shift in both the gender order and class distinctions as a result of market-oriented economic reforms is occurring, with a commensurate lack of protection for social reproduction – both paid and unpaid. It is unlikely that China will return to the pre-reform socialist era; therefore, measures to redress gross injustices need to be found immediately, but also a long-term strategy is necessary to ensure that social reproduction receives the same consideration in public policy as commodity production does.

At the same time, through this study, I hope to call attention to domestic workers' underclass situation in the world. Global capitalism has directly caused the problems of domestic workers. Facilitating domestic service is not an ultimate way to solve care crisis in a country. It takes the concerted efforts of all governments to improve domestic workers' working conditions, take back government's social reproduction responsibilities and ultimately eliminate the division of labour globally.

Appendix 1   Open-ended interview sample questions for domestic workers

Participant's basic information:

Sex
Age
Education level
Where does she/he come from?
How long at this job?
Nature of current job or previous job

Reason for looking for domestic work:

Q. Why do you work as a domestic?

Mechanisms for looking for current job:

Q. How did you find the job? Through relatives, friends or agency?
Q. Have you had any training from your agency? What do they train you to do? Useful or not?
Q. Do you have a contract with your agency? Why? or why not?

Work history:

Q. How many employers have you had? Why did you leave each job?
Q. How long did you stay in the former jobs?
Q. What are your employers' occupations (both male and female)? Who employed you, the male employer or the female employer?

Working conditions:

Q. Have you signed a contract with your employer?
Q. How many hours do you work a day? What time do you get up and go to sleep?
Q. What kind of work do you do? Could you describe your everyday work?
Q. Do you have specified time off work?
Q. Do you have statutory holidays, paid or unpaid?

Q. Have you had work-related injuries, such as burn, cuts? Does your employer pay for your prescriptions?
Q. Have you had any conflicts with your employer? If it happened, what generally do you do? Why?
Q. How much is your pay? Do you have any pay other than your wage?
Q. Do you have any pension, health care or other social insurance? Please specify.
Q. What do you usually do when your employers go to work?
Q. Do you have your own room in the employer's home?
Q. Do you eat the same food with the family?

Other:

Are you satisfied with your job?
What do you think your agency and other institutions should do to protect your rights?
If you did not do domestic work, what would you do?

Appendix 2 Open-ended interview sample questions for employers

Reasons for looking for a domestic worker:

Q. Why do you need a domestic (live-in, live-out, cleaner)? Mechanisms for looking for domestic workers.
Q. How did you find this worker? Through relatives, friends or agency? Why did you look for a worker through them?

Hiring history:

Q. How many workers have you employed? When did they leave? Why?
Q. How many workers do you currently have? Are they male or female? What are their ages? How long have they been working for you?
Q. What is your occupation (both male and female)? Who decided to hire a domestic worker, you or your spouse? Why?

Workers' working conditions:

Q. Have you signed a contract with your worker?
Q. What do you ask your worker to do for you and the family?
Q. How many hours does you worker work a day? Could you describe his/her everyday work?
Q. Does your worker have specified time off?
Q. Does your worker have statutory holidays, paid or unpaid?
Q. What do you do about your worker's work-related injuries, such as burns, cuts? Who pays?
Q. Have you had any conflicts with your worker? If it happened, what generally do you do? Why?
Q. How much do you pay? Do you think the pay is reasonable?
Q. Does your worker have any pension, health care and other social insurance? Who pays for these?
Q. What do you usually ask your worker to do when you are not home?
Q. Does your worker have her own room?
Q. Does your worker eat the same food within the family?

Other:

Are you satisfied with your worker's job?
What rights do you think you and your worker(s) should have by law? Are they adequate? What could be improved by law?
What do you think the agency and other institutions should do to protect you and your worker?

Appendix 3   Open-ended interview sample questions for domestic agencies

1. How does your company recruit workers? What is the procedure?
2. Who comes to your company to look for domestic work? What is the gendered composition of males and females? Why do you think they need such a job?
3. Do you train them regarding working skills and labour rights? What kind of training do they have?
4. How do you support your domestic workers? From what aspects do you support domestic workers?
5. Are there any specific ways that you protect domestic labourers in your organization?
6. Do you receive complaints from domestic workers about their employers or working conditions? How do you deal with these?
7. What do you think your company should do to better protect domestic workers' rights?
8. How do you think your organization can cooperate with domestic workers support groups?
9. Ideally, what labour rights do you think domestic employees in your company should enjoy?

Appendix 4 Open-ended interview sample questions for labour authority and support groups

1. Are there any regulations to protect domestic labourers in your organization?
2. How do you support domestic workers? From what aspects do you support domestic workers?
3. Do you organize any training or events to educate domestic workers recognize their rights?
4. Are there any domestic workers come for help because of mistreatment by their employers? How do you deal with it?
5. Who are these paid domestic workers now? Why do you think they do such a job?
6. Ideally, what labour rights do you think domestic employees should have?
7. What do you think your organization should do to better protect domestic workers' rights?
8. How do you think your organization can cooperate with other domestic workers support groups?

Glossary of Chinese words

ayi   aunt: refers to female domestic workers since the 1930s
baodi   a minimum salary
baomu   nanny: a title for female domestic workers since the 1930s
chongshi   enrichment
cou he   acceptable
dagong   working
dagong mei   working sisters
dajia shuofa   everybody talks about the law
dagongmei zhi jia   The Migrant Women's Club
danwei   work unit
deng   waiting for
funü neng ding banbiantian   women hold up half the sky
gao di gui jian   jobs that are high-end or low-end, or noble or degrading
gonggu   consolidation
hefa quanyi   lawful rights and interests
hetongzhi guanli   contractual administration
hukou   household registration
huohong de niandai   Red era, refers to the Cultural Revolution (1966–76)
jianmin   mean people, including bondservants, together with actors, prostitutes and beggars
jiating fuwu yuan   family service worker
jiazheng fuwu yuan   domestic service worker
jiafa   domestic discipline in a household
jin   Chinese weight unit: 2 jin equals 1 kg
kao   relying on
koumen   stingy
lao shao bian qiong   an overall name for poor regions in China
liangjian   class division in feudal society
liangmin   good people, which included the literati, farmers, craftsmen and merchants (and women in households)
liang tiao tui zou lu   walk on two legs

liudong renkou floating population, refers to anyone who has moved, either temporarily or long-term, away from home without a corresponding transfer of their official household registration or *hukou*
nan zhu wai, nü zhu nei males were primary in the outer; females were primary in the inner
nan zun nü bei men are superior, women are inferior
nei-wai inner–outer distinction, in which females were assigned to the inner, and males, to the outer sphere: *nei* referred to the private/domestic sphere and *wai* referred to the public/social sphere
nüzi wu cai bian shi de a woman without talent is virtuous
san cong three bonds of obedience for women: to obey fathers when young, husbands when married and adult sons when widowed
san nong three rural problems: farming, rural areas and peasants
shebude stingy
suzhi quality
suzhi di low human capital accumulation
tianjia sky-high prices
tiaozheng adjustment
ticheng a percentage of the hourly wage rate
tie fan wan iron rice bowl: a traditional name for permanent employment that provided lifetime employment with guaranteed welfare benefits
tigao improvement
xiagang laid-off
xiao shi gong hourly worker
xiao xifu, da zhangfu little wife, big husband
yang Confucianism aligned the male with the cosmic force of yang with a hierarchical relationship of *yang* presiding over *yin*
yao asking from
yin Confucianism aligned the female with the cosmic force of *yin*
youhua zuhe optimizing regrouping
yuesao domestic workers who specifically do neonatal care for newborns and moms
yuersao domestic workers who specialize in looking after babies that are older than three months or 100 days
yu shijie jiegui closer ties with the world
zeyou shanggang merit employment
zhiyou genggao, meiyou zuigao only higher, no highest
zugui clan conventions

Acronyms and abbreviations

ACFTU	All-China Federation of Trade Unions
ACWF	All-China Women's Federation
BAIC	Beijing Administration for Industry and Commerce
BHSA	Beijing Home Service Association
BUWLSSC	Beijing University Women's Law Study and Services Center
CCP	Chinese Communist Party
CEDAW	Convention on the Elimination of all Forms of Discrimination against Women
CETTIC	China Employment Training Technical Institution Centre
CNSECE	China National Society of Early Childhood Education
CMSs	Cooperative Medical Systems
CWLSLS	Centre for Women's Law Studies and Legal Services of Peking University
EOP	Employer's Orientation Programme
ESA	Employment Standards Act
FPDSC	Fu Ping Domestic Service Centre
HRS	Household Responsibility System
ICCPR	International Covenant on Civil and Political Rights
ICESCR	International Covenant on Economic, Social and Cultural Rights
ILC	International Labour Conference
ILO	International Labour Organization
MWC	Migrant Women's Club
MOF	Ministry of Finance
MOFCOM	Ministry of Commerce
MOHRSS	Ministry of Human Resources and Social Security
MOLSS	Ministry of Labour and Social Security
MOM	Ministry of Manpower of Singapore
NGO	Non-government organization
PRC	People's Republic of China
RCWDR	Research Centre for Women's Development and Rights of Northwestern Polytechnic University
SAIC	State Administration for Industry and Commerce of the People's Republic of China

SBFSC	San Ba Family Service Centre
SOE	State-owned enterprises
UN	United Nations
UNIFEM	United Nations Development Fund for Women
UNTGG	United Nations Thematic Group on Gender
WTO	World Trade Organization
ZLDSC	Zuo Ling Domestic Service Company

Notes

1 Introduction

1 In March 2008, the former Ministry of Labour and Social Security of the People's Republic of China and the former Ministry of Personnel of the People's Republic of China merged and were replaced by Ministry of Human Resources and Social Security of the People's Republic of China.
2 The notion of a human-centred development that aims to transform China into a harmonious and well-off society was first introduced by the Chinese government at the third session of the Sixteenth Chinese Communist Party Congress on 11–14 October 2003. Since then, the Chinese government has been making an effort to create a harmonious society, in which human development is in tune with economic and social development (Chinese Communist Party 2003).
3 Women were expected to live with their husbands' families after marriage and men were considered natural household heads.
4 It should be noted that Sainsbury's model is based on a heterosexual marriage and a nuclear family relationship without considering family form change.

2 Domestic employment regimes in China

1 *Gao di gui jian* in China refers to different social classes of human being and different levels of jobs and other things. In socialist China it is always said that there is no *gao di gui jian* distinction between any jobs or any human beings since, in a socialist country, everyone is supposed to be equal, and whatever job a person does, it is a contribution to the country.
2 The number, 360 professions, refers to a variety of professions. It is not an accurate number.
3 Domestic attendant is the official name of a domestic worker.
4 The Opium War was started in 1840 by the British invaders due to dumping opium in China by force. Therefore, in history, the war was also called the Opium War. After the War, the Chinese government was forced to sign the Treaty of Nanjing, ceding Hong Kong and opening five trading ports, such as Guangzhou, Fuzhou, Xiamen, Ningbo and Shanghai, to British residence and trade. Since then, China began to transform gradually from an independent feudal country into a semi-colonial and semi-feudal country.
5 It was translated by Ma Junwu, a famous scholar and political activist in modern China, and published in serial form in *Xinmin Cong Bao* (*New Citizen Newspaper*) from 11 April 1903.
6 Feminist scholar Cynthia Enloe (2000) has a study about the British in India. In her work, she argues that while the British in India felt themselves to be superior to Indian men as they stopped what they saw as barbaric practices towards women, they

introduced prostitutes for their army and at the same time introduced a new law that banned women from sexually refusing their husbands (Enloe 2000).
7 The feminists formulated 11 political programmes: 1) implement women's equal rights with men; 2) implement universal women's education; 3) improve household customs; 4) prohibit the sale of bondservants; 5) implement monogamy; 6) prohibit prostitution by force; 7) promote women's entrepreneurship; 8) open charities; 9) set bound feet free by force; 10) improve women's clothing; 11) prohibit no-cause divorce (referring to those who got married based on personal freedom).
8 The New Culture Movement sprang from the disillusionment with traditional Chinese culture following the failure of the Chinese Republic to address China's problems. China's intellectual class promoted democracy, science and the destruction of Confucianism that had led China to stagnate and fall under foreign domination. On 4 May 1919, students in Beijing protested the Paris Peace Conference's giving German rights over Shandong to Japan, turning this cultural movement into a political one in what became known as the May Fourth Movement. This movement created conditions for the spread of Marxism in China.
9 It was an economic and social campaign undertaken by the Chinese Communist Party between 1958 and 1960. The aim of the campaign was to rapidly transform the country from an agrarian economy into a modern society through the process of agriculturalization, industrialization and collectivization.
10 For a detailed discussion, see Croll 1978.
11 *Suzhi* or quality has become a discourse widely used in the reform era in China. Individuals or groups of 'high' *suzhi* are seen as deserving more income, power and status than those of 'low' *suzhi* during market economic reforms (Kipnis 2006). Women are the most common targets for *suzhi* discourse. For discussion about *suzhi* in China, *see* Jacka (2009); Kipnis (2006); Judd (2002). For studies highlighting the importance of *suzhi* in discourses relating to rural migrants, see Sun 2009b; Yan 2003a, 2003b.

3 Globalization, economic reforms and paid domestic employment in China

1 For an overview of economic reform in China, see Naughton 1995; White 1993.
2 For more detailed explanation of rationing, see Naughton 1995: 46.
3 Floating population refers to anyone who has moved, either temporarily or long term, away from home without a corresponding transfer of their official household registration or *hukou*.
4 Sen 1999.
5 For discussion of defining and measuring poverty, see Laderchi, Saith and Stewart 2006; Sumner 2006.
6 Economists usually use the Gini coefficient to measure income distribution: the Gini coefficient ranges between 0 and 1 in value, and a Gini coefficient of 0 would represent that income was perfectly equally distributed, while a Gini coefficient of 1 would indicate that all income was concentrated in the hands of a single individual.
7 In 2002, $1 US dollar equalled roughly ¥8; therefore, ¥2,476 was about $310 and ¥7,703 was about $963.
8 *Lao shao bian qiong* areas is an overall name for poor regions in China. *Lao* means old, which refers to the old revolutionary bases such as Shanxi and Jiangxi. *Shao* means ethnic minority. *Bian* means border areas that are less developed. *Qiong* means poor.
9 Chinese workers in state-owned enterprises received amenities such as soap, toilet paper and even theatre tickets from time to time (World Bank 2002).
10 *Danwei* is a general term for state-owned and collective enterprises and different government institutions.

156 *Notes*

11 *Hetong Guanli* refers to a personnel administration approach whereby employers hire workers by employment contract. Both employers and workers have the right to choose whether or not to sign or renew a contract.
12 *Youhua Zuhe* is a management approach to reorganize work to meet strategic business objectives.
13 *Zeyou shanggang* means employers can choose their workers based on workers' performance during their jobs. Only those workers who perform well can remain in the enterprises.
14 CCP 1992.
15 CCP 1997.
16 National Bureau of Statistics of the People's Republic of China 1999; 2005.
17 Some scholars estimated that females comprise about 60 per cent of laid-off workers (Liu 2007).
18 National Bureau of Statistics of the People's Republic of China 1999; 2005.
19 'Registered unemployment rate' refers to the proportion of registered unemployed in urban areas accounting for the total employed and registered unemployed in urban areas. 'Registered employed' refers to only people who are urban residents within the legal labour age (16–64), have employability but no job, but are looking for a job and have registered in local labour administration organizations. It does not include migrant workers from rural areas and actual urban unemployed people who have not registered.
20 In November 1993, the MOLSS promoted The Re-Employment Project nationwide. It aims to mobilize various social forces to serve and help unemployed and laid-off workers re-employed through policy support and employment service.
21 In China, all businesses should register at local industry and commerce bureau and have business licences. Small businesses without registration are illegal.
22 It refers to career interruption.
23 This comes from the author's experience of the organization.
24 The author was one of its two investigators.
25 For example, China signed the Convention on the Elimination of All Forms of Discrimination against Women in 1988 and the Beijing Declaration on the Fourth Women's Conference in 1995.
26 *China Women's News* 2005, 4 January.
27 All-China Women's Federation (N.d.).
28 The lowest monthly wage rate of domestic workers in Beijing is ¥800.
29 A new terminology refers to those people who take care of newborns and their mothers.
30 Jilin Agricultural University and Hebei College of Industry and Technology 2006, 22 June.
31 Interview, 29 November 2007.

4 Childcare crisis after economic reforms

1 Xinhua News Agency N.d.
2 Ibid.
3 China Labour Information N.d.
4 The Shaanxi-Gansu-Ningxia revolutionary base was also called the Shaanxi-Gansu-Ningxia border region. From 1937 to 1947, *Yan'an* was the place where the Shaanxi-Gansu-Ningxia border region government was located. This was the government led by the Chinese Communist Party during the Anti-Japanese War.
5 Calculated by the author through Table 4.1 in Tang 2005: 39.
6 Calculated by author through interview data.
7 Red symbolizes revolution. The 10 years of Cultural Revolution were also called the red era at that time.

8 It is a new fee item that many transformed public childcare centres charge students. The fee is mandatory and should be paid upon acceptance. Generally, it is calculated on a yearly basis, but parents are asked to pay it as one fee. While nursing and teaching fees are a few hundred per month, the size of sponsorship fees is generally from a few thousand to 10 thousand or even more a year. The size differs from centre to centre and from city to city.
 9 The National Education Committee, National Plan Committee, Ministry of Civil Affairs, Ministry of Housing and Urban-Rural Development, National Economy and Trade Committee, ACFTU, and ACWF. Some institutions have changed their names, such as National Education Committee which is the current Ministry of Education (China National Society of Early Childhood Education (CNSECE) 1999).
10 Feng Shiliang 2010.
11 Ibid.
12 *Guangzhou Daily* 2010a.
13 *Guangzhou Daily* 2010b.
14 *Beijing News* 2010b.
15 This was calculated by the author according to Department of Population, and Employment Statistics of National Bureau of Statistics, P.R.C. and Department of Planning and Finance, MOLSS, P.R.C 2005, 2006; and Ministry of Education of the People's Republic of China 2006.
16 In September 1989, the Kindergarten Management Regulations approved by the State Council and issued by the former National Education Committee (now the Ministry of Education), stated that kindergartens should charge parents nursing and education fees to (Article 24). In July 1997, the Implementation Suggestions on 'the Ninth Five Year' Development Goals of Early Childhood Education issued by the former National Education Committee further mentioned that early childhood education is not compulsory and 'parents who send their children to childcares should pay fees' (China National Society of Early Childhood Education 1999).
17 National Bureau of Statistics of the People's Republic of China 1999, 2005.
18 *Beijing News* 2010a.

5 Domestic labour as precarious work in China

 1 All-China Federation of Trade Unions N.d.
 2 Peking University Centre for Legal Information N.d.
 3 *Findlaw.cn.* 2010.
 4 *Xinhua News Agency* 2003, 4 May.
 5 *People's Court Daily* 2006, 31 August.
 6 Central People's Government, China 2007, 29 June.
 7 Paraphrased by the author.
 8 Paraphrased by the author.
 9 According to the Beijing Statistics Bureau, the average annual wage of staff and employees in urban work units in Beijing was ¥39,867 in 2007. Therefore, the average monthly wage was ¥3,322.25 (¥39,867 per annum) for Beijing city residents in 2007 (Beijing Statistical Information Net 2008, 25 March).
10 For an overview of health care reform and its gendered impact in China see Chen and Standing 2007.
11 *Xinhua News Agency* 2009, 3 January.
12 For the full story see China Labour Market 2004, 26 March.
13 Guangdong Satellite TV 2006.
14 For the full story see Guangdong Satellite TV 2006.
15 Sina Jilin 2010, 19 and 20 September.
16 Sang Lan 2009, 5 September.

158 Notes

17 Sang Lan 2009, 7 September.
18 The company gives regular clients options to pre-pay the service fee. Once they pre-pay the fee, each client is registered with a service card with their names and pay information on it. Every time the company sends any cleaner(s) (cleaners are usually sent in pairs) to work, the pre-pay clients only need to sign on the service card and the company will deduct the fee each time till it is used up.

6 From individual resistance to unionized negotiation

1 Foucault 2001: 267, and 1976: 126.
2 Foucault 2001: 267.
3 Foucault 2007: xx–xxiii.
4 Examples in developed countries, such as Canada, show that low union coverage among workers in precarious employment is most pronounced (Cranford *et al.* 2005).
5 Paraphrased by the author.
6 Generally, domestic workers do not want their employers' house to be too large because, while their pay does not increase much along with employers' house sizes, their living space does not increase along with employers' house sizes either. No matter how big and luxurious an employer's house is, the domestic workers' room is always 5–6 sq. m or even less. This is only enough room for a single bed and it is hidden in the least visible corner, like a pigeon's cage (*gezi long*, a commonly used word that refers to a very small sized room in China).
7 Chinese weight unit: 2 *jin* equals 1 kg.
8 See the Central People's Government, China 2005, 12 August.
9 Beijing Second Intermediate People's Court 2007.
10 Xiang, F. H. 2010.
11 This emergency aid programme is funded by donation. Relatively few migrant workers receive aid from this fund both because few know of its existence and its general limited capability to deal with large numbers of women.
12 Migrant Women's Club (N.d.).
13 All-China Federation of Trade Unions (N.d.).
14 The description to safeguard employers' rights and interests has an inseparable relationship with this union's focus. Since the union's emphasis is on the recreation and education of domestic workers, it organizes various recreational activities and educational workshops and even includes cooking skills training. The presupposition is that if workers can relax in the recreational activities and learn more subjects and skills, they can then work better for employers.
15 In terms of unionizing precarious workers, some international strategies might be referenced. Several countries in Europe, such as Sweden and Germany, have begun to improve unionization in the temporary sector (Anderson, Beaton and Laxer 2005). Various unionization solutions, such as community unionism and sectorial and general unions, have been offered to organize precarious workers (Cranford *et al.* 2005).

7 Establishing domestic workers' rights

1 Hu Jintao 2007: N.p.
2 ILO 2010.
3 Department of Labour and Employment, Philippines N.d.
4 Labour Department, Hong Kong 2009, 25 August.
5 Ministry of Labour, British Columbia Government, Canada N.d.
6 Ministry of Labour, Ontario Government, Canada 2008.
7 In the example of Canada, because of less effective enforcement of the ESA, many domestic workers are still treated badly (Pratt 2003).

8 Labour Department, Hong Kong 2008, July.
9 Citizenship and Migration Canada N.d.
10 Ministry of Manpower, Singapore 2007, 1 February.
11 Labour Contract Law N.d.
12 See the introduction of Beijing Domestic Service Contract on the official website of the Beijing municipal government (Beijing Government 2006, 20 December).
13 Ministry of Civil Affairs 2005.
14 *People's Daily* 2010, 2 September.

Bibliography

ACWF and ILO (2009, 2 November) Situational analysis of domestic work in China. Online. Available <http://www.ilo.org/asia/whatwedo/publications/lang--en/docName--WCMS_114261/index.htm> (accessed 23 August 2010).
All-China Federation of Trade Unions (ACFTU) (N.d.) *Zhonghua renmin gonghegong laodong fa* [Labour Law the People's Republic of China]. Online. Available <http://www.acftu.org/template/10004/file.jsp?cid=69&aid=690> (accessed 21 October 2008).
All-China Women's Federation (ACWF) (N.d.) *Jinguo Shequ Fuwu Gongcheng* [Women's Community Service Project]. Online. Available <http://www.women.org.cn/jingdianhuodong/4gongcheng/fuwu.htm> (assessed 21 August 2007).
—— (1988) *Mao Zedong, Liu Shaoqi, Zhou Enlai, Zhu De lun funü jiefang* [Mao Zedong, Liu Shaoqi, Zhou Enlai, Zhu De talk about the liberation of women], Beijing: *Zhongguo Funü Chubanshe* [China Women Publishing House].
Anagnost, A. (2004) 'The corporeal politics of quality (*suzhi*)', *Public Culture*, 16, 2: 189–208.
Anderson, B. (2000). *Doing the Dirty Work? The Global Politics of Domestic Labour*. New York: Zed Books.
Anderson, J., Beaton, J. and Laxer, K. (2005) 'The union dimension: Mitigating precarious employment?', in L. F. Vosko (ed.) *Precarious Employment: Understanding Labour Market Insecurity in Canada*, Montreal: McGill-Queen's University Press.
Anonymous interviews (October 2007–January 2008).
Appleton, S., Knight, J., Song, L. N. and Xia, Q. J. (2002) 'Labour retrenchment in China: Determinants and consequences', *China Economic Review*, 13: 252–75.
Arat-Koc, S. (1989) 'In the privacy of our own home: Foreign domestic workers as solution to the crisis in the domestic sphere in Canada', *Studies in Political Economy*, 28: 33–58.
Basu, A. (ed.) (1995) *The Challenge of Local Feminisms: Women's Movements in Global Perspectives*, Boulder: Westview Press.
Beijing Municipal Government (2006, 20 December) *2001 Nian 1 Yue 1 Ri qi zhengshi tuixing Beijing Shi Jiazheng Fuwu Hetong* [Beijing Domestic Service Contract will be officially implemented 1 January 2001]. Online. Available <http://www.beijing.gov.cn/ggfw/jm/jmsy/shxx/t708592.htm> (accessed 8 August 2007).
Beijing Home Service Association (BHSA) (2007) Director's speech, 15 November: N.p.
Beijing News (2010) N.T. Online. Available <http://epaper.bjnews.com.cn/html/2010-09/01/content_142977.htm?div=-1> (accessed 1 September 2010).
—— (2010b) N.T. Online. Available <http://epaper.bjnews.com.cn/html/2010-09/03/content_143807.htm?div=-1> (accessed 3 September 2010).

Beijing Second Intermediate People's Court (2007) Civil mediation agreement No.11336.
Beijing Statistical Information Net (2008, 25 March). *2007 nian Beijing shi zhigong pingjun gongzi* [The average annual wage of staff and employees in Beijing in 2007]. Online. Available <http://www.bjstats.gov.cn/tjzn/mcjs/200901/t20090103_133658. htm> (accessed 22 Feburary 2010).
Beneria, L. (2003) *Gender, Development and Globalization: Economic As If All People Mattered*, London: Routledge.
Berik, G. (1997) 'The need for crossing the method boundaries in economics research', *Feminist Economics*, 3, 2: 121–5.
Bezanson, K. (2006) 'The neo-liberal state and social reproduction: Gender and household insecurity in the late 1990s', in K. Bezanson and M. Luxton (eds.) *Social Reproduction: Feminist Political Economy Challenges Neo-liberalism*, Montreal and Kingston: McGill-Queen's University Press.
—— and Luxton, M. (2006) 'Introduction: Social reproduction and feminist political economy', in K. Bezanson and M. Luxton (eds.) *Social Reproduction: Feminist Political Economy Challenges Neo-Liberalism*, Montreal and Kingston: McGill-Queen's University Press.
Blackett, A. (1998) *Making Domestic Work Visible: The Case for Specific Regulation*, Geneva: International Labour Office.
—— (2010) Making domestic work visible: The case for specific regulation. Online. Available <http://www.ilo.org/public/english/dialogue/ifpdial/publ/infocus/domestic/> (accessed 23 August 2010).
Brodie, J. (2007) 'Canada's three Ds: The rise and decline of the gender-based policy capacity', in M. G. Cohen and J. Brodie (eds.) *Remapping Gender in the New Global Order*, London and New York: Routledge.
Broomhill, R. and Sharp, R. (2007) 'The problem of social reproduction under neoliberalism: Reconfiguring the male-breadwinner model in Australia', in M. G. Cohen and J. Brodie (eds.) *Remapping Gender in the New Global Order*, London; New York: Routledge.
Bujra, J. (2000) *Serving Class: Masculinity and the Feminisation of Domestic Service in Tanzania*, Edinburgh: Edinburgh University Press Ltd.
Cameron, B. (2006) 'Social reproduction and Canadian federalism', in K. Bezanson and M. Luxton (eds.) *Social Reproduction: Feminist Political Economy Challenges Neo-liberalism*, Montreal and Kingston: McGill-Queen's University Press.
Cao, J. C. (2001) '*Guanyu lanyin hukou wenti de sikao*' ['Some thoughts on the blue-stamp hukou'], *Population and Economics*, 6, 66: 15–21.
Central People's Government, China (2005, 12 August) *Guowuyuan bangongting guanyu zuohao nongmin jincheng wugong jiuye guanli he fuwu gongzuo de tongzhi* [The notice on improving rural migrant labour's employment management and service]. Online. Available <http://www.gov.cn/zwgk/2005-08/12/content_21839.htm> (accessed 10 October 2008).
—— (2007, 29 June) *Zhonghua renmin gongheguo laodong hetong fa* [Labour Contract Law of the People's Republic of China]. Online. Available <http://www.gov.cn/jrzg/2007-06/29/content_667720.htm> (accessed 4 December 2008).
—— (2007, 24 October) Hu Jintao's report at Seventeenth Party Congress. Online. Available <http://english.gov.cn/2007-10/24/content_785505.htm> (accessed 25 August 2010).
Centre for Women's Law Studies and Legal Services of Peking University (CWLSLS) (2006, 16 October) Introduction, Online. Available <http://www.woman-legalaid.org/article.php/5> (accessed 26 March 2009).

—— (2007, 23 August) 'Domestic workers labour rights' Project in Guangzhou, Online. Available <http://www.woman-legalaid.org/article.php/183> (accessed 26 March 2009).

China Employment Training Technical Instruction Centre (CETTIC), MOLSS (2004) *Jiazheng fuwu baipishu* [The white paper on domestic service], Beijing, China.

—— (2006) *Jiazheng fuwu yuan – Jichu zhishi* [*The Basic Knowledge for Domestic Service Workers*], Beijing: *Zhongguo Laodong Shehui baozhang Chuban she* [China Labour and Social Security Press].

Chang, K. A. and Ling, L. H. M. (2000) 'Globalization and its intimate other: Filipina domestic workers in Hong Kong', in M. H. Marchand and A. S. Runyan (eds.) *Gender and Global Restructuring: Sightings, Sites and Resistances*, London: Routledge.

Chen, H. (1999) '*Zhongguo laodongli shichang zhengce de zhuyao zhixiang*' [The main trend of the Chinese labour market policies], *Guanli Shijie* [*Management World*], 5: 64–6, 97.

Chen, L. Y. (2008) *Gender and Chinese Development: Towards an Equitable Society*, London: New York: Routledge.

Chen, L. Y. and Standing, H. (2007) 'Gender equality in transitional China's healthcare policy reforms', in *Feminist Economics*, 13, 3–4: 189–212.

Chen, S. Y. (1996) *Social Policy of the Economic State and Community Care in Chinese Culture*, Aldershot, Hants, England; Brookfield, Vt.: Avebury.

Chen, W. Q. (2008) '*Shequ gonghui de xianshi yiyi yu kunjing*' ['The realistic meaning and dilemma of community unions'], *Shequ* [*Community*], 5: 36–7.

Cheung, L. (2006). 'Living on the edge: Addressing employment gaps for temporary migrant workers under the live-in caregiver program', unpublished MA thesis, Burnaby, B.C.: Simon Fraser University.

Chin, C. B. N. (1998) *In Service and Servitude: Foreign Female Domestic Workers and the Malaysian 'Modernity' Project*, New York: Colombia University Press.

China Labour Information (N.d.) Regulations Governing the Treatment of Occupational Diseases. Online. Available <http://law.51labour.com/lawshow-68109.html>.

China Labour Market (2004, March 26). *Cong Zhou Dailan shangcan toushi shebao queshi* [From the Zhou Dailan case to look at the missing social insurance]. Online. Available <http://www.lm.gov.cn/gb/news/2004-03/26/content_24963.htm> (accessed 4 December 2008).

China National Society of Early Childhood Education (CNSECE) (1999) *Zhonghua renmin gongheguo youer jiaoyu zhongyao wenxian huibian* [*The collection of important literature on early child education in the Chinese People's Republic of China*], Beijing: *Beijing Shifan Daxue Chubanshe* [Beijing Normal University Press].

—— (2003) *Bai nian zhongguo youjiao* [*The centenary Chinese preschool education*], Beijing: *Jiaoyu Kexue Chubanshe* [Educational Science Publishing House].

China Women's News (2005, 4 January) *Tianjin: Xiao e xindai jiang cheng 'funü yinhang'* [Tianjin: Microcredit loans will turn into 'a women's bank';]. Online. Available <http://www.women.org.cn/allnews/0705/223.html> (accessed 20 August 2008).

Chinese Communist Party (1992, 12 October) *Jiakuai gaige kaifang he xiandaihua jianshe bufa, zhengqu you zhongguo tese shehui zhuyi shiye de geng da shengli* [Accelerating the pace of reform and opening up and the construction of modernization, to win the greater victory of socialism with Chinese characteristics], The report of President Jiang Zemin at the 14th National Congress.

—— (1997, 12 September) *Gaoju Deng Xiaoping lilun weida qizhi, ba jianshe you zhongguo teshe shehui zhuyi quanmian tui xiang ershiyi shiji* [Hold high the great banner of Deng Xiaoping theory, fully push the construction of socialism with Chinese characteristics into the twenty-first century], The report of President Jiang Zemin at the 15th National Congress.

—— (2003, 14 October). *Zhonggong zhongyang guanyu wanshan shehui zhuyi shichang jingji tizhi ruogan wenti de jueding* [The decision of a number of issues on perfecting the socialist market economic system by the CCP Central Committee], The decision passed on the third session of the 16th National Congress.

—— (2007, 15 October). *Gaoju zhongguo tese shehuizhuyi weida qizhi, wei zhengqu quanmian jianshe xiaokang shehui xin shengli er fendou* [Hold High the Great Banner of Socialism with Chinese Characteristics and Strive for New Victories in Building a Moderately Prosperous Society in all Respects], The report of President Hu Jintao at the 17th National Congress.

Chow, G. (2009) 'Rural poverty in China: Problem and solution', in R. Kanbur and X. B. Zhang (eds.) *Governing Rapid Growth in China: Equity and Institutions*, London; New York: Routledge.

Chow, N. and Xu, Y. (2001) *Socialist Welfare in a Market Economy – Social Security Reforms in Guangzhou, China*, Hampshire, England: Ashgate Publishing Limited.

Chu, G. S. (1995) *Nubi shi: Zhongguo nubi wenti de lishi sikao* [A history of servants: A historical examination of the servant question in China], Shanghai: Shanghai Wenyi Chuban She [Shanghai Literature and Art Publishing Press].

Chu, Y. and So, A. Y. (2010) 'State neoliberalism: The Chinese road to capitalism', in Y. Chu (ed.) *Chinese Capitalisms: Historical Emergence and Political Implications*, Basingstoke (England), New York: Palgrave Macmillan.

Citizenship and Migration Canada (N.d.) Live-in Caregiver Program: Sample contract. Online. Available <http://www.cic.gc.ca/english/work/caregiver/sample-contract.asp> (accessed 13 May 2009).

Clarkson, S. (2002). *Uncle Sam and Us: Globalization, Neoconservatism, and the Canadian State*, Toronto: University of Toronto Press; Washington, DC: Woodrow Wilson Center Press.

Cockburn, C. (1983) *Brothers: Male Dominance and Technological Change*, London: Pluto Press.

Cohen, M. G. (1994) 'The implications of economic restructuring for women: The Canadian situation', in I. Bakker (ed.) *The Strategic Silence Gender and Economic Policy*, London, UK; Atlantic Highlands, N.J., USA: Zed Books in association with the North-South Institute.

—— (1996) 'New international trade agreements: Their reactionary role in creating markets and retarding social welfare', in I. Bakker (ed.) *Rethinking Restructuring: Gender and Change in Canada*, Toronto; Buffalo; London: University of Toronto Press.

—— (1997) 'From welfare state to vampire capitalism', in P. Evans and G. Wekerle (eds.) *Women and the Canadian Welfare State*, Toronto: University of Toronto Press.

—— and Brodie, J. (2007) 'Remapping gender in the new global order', in M. G. Cohen and J. Brodie (eds.) *Remapping Gender in the New Global Order*, London; New York: Routledge.

—— Ritchie, L., Swenarchuk, M. and Vosko, L. (2000) 'Globalization implications and strategies for women', *Canadian Women's Studies*, 21, 22, 4, 1: 5–14.

Cohen, R. and Kennedy, P. (2007) *Global Sociology*, 2nd edn, Basingstoke, UK; New York: Palgrave Macmillan.

Cox, R. (2006) *The Servant Problem: Domestic Employment in a Global Economy*, London and New York: I. B. Tauris.

Cranford, C. J., Das Gupta, T., Ladd, D. and Vosko, L. F. (2005) 'Thinking through community unionism', in L. F. Vosko (ed.) *Precarious Employment: Understanding Labour Market Insecurity in Canada*, Montreal: McGill-Queen's University Press.

Cranmer-Byng, J. L. (ed.) (1958) *The Saying of Confucius: A Translation of the Greater Part of the Confucian Analects with Introduction and Notes by Lionel Giles*, New York: Grove Press.

Croll, E. (1978) *Feminism and Socialism in China*, London; Boston: Routledge & K. Paul.

—— (1983) *Chinese Women since Mao*, London: Zed Books; Armonk, N.Y.: M.E. Sharpe.

—— (2006) *China's New Consumers: Social Development and Domestic Demand*, London; New York: Routledge.

Davin, D. (1975) 'The implications of some aspects of CCP policy toward urban women in the 1950s', *Modern China*, 1, 4: 363–78.

Day, S. and Brodsky, G. (1998) *Women and the Equality Deficit: The Impact of Restructuring Canada's Social Programs*, Ottawa: Status of Women Canada.

Department of Labour and Employment, Philippines (N.d.). Labour Code of the Philippines. Online. Available <http://www.dole.gov.ph/labor_codes.php> (accessed 11 May 2009).

Department of Population and Employment Statistics of National Bureau of Statistics, P.R.C. and Department of Planning and Finance, MOLSS, P.R.C (2005) *China Labour Statistics Yearbook 2005*, Beijing: China Statistics Press.

—— (2006), *China Labour Statistics Yearbook 2006*, Beijing: China Statistics Press.

Dong, X. Y., Du, F. L., Liu, J., Liu, L. and Wang, H. (2009, March) *Toward Gender Equality in China's Economic and Social Transformation: Unpaid Care for Children and the Elderly and its Impacts on Women and Children during China's Economic Transition*, Beijing: The Heinrich Böll Foundation.

Du, F. L. (2008) '*Jiating jiegou, ertong kanhu yu nüxing laodong canyu: Laizi zhongguo fei nongcun de zhengju*' ['Family structure, childcare and women's labour participation: The evidence of non-agricultural areas in China'], *Shijie Jingji Wenhui* [*World Economic Papers*], 2, April: 1–12.

—— and Dong, X. Y. (2008) 'Why do women have longer durations of unemployment than men in post-structuring urban China?', *Cambridge Journal of Economics*, 33: 233–52.

Elson, D. (1988) 'Market socialism or socialization of the market?', *New Left Review*, I/172: 3–44.

—— (1999) 'Labour markets as gendered institutions: Equality, efficiency and empowerment issues', *World Development*, 27, 3: 611–27.

Emerson, J. P. (1968) 'Employment in mainland China: Problems and prospects', in W. Proxmire (Foreword), *An Economic Profile of Mainland China*, New York: Praeger.

Engels, F. (1972) *The Origin of the Family, Private Property and the State*, New York: New World Paperbacks.

England, P. and Folbre, N. (1999) 'The cost of caring', *ANNALS of the American Academy of Political and Social Science by SAGE Journals Online*, 561: 39–51.

Enloe, C. (2000) *Bananas, Beaches and Bases: Making Feminist Sense of International Politics*, Berkeley: University of California Press.

Fan, C. (2008) 'Migration, *hukou*, and the city', in S. Yusuf and T. Saich (eds.), *China Urbanizes: Consequences, Strategies, and Policies*, World Bank Publications.

Fang, Y. Q., Granrose, C. S. and Kong, R. V. (2006) 'National policy influences on women's careers in the People's Republic of China', in C. S. Granrose (ed.) *Employment of Women in Chinese Culture: Half the Sky*, Northampton, Mass.: Edward Elgar Publishing.

Feng, S. L. (2010, 3 March) Blog. *Tian jia youeryuan ling baixing hanxin – jianyi dui youeryuan shoufei shixing xianjia* [Tian jia childcare made common people upset – suggest to impose price limits to childcare]. Available <http://blog.people.com.cn/blog/c7/s83375,w1267597928152458>.

Findlaw.cn. (N.d.) *Laodongbu guanyu yinfa guanyu guanche zhixing Zhonghua Renmin Gonghegong Laodong Fa ruogan wenti de yijian* [The Opinion on Certain Questions during the Enforcement of the People's Republic China Labour Law]. Online. Available <http://china.findlaw.cn/fagui/sh/23/46939.html> (accessed 10 October 2008).

Folbre, N. (1994) *Who Pays for the Kids?* London and New York: Routledge.

—— and Weisskofp, T. (1998) 'Did father know best? Families, markets and the supply of caring labour', in A. Ben-Ner and L. Putterman (eds.) *Economics, Values and Organizations*, New York: Cambridge University Press.

Foucault, M. (1976) *Histoire de la sexualité, Vol. 1, La Volonté de savoir*, Paris: Gallimard.

—— (1978) *The History of Sexuality Vol. 1: An Introduction*, trans. R. Hurley, New York: Vintage.

—— (2001) 'Non au sexe roi', in *Dits et ecrits II, 1976–88*, Paris: Gallimard.

—— (2007) 'Introduction', in M. Foucault, M. Senellart and A. I. Davidson, *Security, Territory, Population: Lectures at the Collège de France, 1977–8*, Basingstoke; New York: Palgrave Macmillan.

Fox, C. (2005) 'Mexico's domestic workers are "doing it for themselves" ', *Contemporary Review E-Journal*, 287, 1675: 92–94.

Fraser, N. (1997) *Justice Interruptus: Critical Reflections on the 'Postsocialist' Conditions*, London: Routledge.

Frazier, M. W. (2002) *The Making of the Chinese Industrial Workplace: State, Revolution, and Labour Management*, New York: Cambridge University Press.

—— (2010) *Socialist Insecurity: Pensions and the Politics of Uneven Development in China*, Ithaca: Cornell University Press.

Frobel, F., Heinrichs, J. and Kreye, O. (2007) 'The new international division of labour in the world economy' [1980], in J. T. Roberts and A. B. Hite (eds.) *The Globalization and Development Reader: Perspectives on Development and Global Change*, Malden, Mass.: Blackwell Publishing.

Gaetano, A. M. (2004) 'Filial daughters, modern women: Migrant domestic workers in post-Mao Beijing', in A. M. Gaetano and T. Jacka (eds.) *On the Move: Women in Rural-to-Urban Migration in Contemporary China*, New York: Columbia University Press.

Gao, X. X. (1999) '*Funü yu fazhan zai zhongguo: dui shijian de fenxi yu zai renshi*' ['Women and development in China: The analysis and re-recognition of practice'], *Zhongguo Fuyun* [*Chinese Women's Movement*], 3: 15–17.

—— (2007) 'The silver flower contest: Rural women in 1950s China and the gendered division of labour', in D. Ko and Z. Wang (eds.) *Translating Feminisms in China: A Special Issue of Gender and History*, Malden, MA; Oxford: Blackwell.

Ge, S. N. (1997, September 8) '*Ba funü jiuye naru jingji fazhan zhuliu*' ['Put women's employment into the mainstream of economic development'], *Zhongguo Funü Bao* [*China Women's News*].

Geiger, S. N. G. (1986) 'Women's life histories: Method and content', *Signs: Journal of Women, Culture and Society*, 11, 2: 334–5.

Gilbert, A. (2008) 'The new international division of labour', in V. Desai and R. B. Potter (eds.) *The Companion to Development Studies*, London: Hodder Education.

Glenn, E. N. (1992) 'From servitude to service work: Historical continuities in the racial division of paid reproductive labour', *Signs*, 18, 1: 1–43.

—— (2010) *Forced to Care: Coercion and Caregiving in America*, Cambridge, Mass.: Harvard University Press.

Government of British Columbia (N.d.) Information for Domestic Workers and Employers. Online. Available <http://www.labour.gov.bc.ca/esb/domestics/>.

Gregson, N. and Lowe, M. (1994) *Servicing the Middle Classes: Class, Gender and Waged Domestic Labour in Contemporary Britain*, London and New York: Routledge.

Guangdong Satellite TV (N.d.) *Ren Zai Ta Xiang: Cengjing Na Me Meili de Cai Minmin (zu tu)* [All alone in a place far from home: Once was so beautiful Cai Minmin] (group pictures). Online. Available <http://gd.news.sina.com.cn 2006-03-14 14:43> (accessed 16 May 2010).

Guangdong Sina News (2006) *Ren zai taxiang: Cengjing na me meili de Cai Minmin* [People living in another place: Cai Minmin was once such a beautiful girl]. Online. Available <http://gd.news.sina.com.cn/social/2006-03-14/2786699.html> (accessed 4 Feburary 2008).

Guangzhou Daily (2010a) *Si sui nühai 'xiao ba' che nei mensi* [A four-year-old girl suffocated to death in school bus]. Online. Available <http://gzdaily.dayoo.com/html/2010-05/22/content_972423.htm> (accessed 22 May 2010).

—— (2010b). *You shi daoyan daren shipin, zhihui nütong zhanggua nantong* [Daycare teacher directed human-beating and videotaped, led a girl to slap a boy]. Online, A6. Available <http://gzdaily.dayoo.com/html/2010-05/16/content_965379.htm> (accessed 16 May 2010).

Guo, J. P., Tan, L. and Zhu, X. J. (2009) '*Zhongguo xin xing nongcun hezuo yiliao zhidu jiqi shishi guocheng de shehui xingbie fenxi*', ['The new rural cooperative medical service in China and the gender analysis in its implementation'] in L. Tang and X. H. Jiang (eds.) *Funü/xingbie lilun yu shijian – Funü Yanjiu Luncong jicui (2005–2009)* [*Theory and Practice on Women and Gender – The Articles Selected from the Collection of Women's Studies*], Beijing: Shehui Kexue Wenxian Chubanshe [Social Sciences Academic Press].

Gustafsson, B., Li, S. and Sicular, T. (2008) 'Inequality and public policy in China: Issues and trends', in B. A. Gustafsson, S. Li and T. Sicular (eds.) *Inequality and Public Policy in China*, Cambridge; New York: Cambridge University Press.

Ha, W., Yi, J. J. and Zhang, J. S. (2009) Internal Migration and Income Inequality in China: Evidence from Village Panel Data, UNDP Human Development Research Paper 2009/27. Online. Available <http://hdr.undp.org/en/reports/global/hdr2009/papers/HDRP_2009_27.pdf> (accessed 8 February 2008).

Hamilton, R. (2005) *Gendering the Vertical Mosaic: Feminist Perspectives on Canadian Society*, Toronto: Pearson Prentice Hall.

Han, H. M. (2006) '*Jiazheng fuwu yuan xing saorao wenti de zhiye tedian*' ['The characteristics of sexual harassment against domestic workers'], *Funü Yanjiu Luncong* [*Collection of Women's Studies*], 74: 68–70.

Harding, S. (ed.) (1987) *Feminism and Methodology*, Milton Keynes: Open University Press.

Hardt, M. and Negri, A. (2004) *Multitude: War and Democracy in the Age of Empire*, New York: The Penguin Press.

Hartmann, H. I. (1979). 'Capitalism, patriarchy and job segregation by sex', in Z. R. Eisenstein (ed.) *Capitalist Patriarchy and the Case for Socialist Feminism*, New York: Monthly Review Press.

—— (1981) 'The unhappy marriage of Marxism and feminism: Towards a more progressive union', in L. Sargent (ed.) *Women and Revolution: A Discussion of the Unhappy Marriage of Marxism and Feminism*, Montreal: Black Rose Books.

Haspels, N. (2010, 28 January) 'International Labour Standard Setting and Decent Work for Domestic Workers', Speech on International Seminar on Development of Domestic Service Sector, Beijing, China.

He, J. H. and Jiang, Y. P. (2007) '*Cong zhichi funü pingheng jiating gongzuo shijiao kan zhongguo tuoyou zhengce ji xianzhuang*' ['From the perspective of supporting women's work-life balance to look at current childcare situation and policies'] , *Xueqian Jiaoyu Yanjiu* [*Studies in Preschool Education*], 8, December: 3–6.

Hebei College of Industry and Technology (2006, 22 June) *Huanying baokao jiazheng fuwu zhuanye* [Welcome to apply for Home Service Major]. Online. Available <http://www.hbcit.edu.cn/newweb/fljj.asp?id=1384> (accessed 9 May 2007).

Henderson, C. (1988) 'Human rights and regimes: A bibliographical essay', *Human Rights Quarterly*, 10, 4: 525–43.

Hershatter, G. (2007) *Women in China's Long Twentieth Century*, London: University of California Press.

Himmelweit, S. (1999) 'Caring labour', *Annals of the American Academy of Political and Social Science by SAGE Journals Online*, 561: 28–38.

Hochschild, A. R. (1983) *The Managed Heart: Commercialization of Human Feeling*, Berkeley: University of California Press.

—— (2000) 'Global care chains and emotional surplus value', in W. Hutton and A. Giddens (eds.) *On the Edge: Living with Global Capitalism*, London: Jonathan Cape.

Hondagneu-Sotelo, P. (2001) *Domestica: Immigrant Workers Cleaning and Caring in the Shadows of Affluence*, London: University of California Press.

Honig, E. (2000) 'Iron girls revisited: Gender and the politics of work in the Cultural Revolution, 1966–76', in B. Entwisle and G. E. Henderson (eds.) *Re-drawing Boundaries: Work, Households, and Gender in China*, Berkeley: University of California Press.

Hou, H. L. (2005) '*Shichang zhuanxing shiqi nongye qianyi nüxing de zhiye diwei huode – Dui wu chengshi liudong yimin shequ de yanjiu*' ['Occupational Status Improvement of Women in Rural Immigrants in Market Transition – Research on Rural Immigrants Communities in Five Cities in China'], *Shichang Yu Renkou Fenxi* [*Market and Demographic Analysis*], 11, 01: 15–21.

Hou, L. M. (2004) '*Bai nian zhongguo youjiao shiye de bianhua ji fazhan*' ['Changes and development of China early child education in one hundred years'], *Youer jiaoyu* [*Early child education*], 2: 14–15.

Hu, A. G. (ed.) (2000) *Zhongguo Zouxiang* [*China Direction*], Hangzhou: *Zhejiang Renmin Chubanshe* [Zhejiang People's Publishing House].

Hu, J. T. (2007, 15 October) *Gaoju zhongguo tese shehuizhuyi weida qizhi, wei zhengqu quanmian jianshe xiaokang shehui xin shengli er fendou* [Hold High the Great Banner of Socialism with Chinese Characteristics and Strive for New Victories in Building a Moderately Prosperous Society in all Respects], Report to the Seventeenth National Congress of the Communist Party.

Huang, J. J. (2005) 'Shanghai zhuanzhi youeryuan guanli tizhi yu ban yuan jizhi xianzhuang diaoyan baogao' ['The study report of the management system and operation status of reformed childcare centres in Shanghai'], *Jiaoyu fazhan yanjiu* [*Exploring education development*], 6: 36–40.

Huang, P. (2000) 'When young farmers leave the farm: What will happen to rural development in China when rural-urban migration takes place at a high pace under impacts of globalization?', in C. Lindqvist (ed.) *Globalization and Its Impact*, Stockholm: FRN.

Huang, S., Yeoh, B. S. A. and Rahman, N. A. (eds.) (2005) *Asian Women as Transnational Domestic Workers*, Singapore: Marshall Cavendish Academic.

Hussain, A. (2007) 'Social security in transition', in V. Shue and C. Wong (eds.) *Paying for Progress in China: Public Finance, Human Welfare and Changing Patterns of Inequality*, Oxon, UK; New York, NY: Routledge.

ILO (International Labour Organization) (1972) Employment, Incomes and Equality: A Strategy for Increasing Productive Employment in Kenya, Geneva: ILO.

—— (1993, January) Fifteenth International Conference of Labour Statisticians (ICLS). Online. Available <http://www.ilo.org/public/english/bureau/stat/download/compres.pdf>.

—— (2002) Decent work and the informal economy. Online. Available <http://www.ilo.org/public/english/standards/relm/ilc90/pdf/rep-vi.pdf> (accessed 26 March 2008).

—— (2004) China employment agenda: Background information of China Employment Forum. Online. Available <http://www.labournet.com.cn/jylt/file.htm> (accessed 17 October 2008).

—— (2007) ABC of Women Workers' Rights and Gender Equality, Geneva: ILO.

—— (2010) Decent work for domestic workers. Online. Available <http://www.ilo.org/asia/whatwedo/publications/lang–en/docName–WCMS_114257/index.htm> (accessed 23 August 2010).

——, UNIFEM and Beijing University Women's Law Study and Services Center (BUWLSSC) (2009) China: Specialist Recommendation Report on the Questionnaire on Decent Work for Domestic Workers. Online. Available <http://www.ilo.org/asia/whatwedo/publications/lang–en/docName–WCMS_114262/index.htm> (accessed 23 August 2010).

Institute for Labour Science Studies, MOLSS (2001, July) *Linghuo duoyang jiuye xingshi wenti yanjiu baogao (neibu ziliao)* [The study report of flexible employment forms (restricted data)].

International Gender and Trade Network (2009) IGTN declaration to the 7th WTO ministerial. Online. Available http://web.igtn.org/home/ (accessed 11 December 2009).

Jacka, T. (1997) *Women's Work in Rural China: Changes and Continuity in an Era of Reform*, Cambridge; New York: Cambridge University Press.

—— (2009) 'Cultivating citizens: *Sushi* (quality) discourse in the PRC', *Positions* 17, 3: 523–35.

Jackson, A., Baldwin, B., Wiggins, C. and Robinson, D. (2000) *Falling Behind: The State of Working Canada*, Ottawa: Canadian Centre for Policy Alternatives.

Ji, Y. L. and Bai, L. (2006) 'Jingcheng diyi jia shequ baomu gonghui ruhe yunzhuan yu fuwu' ['How does the first community domestic workers' union run and provide service in Beijing'], *Renmin Ribao* [*Peoples' Daily*], 28 November.

Jiang, Y. P. (2005a) '*Funü jiuye*' ['Female employment'], in Y. Jun (ed.) 2005 *Zhongguo jiuye baogao – Tongchou chengxiang jiuye* [*China Employment Report – To Make an Overall Plan for Rural and Urban Employment*], Beijing: *Zhongguo laodong he shehuibaozhang chubanshe* [China Labour and Social Security Publishing House].

Jiang, Y. P. (2005b) 'The cross-century debate on "life-cycle employment" and women going home', in L. Tan and B. H. Liu (eds.) *Review on the Chinese Women's Studies in*

Recent 10 Years: Response to the Beijing Platform for Action, Beijing: Social Sciences Academic Press.

Jilin Agricultural University (2006, 22 June) *Jilin Nongye daxue jiazhengxue zhuanye jieshao* [The Introduction of Home Economics of Jilin Agricultural University]. Online. Available <http://col.jlau.edu.cn/renwen/subject.asp?a=3> (accessed 9 May 2007).

Jin, Y. H. (1998) '*Feinonghua zhuanyi guocheng zhong de nongcun funü*' ['Rural women in non-agricultural migration'], in Jin, Y. H. and Liu, B. H. (eds) *Shiji zhi jiao de zhongguo funü yu fazhan – Lilun, jingji, wenhua, jiankang* [*Women and Development in China at the Turn of the Century – Theory, Economy, Culture, Health*], Nanjing: Nanjing Daxue Chubanshe [Nanjing University Press].

—— (2004) '*Funü jiuye yanjiu zongshu*' ['The literature review of studies on women's employment'], in Women's Studies Institute of China (ed.) *Zhongguo funü yanjiu nianjian* [*Almanac of Chinese women's studies*], Beijing: *Zhongguo Funü Chubanshe* [China Women Publishing House].

Johnson, K. A. (1983) *Women, the Family and Peasant Revolution in China*, Chicago and London: The University of Chicago Press.

Judd, E. R. (1994) *Gender and Power in Rural North China*, Stanford, California: Stanford University Press.

—— (2002) *The Chinese Women's Movement: Between State and Market*, Stanford, CA: Stanford University Press.

Kelly, L., Burton, S. and Regan, L. (1994) 'Researching women's lives or studying women's oppression? Reflections on what constitutes feminist research', in M. Maynard and J. Purvis (eds.) *Researching Women's Lives from a Feminist Perspective*, London: Taylor & Francis.

Kipnis, A. (2006) 'Suzhi: A keyword approach', *China Quarterly*, 186: 295–313.

Koggel, C. M. (2003) 'Globalization and women's paid work: Expanding freedom?', *Feminist Economics*, 9, 2–3: 163–83.

Krasner, S. D. (1982) 'Structural causes and regime consequences: Regimes as intervening variables', *International Organization*, 36, 2: 185–205.

Kremer, M. (2005) *How Welfare States Care: Culture, Gender and Citizenship in Europe*, Tekst: Proefscherift Universiteit Utrecht.

Labour Contract Law (N.d.) Central People's Government of the People's Republic of China. Online. Available <http://www.gov.cn/flfg/2007-06/29/content_669394.htm>.

Labour Department, Hong Kong (2008, July) Foreign domestic helpers rights and protection under the Employment Ordinance. Online. Available <http://www.labour.gov.hk/eng/public/wcp/FDHLeaflet_Eng.pdf> (accessed 11 May 2009).

—— (2009, 25 August) The Employment Ordinance. Online. Available <http://www.labour.gov.hk/eng/public/ConciseGuide.htm> (accessed 25 August 2009).

Laderchi, C, Saith, R. and Stewart, F. (2006) 'Does it matter that we do not agree on the definition of poverty? A comparison of four approaches', in M. McGillivray and M. Clarke (eds.), *Understanding Human Well-being*, New York: United Nations University Press.

Lang, O. (1968) *Chinese Family and Society*, Hamden: Archon Books.

Lee, C. K. (2009) 'Labour reform and livelihood insecurity in China', in S. Razavi (ed.) *The Gendered Impacts of Liberalization: Towards 'Embedded Liberalism'?* New York: Routledge.

—— (2010) 'Pathways of labour activism', in E. J. Perry and M. Seldon (eds.) *Chinese Society: Change, Conflict and Resistance*, 3rd edn, London; New York: Routledge.

Lee, P. N. S. (1995) 'Housing privatization with Chinese characteristics', in L. Wong and S. MacPherson (eds.) *Social Change and Social Policy in Contemporary China*, Aldershot, England: Avebury; Brookfield, Vermont USA: Ashgate.

Letherby, G. (2003) *Feminist Research in Theory and Practice*, Philadelphia, PA: Open University Press.

Lewis, J. (1992) 'Gender and the development of welfare regimes', *Journal of European Social Policy*, 2, 3: 159–73.

Li, D. J. (2007, November 15) Speech on the Workshop of Seeking the Healthy Development of Home Service Industry, Beijing.

Li, J. F. (2006) 'Zai kunjing zhong weiquan nuli jin wo men de zeren' ['Safeguard rights in difficulties and try our best to fulfil our responsibilities'], in *Dagongmei shi zhounian qingdian ji di sijie quanguo dagongmei quanyi wenti yantaohui 'Jiazheng Fuwuyuan Quanyi Wenti Luntan' lunwen ji* [*Proceedings of the Forum on Issues of Domestic Workers' Rights and Interests on the Tenth Anniversary Celebration of the Migrant Women's Club and the Fourth National Workshop on Migrant Women's Rights and Interests*], Beijing: The Cultural Centre for Rural Women.

Li, X. Y., Zhang, X. M. and Tang, L. X. (2005) 'Dangqian zhongguo nongcun de pinkun wenti' ['Situation of rural poverty in China'], *Zhongguo nongye daxue xuebao* [*Journal of China Agricultural University*], 10, 4: 67–74.

Li, Y. L. and Feng, X. N. (2005) 'Jiazheng nugong xiaozu "chongquan" guocheng fenxi' ['The analysis of the "empowerment: process for female domestic workers' groups'], in H. M. Guo (ed.) *Shehui xingbie yu laodong quanyi* [*Gender and labour rights*], Xi'an: Xibei Gongye Daxue Chubanshe [Northwestern Polytechnical University Press].

Li, Y. L. and He, M. (2004, 27 December) *Xibei Gongye Daxue Funü Fazhan Yu Quanyi Yanjiu Zhongxin Xingdong Jihua* [*The Action Plan of The Centre for Women's Development and Rights of Northwestern Polytechnical University*]. Online. Available <http://www.china-gad.org/HR_NewsDetail.asp?strDetailId=9247> (accessed 17 February 2009).

Li, Y. L. (2006) 'Jiazheng shichang huhuan guifan guanli' ['Domestic service market calls for formal management'], in *Dagongmei shi zhounian qingdian ji di sijie quanguo dagongmei quanyi wenti yantaohui 'Jiazheng Fuwuyuan Quanyi Wenti Luntan' lunwen ji* [*Proceedings of the Forum on Issues of Domestic Workers' Rights and Interests on the Tenth Anniversary Celebration of the Migrant Women's Club and the Fourth National Workshop on Migrant Women's Rights and Interests*], Beijing: The Cultural Centre for Rural Women.

Li, Z. and Chen, Y. (1999) 'Jiejue wo guo jiuye wenti duice zongshu' ['Review of policy solutions on solving employment problems in China'], *Hongguan Jingji Yanjiu* [*Macro Economics Studies*], 10: 49–52.

Liang, Z. and Chen Y. P. (2004) 'Migration and gender in China: An origin-destination linked approach', *Economic Development and Cultural Change*, 52, 2: 423–43.

Li-Hsiang, L. R. (2006) *Confucianism and Women: A Philosophical Interpretation*, Albany State: University of New York Press.

Lin, K. C. (2009) 'Class formation or fragmentation? Allegiances and divisions among managers and workers in state-owned enterprises', in T. B. Gold, W. J. Hurst, J. Won and Q. Li (eds.) *Laid-off Workers in a Workers' State: Unemployment with Chinese Characteristics*, New York: Palgrave Macmillan.

Liu, B. H., Zhang, Y. Y. and Li, Y. N. (2008) *Reconciling Work and Family: Issues and Policies in China*, Beijing Office, China: ILO.

—— (2010) 'Work-family balance: Public policy reform and development', in X. Y. Dong and S. Lin (eds.) *Gender Equality and China's Economic Transformation: Informal Employment and Care Provision*, Beijing: Economic Science Press.
Liu, G. G., Yuen, P., Hu, T. W., Li, L. and Liu, X. Z. (2004) 'Urban health insurance reform: What can we learn from the pilot experiments?', in A. M. Chen, G. G. Liu and K. H. Zhang (eds.) *Urbanization and Social Welfare in China*, Aldershot, England; Burlington, VT: Ashgate.
Liu, J. Y. (2007) 'Gender dynamics and redundancy in urban China', *Feminist Economics*, 13, 3–4: 125–58.
Liu, X. D. (2000) 'Zhang Zuoji shuo jiazhengye shi zaijiuye zhugong fangxiang' ['Zhang Zuoji said that domestic service should be the main area for re-employment'], *Zhenggong Yanjiu Dongtai* [*News for Research on Political Work*], 13.
Lu, D. and Wang, N. (2004) *Shehui de you yi cengmian: Zhongguo jindai nüyong* [*Another Dimension of Society: Female Servants in China's Near-Modern Times*], Shanghai: Xuelin Chubanshe [Xuelin Press].
Lu, X. H. and Wang, Y. G. (2006) 'Zhongguo chengxiang renkou qianyi guimo de cesuan yu fenxi' ['Rural urban migration in China: Estimation and analysis'], *Xibei renkou* [*Northwest Population*], 1: 14–16.
Lu, X. Y. (2003) 'Nongmingong wenti yao cong genben shang zhili' ['Rural migrant worker's issues should be managed from the root'], *Tequ lilun yu shjian* [*Practice and Theory of Special Economic Zones*], 7, 31–6.
Lu, Y. J. and Liu, Z. (2001, 29 August) 'Beijing: Jiaoyu cong lingsui kaishi' ['Beijing: Education starts from 0-year old'], *Xinxi Ribao* [*Information Daily*]: A03.
Luxton, M. (2002) *Feminist Perspectives on Social Inclusion and Children's Wellbeing*, Toronto: Garamond Press.
—— (2006) 'Feminist political economy in Canada and the politics of social reproduction', in K. Bezanson and M. Luxton (eds.) *Social Reproduction: Feminist Political Economy Challenges Neo-liberalism*, Montreal and Kingston: McGill-Queen's University Press.
Lü, M. Y., Jiang, M. H., Zhang, L. B. and Zheng, Y. F. (2008). 'Funü yundong de yunniang yu xingqi 1898–1995' ['The preparation and rise of women's movement 1898–1915'], in X. L. Gu (ed.) *Er shi shiji zhongguo funü yundong shi (shang juan)* [*The History of Women's Movement in the 20th Century in China (Upper volume)*], Beijing: Zhongguo Funu Chubanshe [China Women Publishing House].
MacPhail, F. and Dong, X. (2007) 'Women's market work and household status in rural China: Evidence from Jiangsu and Shandong in the late 1990s', *Feminist Economics*, 13, 3–4: 93–124.
Marchbank, J. (2000) *Women, Power and Policy – Comparative Studies of Childcare*, London and New York: Routledge.
Marx, K. and Engels, F. (1999) *The Communist Manifesto: With Related Documents*, ed. J. E. Toews, Boston: Bedford/St. Martin's.
McBride, S. (1992) *Not Working: State, Unemployment and Neo-conservatism in Canada*, Toronto: University of Toronto Press.
—— (2001) *Paradigm Shift: Globalization and the Canadian State*, Halifax: Fernwood Publishing.
—— and Wiseman, J. (2000) *Globalization and its Discontents*, New York: St. Martin's Press.
McKay, D. (2002) 'Filipina identities: Geographies of social integration/exclusion in the Canadian metropolis', Research on Immigration and Integration in the Metropolis

Working Paper Series, Burnaby, B.C.: Vancouver Centre of Excellence with the Philippine Women Centre.

Meng, X. (2000) *Labor Market Reform in China*, Cambridge: Cambridge University Press.

Migrant Women's Club (MWC) (2009a, October 29) *Zhongguo diyijia jiazhenggong jiemei zujian de jiazhenggong hezuoshe zai jing gua pai* [*The first domestic workers' cooperative organized by domestic workers opened in Beijing*]. Online. Available <http://www.nongjianv.org/web/Html/jiazh/2009-10/29/1029160124.html> (accessed 30 August 2010).

—— (2009b, Feburary 26) *Jinrong weiji li ni you duoyuan* [*How far is the financial crisis from you*]. Online. Available <http://www.nongjianv.org/web/Html/jiazh/2009-3/30/0330172917.html> (accessed 9 August 2010).

—— (2006) About us: Migrant Women's Club. Online. Available <http://www.nongjianv.org/web/english/aboutus/club.html> (accessed 24 March 2009).

Ministry of Civil Affairs, China (2005). Online. Available <http://dbs.mca.gov.cn/article//csdb/zcfg/200712/20071200005641.shtml> (accessed 14 December 2005).

Ministry of Education of the People's Republic of China (2006) *Educational Statistics Yearbook of China* (2006), Beijing: People's Education Press.

Ministry of Labour, BC Government, Canada (N.d.) Information for domestic workers and employers. Online. Available <http://www.labour.gov.bc.ca/esb/domestics/> (accessed 13 May 2009).

Ministry of Labour, Ontario Government, Canada (2008, June) Domestic workers Employment Standards Fact Sheet. Online. Available <http://www.labour.gov.on.ca/english/es/pdf/fs_domestics.pdf> (accessed 13 May 2009.

Ministry of Manpower, Singapore (2007, 1 February) Employers' Guidelines. Online. Available <http://www.mom.gov.sg/publish/momportal/en/communities/work_pass/foreign_domestic_workers/employers__guidelines.html> (11 May 2009).

MOLSS (Ministry of Labour and Social Security, China) (2000) *China National Occupational Standards of Domestic Workers*, Beijing: China Labour and Social Security Publishing House.

NAC (National Action Committee on the Status of Women in Canada) (1995) *A Decade of Deterioration in the Status of Women in Canada: A Summary Report*, Toronto, Canada.

National Bureau of Statistics of the People's Republic of China (1999, 2003, 2005, 2007) *China Statistics Yearbook*, Beijing: China Statistics Publishing House.

Naughton, B. (1995) *Growing Out of the Plan: Chinese Economic Reform, 1978–1993*, New York, NY: Cambridge University Press.

—— (2007) *The Chinese Economy: Transitions and Growth*, Cambridge, Massachusetts; London, England: The MIT Press.

Neysmith, S., Bezanson, K. and O'Connell, A. (2005) *Telling Tales: Living the Effects of Public Policy*, Halifax: Fernwood.

Ngai, P. (2005) *Made in China: Women Factory Workers in a Global Place*, Durham, NC: Duke University Press; Hong Kong: Hong Kong University Press.

—— (2009) 'The making of a global dormitory labour regime: Labour protection and labour organizing of migrant women in South China', in R. Murphy (ed.) *Labour Migration and Social Development in Contemporary China*, Abingdon, Oxon; New York, NY: Routledge.

O'Brien, K. J. and Li, L. J. (2006) *Rightful Resistance in Rural China*, Cambridge; New York: Cambridge University Press.

O'Connor, J., Orloff, A. S and Shaver, S. (1999) *State, Markets, Families: Gender, Liberalism and Social Policy in Australia, Canada, Great Britain and the United States*, Cambridge: Cambridge University Press.

Ostner, I. and Lewis, J. (1995) 'Gender and the evolution of European social policies', in S. Leibfried and P. Pierson (eds.) *European Social Policy: Between Fragmentation and Integration*, Washington, DC: Brookings.

Pan, Z. F. and Huang, A. X. (2005) 'Dangqian nongcun yihun funü waichu jiuye dongyin de shehuixue fenxi – Yi pancun de ge an yanjiu wei li' ['A sociological analysis of the motivating factors of rural married women finding employment out of home village – A case study of Pancun village'], *Collection of Women's Studies*, 02: 20–5.

Parrenas, R. S. (2001) *Servants of Globalization: Women, Migration and Domestic Work*, Stanford, California: Stanford University Press.

Party History Research Centre of the CCP Central Committee (2009, 4 October). *Zhonghua renmin gongheguo dashiji (1949 nian 10 yue – 2009 nian 9 yue)* [*The record of big events in the People's Republic of China (October 1949 – September 2009)*]. *People's Daily*. Online. Available http://dangshi.people.com.cn/GB/85039/10154059.html (accessed 20 September 2010).

Pei, M. X. (2010) 'Rights and resistance: The changing contexts of the dissident movement', in E. J. Perry and M. Seldon (eds.) *Chinese Society: Change, Conflict and Resistance*, 3rd edn, London: New York: Routledge.

Peking University Centre for Legal Information (N.d.) *Laodongbu bangongting guanyu yinfa guanyu Laodong Fa ruogan tiaowen de shuoming* [*The explanation of certain articles of the Labour Law by the Ministry of Labour*]. Online. Available http://vip.chinalawinfo.com/newlaw2002/slc/slc.asp?db=chl&gid=27173 (accessed 12 January 2008).

Peng, X. Z. and Yao, Y. (2004) 'Liqing Fei Zhenggui Jiuye Gainian Tuidong Fei Zhenggui Jiuye Fazhan' ['Clarify Informal Employment Concept and Promote Informal Employment Development'], *Shehui Kexue* [*Social Science*], 07: 63–72.

People's Court Daily (2006, August 31) *Zuigao Renmin Fayuan guanyu shenli laodong zhengyi anjian shiyong falu ruogan wenti de jieshi* [*The Supreme Court of the People's Republic of China Interpretation of Certain Issues on the Applicable Laws about Hearing of Cases of Labour Disputes*]. Online. Available <http://rmfyb.chinacourt.org/public/detail.php?id=100328> (accessed 4 February 2008).

People's Daily (2010, September 2) *Wen Jiabao zhuchi zhaokai guowuyuan changwu huiyi: Yanjiu bushu fazhan jiating fuwuye de zhengce cuoshi* [*Wen Jiabao chaired a State Council executive meeting: Study and plan the policies and measures to develop domestic service industry*]. Online. Available <http://politics.people.com.cn/GB/1024/12610468.html> (accessed 10 September 2010).

Pratt, G. (1999). 'Is this Canada? Domestic workers' experiences in Vancouver, B.C.', in J. H. Momsen (ed.) *Gender, Migration and Domestic Service*, London and New York: Routledge.

—— (2003) 'From migrant to immigrant: Domestic workers settle in Vancouver, Canada, Research on Immigration and Integration in the Metropolis Working Paper Series', Burnaby, B.C.: Vancouver Centre of Excellence with the Philippine Women Centre.

Qin, L. (2006a) 'Baomu Hangye de Xianzhuang, Fazhan Fangxiang Jiqi Lifa Sikao' ['The situation, development direction and legal thoughts on nanny industry'], *Xingzheng yu Fa* [*Administration and Law*], March: 77–9.

—— (2006b) 'Baomu Hangye de Weiji, Chulu Jiqi Lifa Tiaozheng' ['The crisis, solutions and legal adjustment on nanny industry'], *Gansu Zhengfa Chengrenjiaoyu Xueyuan*

Xuebao [*Journal of Adult Education of Gansu Political Scienced and Law Instititue*], March: 73–5.

Ramirez-Machado, J. M. (2003) 'Domestic work, conditions of work and employment: A legal perspective', in *Conditions of Work and Employment Series No. 7*, Geneva: ILO.

Ran, J. F. (2009) *Nongmin, mingong yu quanli baohu – falu yu pingdeng de yige shijiao* [*Farmers, migrant workers and rights and interests protecting – a perspective on law and equality*]. Online. Available <http://www.iolaw.org.cn/shownews.asp?id=9925> (accessed 16 January 2009).

Ray, D. (1998) *Development Economics*, Princeton, NJ: Princeton University Press.

RCWDR (Research Centre for Women's Development and Rights and Interests of Northwestern Polytechnical University) (2008, 18 November) About us: The Centre for Women's Development and Rights and Interests of Northwestern Polytechnical University. Online. Available <http://www.genderandlaborrights.com/show.asp?id=3215> (accessed 26 March 2009).

Reinharz, S. (1992) *Feminist Methods in Social Research*, Oxford: Oxford University Press.

Riskin, C. and Li, S. (2001) 'Chinese rural poverty inside and outside the poor regions', in C. Riskin, R. W. Zhao and S. Li (eds.) *China's Retreat from Equality: Income Distribution and Economic Transition*, Armonk, NY: M.E. Sharpe.

Robinson, J. C. (1985) 'Of women and washing machines: Employment, housework, and the reproduction of motherhood in socialist China', *The China Quarterly*, 101, March: 33–57.

Romero, M. (1992) *Maid in the USA*, New York: Routledge, Chapman & Hall.

Rowbotham, S. (1992) *Women in Movement: Feminism and Social Action*, New York: Routledge.

Rubin, G. (1975). 'The traffic in women: Notes on the "political economy" of sex', in R. R. Rapp (ed.) *Toward an Anthropology of Women*, New York: Monthly Review Press.

Sainsbury, D. (1994) 'Women's and men's social rights: Gendering dimensions of welfare state', in D. Sainsbury (ed.) *Gendering Welfare States*, London: Thousand Oaks, Calif.: Sage Publications.

—— (1996) *Gender, Equality and Welfare States*, Cambridge: Oxford University Press.

Sang, L. (2009, 5 September) *Shenme Shi Jiazheng Fuwu* [*What is Domestic Service* (the first half)]. Blog. Available <http://blog.sina.com.cn/s/blog_47420b930100eudy.html>.

—— (2009, 7 September) *Shenme Shi Jiazheng Fuwu* [*What is Domestic Service* (the second half)]. Blog. Available <http://blog.sina.com.cn/s/blog_47420b930100eux3.html>.

Sassen, S. (1996) *Losing Control? Sovereignty in an Age of Globalization*, New York: Columbia University Press.

Schecter, T. (1998) *Race, Class, Women and the State: The Case of Domestic Labour in Canada*, Montreal: Black Rose Books.

Selden, M. and Perry, E. J. (2010) 'Introduction', in E. J. Perry and M. Selden (eds.) *Chinese Society: Changes, Conflict and Resistance*, 3rd edn, London and New York: Routledge.

Sen, A. (1999) *Development as Freedom*, New York: Knofp.

Sidel, R. (1972) *Women and Childcare in China: A First Hand Report*, New York: Hill & Wang.

Sina Jilin (2010, September 19) 'Jiangcheng "baomu shashou" zizhao suo 8 ming' ['*Baomu* killer' self confessed to have murdered 8 people]. Online. Available <http://www.jlsina.com/news/2010-09-19/112408.shtml> (accessed 9 October 2010).

—— (2010, 20 September) 'Baomu shashou' pan jinkuai shoushen ['Baomu killer' is expecting to be on trial soon]. Online. Available <http://www.jlsina.com/news/2010-09-20/112548.shtml> (accessed 9 October 2010).
Sina News (2006, 14 January). *Qingxiu xiaobaomu shou guzhu nuedai wu nian can zao huirong* [Pretty little *baomu* was abused for five years and was disfigured]. Online. Available <http://news.sina.com.cn/s/2006-01-14/13217982967s.shtml> (accessed 4 Feburary 2008).
Solinger, D. J. (2010) 'A question of confidence: State legitimacy and the new urban poor', in P. H. Gries and S. Rosen (eds.) *Chinese Politics: State, Society and the Market*, London: New York: Routledge.
Song, S. P. (2007) 'The state discourse on housewives and housework', in M. Leutner (ed.) *Rethinking China in the 1950s*, Berlin: LIT Verlag Fresnostr.
Stiell, B. and England, K. (1999) 'Jamaican Domestics, Filipina Housekeepers and English Nannies: Representations of Toronto's Foreign Domestic Workers', in J. H. Momsen (ed.) *Gender, Migration and Domestic Service*, London and New York: Routledge.
Su, B. (2004, September 24) 'Xi'an shi jiangzheng gong gonghui zuo chengli Xi'an jiazheng gong you le "jia"', ['Xi'an domestic workers' union was founded yesterday and domestic workers have a "home" in Xi'an'], *Huashang Bao* [*Chinese Business View*], *Huashang Baoshe* [Chinese Business News Press].
Sumner, A. (2006) 'Economic well-being and non-economic well-being', in M. McGillivray and M. Clarke (eds.) *Understanding Human Well-being*, New York: United Nations University Press.
Sun, L. (2002) 'Fei yong jin Shanghai' ['Filipino domestic workers come to Shanghai'], *Xinwen Zhoukan* [*News Weekly*], 9 September: 48–51.
Sun, W. N. (2009a) *Maid in China: Media, Morality, and Cultural Politics of Boundaries*, London: New York: Routledge.
—— (2009b) 'Suzhi on the move: Body, place, and power', *Positions*, 17, 3: 617–42.
Tan, L. and Li, J. F. (2003) 'Woguo fei zhengui jiuye de xingbei tezheng fenxi' ['A gendered analysis of informal employment in China'], *Renkou Yanjiu* [*Population Research*], 27, 5, 11–18.
Tan, S. (1998) 'Zhujiang sanjiaozhou wailai dagongmei de xianzhuang yu fazhan' ['The current situation and development of rural migrant women in the Pearl River delta'] in Y. H. Jin and B. H. Liu (eds) *Shiji zhi jiao de zhongguo funü yu fazhan – Lilun, jingji, wenhua, jiankang* [*Women and Development in China at the Turn of the Century – Theory, Economy, Culture, Health*], Nanjing: Nanjing Daxue Chubanshe [Nanjing University Press].
Tang, S. (2005) 'Zhongguo nongcun youer jiaoyu de fazan yu biange' ['The development and reform of early child education in rural China'], *Xueqian Jiaoyu Yanjiu* [*The Study of Pre-school Education*], 6: 38–40.
—— and Kou, C. L. (2003) '*1889–949 zhongguo xueqian ertong jiaoyu dashi ji*' ['The big events of Chinese pre-school children education 1889–1949'], in *Xueqian Jiaoyu Yanjiu* [*The Study of Pre-school Education*], 10: 23–24; 12: 19–20.
Tao, C. F. and Gao, X. X. (eds.) (1991) *Zhongguo funü tongji ziliao: 1949–1989* [*Statistics on Women in China: 1949–1989*], Beijing: *Zhongguo Tongji Chubanshe* [China Statistics Publishing House].
Therborn, G. (2003) 'Classed and states: welfare state developments, 1881–1981', in C. Andrew *et al.* (eds) *Studies in Political Economy: Developments in Feminism*, Toronto: Women's Press.

Tomba, L. (2002) *Paradoxes of Labour Reform: Chinese Labour Theory and Practice from Socialism to Market*, London: Routledge Curzon.

UN (United Nations) (1948) The Universal Declaration of Human Rights, New York: United Nations.

—— (1966a) The International Covenant on Civil and Political Rights (ICCPR), New York: United Nations.

—— (1966b) The International Covenant on Economic, Social and Cultural Rights (ICESCR), New York: United Nations.

—— (1979) The Convention on the Elimination of all Forms of Discrimination against Women (CEDAW), New York: United Nations.

—— (1990) The International Convention on the Protection of the Rights of all Migrant Workers and Members of their Families, New York: United Nations.

—— (1993) The Declaration on the Elimination of Violence against Women, New York: United Nations.

—— (1995) The Beijing Declaration and Platform for Action, New York: United Nations.

—— (1999) The Convention on the Elimination of all Forms of Discrimination against Women (CEDAW) First Optional Protocol, New York: United Nations.

—— (2000) The Millennium Development Goals. Online. Available <http://www.un.org/millenniumgoals/> (accessed 20 September 2010).

Waller, D. J. (1981) *The Government and Politics of the People's Republic of China*, London: Hutchinson.

Wallerstein, I. (1974) *The Modern World System: Capitalism, Agriculture and the Origins of the European World-Economy in the Sixteenth Century*, New York: Academic Press.

—— (1979) 'The rise and future demise of the world capitalist system: concepts for comparative analysis', in I. Wallerstein (ed.) *The Capitalist World-Economy*, Cambridge: Cambridge University Press.

Wang, C. G. and Liu, Z. (2009, 26 August) *Xiaochu pinkun yongbao xiaokang zouxiang fanrong – 60 nian jianzheng xin zhongguo fuxing* [*Eradicate poverty, embrace well-off, walk toward prosperity – 60 years' witness of new China's economic renaissance*]. Online. Available <http://theory.people.com.cn/GB/9932656.html> (accessed 20 September 2010).

Wang, D. J. (2004) 'Wanshan laodong shehui baozhang zhidu cujin linghuo jiuye jiankang fazhan' ['Perfect labour and social security system and promote the healthy development of flexible employment'], *Jingji yu Guanli Yanjiu* [*Economy and Management Study*], 3: 7–12.

Wang, F. L. (2005) *Organizing through Division and Exclusion: China's Hukou System*, Stanford: Stanford University Press.

Wang, H. (2003) *China's New Order: Society, Politics and Economy in Transition*, Cambridge, Mass.: Harvard University Press.

—— (2009) *The End of the Revolution: China and the Limits of Modernity*, London; New York: Verso.

Wang, H. and Lan, G. (2006, April) 'Wo Guo Nuxing Feizhenggui Jiuye de Diaocha yu Kunjing Fenxi' ['The Survey and Analysis on the Problematic Situation of Female Informal Employment in China'], *Jiangxi Xingzheng Xueyuan Xuebao* [*Journal of Jiangxi Administration Institute*], 8, 2: 56–8.

Wang, H. F. (2006) 'Fei zhenggui jiuye – jiazheng fuwu yuan quanyi wenti yanjiu' ['Informal employment – The study of the rights and interests of domestic workers]', *Chongqing Daxue Xuebao* [*Journal of Chongqing University*], 12, 2: 72–8.

Wang, J. F., Si, M. and Chen, Y. X. (2010) 'Domestic workers' access to social security in Shanghai', in X. Y. Dong and S. Cook (eds.) *Gender Equality and China's Economic Transition: Informal Employment and Care Provision*, Beijing: Economic Science Press.

Wang, M. X. (2001) 'Zhongguo jindai shehui zhuanxing yu nüzi jiaoyu de fazhan' ['Social conversion in modern China and development of women's education'], *Beijing Daxue Xuebao* [*Journal of Peking University: Humanities and Social Sciences*], 38, 3: 87–94.

Wang, S. M. and Hu, X. Y. (1997) 'Chengshi funü jiuye dongji yu shengyu qijian de jiuye yiyuan' ['Urban women's employment motivation and employment needs after giving birth'], *Zhejiang Xuekan* [*Zhejiang Academic Journal*], 5: 78–84.

Wang, S. M. (2006) 'Shehui zhuanxing yu xingbie shijiao xia de shenghuo fangshi' ['Social transition and life style under gender perspective'], in Women's Studies Institute of China (eds.) *Zhongguo shehui zhuanxing zhong de funü shehui diwei* [*Women's Social Status under Social Transition*], Zhongguo Beijing: *Funü Chuban She* [China Women Press].

Wang, W. (2006) 'Jiangzheng gong shengcun tansuo – zuzhi qi lai' ['The exploration of survival strategies of domestic workers – get organized'], *Dagongmei shi zhounian qingdian ji di sijie quanguo dagongmei quanyi wenti yantaohui Jiazheng Fuwuyuan Quanyi Wenti Luntan' lunwen ji* [*Proceedings of the Forum on Issues of Domestic Workers' Rights and Interests on the Tenth Anniversary Celebration of the Migrant Women's Club and the Fourth National Workshop on Migrant Women's Rights and Interests*], Beijing: The Cultural Centre for Rural Women.

Wang, Y. P. (2003) 'Progress and problems of urban housing reform', in C. J. Finer (ed.) *Social Policy Reform in China: Views from Home and Abroad*, Aldershot, Hants; Burlington, VT: Ashgate.

Wang, Z. Q. (2007, 8 December) Speech on the Workshop on the Protection of Domestic Workers' Labour Rights, Available upon request to author.

Wei, Q. Y., Wu, Q. Y and Lu, S. (1982) *Qing dai nubi zhidu* [*Bondservant System in Qing Dynasty*], Beijing: Zhongguo Renmin Daxue Chubanshe [China Renmin University Press].

Wen, T. J. (2008) 'How China's migrant labourers are becoming the new proletariat', in A. Bieler, I. Lindberg and D. Pillary (eds.) *Labour and the Challenges of Globalization: What Prospects for Transnational Solidarity*, London; Ann Arbor, MI: Pluto Press; Scottsville, South Africa: University of KwaZulu-Natal Press.

White, G. (1993) *Riding the Tiger: The Politics of Economic Reform in Post-Mao China*, London: Macmillan.

Whyte, M. K. (2010) 'Do Chinese citizens want the government to do more to promote equality?', in P. H. Gries and S. Rosen (eds.) *Chinese Politics: State, Society and the Market*, London; New York: Routledge.

Wong, L. and Huen, W. P. (1998) 'Reforming the household registration system: A preliminary glimpse of the blue chop household registration system in Shanghai and Shenzhen', *International Migration Review*, 32, 4: 974–94.

Wong, L. (2001) 'Welfare policy reform', in L. Wong and N. Flynn (eds.) *The Market in Chinese Social Policy*, New York: Palgrave.

Woo, M. Y. K. (2002) 'Law and the gendered citizen', in M. Goldman and E. J. Perry (eds.) *Changing Meaning of Citizenship in Modern China*, Cambridge, Mass.; London, England: Harvard University Press.

World Bank. (2002) *China Country Gender Review*, Washington, DC: World Bank.

Xiang, F. H. (2010) 'Baomu yaoqiu guoqingjie san bei gongzi, guanyuan cheng bu shiyong laodong fa' ['*Baomu* claimed triple pay for National Day holiday, labour officer said it was not applicable to the Labour Law'], in *Xiandai Kuaibao* [*Modern Daily*] Online. Available <http://news.xinhuanet.com/employment/2010-10/07/c_12633728.htm> (accessed 7 October 2010).

Xinhua News Agency (N.d.) *Regulations Governing Labour Insurance in the People's Republic of China (1951)*. Online. Available <http://news.xinhuanet.com/ziliao/2004-12/17/content_2347271.htm> (accessed 4 December 2008).

—— (N.d.) (2003, May 4) *Gongshang baoxian tiaoli (quanwen)* [*The regulation on the insurance of the Regulation on the Insurance of Workplace Injury*]. Online. Available <http://news.xinhuanet.com/fortune/2003-05/04/content_857553.htm> (accessed 4 December 2008).

—— (N.d.) (2009, 3 January) *Zenyang gonggu he fazhan xinxing nongcun hezuo yiliao zhidu* [*How to consolidate and develop the new cooperative medical system*]. Online. Available <http://news.xinhuanet.com/newscenter/2009-01/03/content_10596005.htm> (accessed 2 March 2009).

Xu, M. (2000) '*Bian tiaozhan wei jiyu*' ['Change challenges into opportunities'], *Zhongguo funü bao* [*China Women's News*], July 25.

Yan, H. R. (2003a) 'Neoliberal governmentality and neohumanism: Organizing *suzhi*/ value flow through labour recruitment networks', *Cultural Anthropology*, 18, 4: 493–523.

—— (2003b) 'Spectralization of the rural: Reinterpreting the labour mobility of rural young women in post-Mao China', *American Ethnologist*, 30, 4: 1–19.

—— (2007) 'Rurality and labour process autonomy: The waged labour of domestic service', in C. K. Lee (ed.) *Working in China: Ethnographies of Labour and Workplace Transition*, London and New York: Routledge.

—— (2008) *New Masters, New Servants: Migration, Development, and Women Workers in China*, Durham, NC: Duke University Press.

Yeates, N. (2005) *Global Care Chains: A Critical Introduction, Global Migration Perspectives No. 44*, Global Commission on International Migration, Geneva.

Yeoh, B. S. A. and Huang, S. (1999) 'Singapore Women and Foreign Domestic Workers: Negotiating Domestic Work and Motherhood', in J. H. Momsen (ed.) *Gender, Migration and Domestic Service*, London and New York: Routledge.

Yeoh, B. S. A., Huang, S. and Devasahayam, T. W. (2004) 'Diasporic subjects in the nation: Foreign domestic workers, the reach of law and civil society in Singapore', *Asian Studies Review*, 28: 7–23.

Young, I. (1981) 'Beyond the unhappy marriage: A critique of the dual systems theory', in L. Sargent (ed.) *Women and Revolution: A Discussion of the Unhappy Marriage of Marxism and Feminism*, Montreal: Black Rose Journals.

Yu, E. H. and Liu, D. Z. (1999) 'Zhongguo jiuye wenti yanjiu zongshu' ['Review of studies on employment issues in China'], *Jingjixue Dongtai* [*Economic Perspectives*], 4: 39–47.

Yuen-Tsang, A. W. K. (1997) *Toward a Chinese Conception of Social Support: A Study on the Social Support Networks of Chinese Working Mothers in Beijing*, Alershot; Brookfield USA; Singapore; Sydney: Ashgate.

Zhang, C. H. (1999) 'Jiangdi funü canyulü bu kexing' ['It is not appropriate to decrease women's labour participation rate'], *Zhongguo Funü Bao* [*China Women's News*], April 13.

Zhang, H. and Liu, Y. (2001) 'Tuoyou yuan suo guanli xianzhuang ji fazhan fangxiang' ['The current situation and future development of the management of nurseries and childcare centres'], *Beijing Wujia* [*Beijing Commodity Price*], 8: 10–11.

Zhang, J. G. (2005) 'Youer jiaoyu ying yinru shichang jizhi' ['Market system should be introduced to early child education'], in L. Y. Xing and Y. Zhang (eds) *Youer jiaoyu guanli lilun yu shijian* [*The Theories and Practice of Early Child Education Management*], Beijing: Beijing Normal University Press.

Zhang, M. M. and Wang, W. T. (2004, May 8) *Baomu gonghui' neng zhenzheng weihu baomu de hefa quanyi* [*Can 'Domestic Workers' Union' really safeguarding domestic worker's rights and interests*]? Online. Available <http://news.xinhuanet.com/focus/2004-05/08/content_1456126.htm> (accessed 26 Feburary 2009).

Zhang, Y. and Wu, Y. (2006) 'Beijing shi jiedao youeryuan fazhan licheng de huigu yu fansi' ['The review and reflection of the development process of neighbourhood childcare centres in Beijing'], *Xueqian jiaoyu yanjiu* [*The study of pre-school education*], 6: 38–41.

Zhang, Y. R. and Zhang, Y. Q. (eds.) (1992) *Fangdichanye gaige juan* [The journal on housing and real estate reform], Dalian: Dalian chubanshe [Dalian Publishing House].

Zhao, Q. (2009) 'Jiang xingbie pingdeng guannian naru nongcun fan pinkun zhengce yu shijian de zhuliu' ['Gender mainstreaming anti-poverty policies and practices'] [2005], in L. Tang and X. H. Jiang (eds.) *Funü/xingbie lilun yu shijian – Funü Yanjiu Luncong jicui (2005–2009)* [*Theory and Practice on Women and Gender – The Articles Selected from the Collection of Women's Studies*], Beijing: Shehui Kexue Wenxian Chubanshe [Social Sciences Academic Press].

Zhao, R. W. (2001) 'Increasing income inequality and its causes in China', in C. Riskin, R. W. Zhao and S. Li (eds.) *China's Retreat from Equality: Income Distribution and Economic Transition*, Armonk, N.Y.: M.E. Sharpe.

Zheng, Z. Z. and Xie, Z. M. (eds.) (2004) *Renkou liudong yu nongcun funü fazhan* [*Floating Population and the Development of Rural Women*], Beijing: Shehui Kexue Wenxian Chubanshe [Social Sciences Academic Press].

Zhong, P. R. (1998) *Shui Wei Zhongguoren Zao Fanwan* [*Who makes rice bowls for the Chinese People*], Beijing: Zhongguo Jingji Chubanshe [China Economy Publishing House].

Zhong, W. and Gustafsson, B. (2008) 'Inequity in financing China's health care', in B. A. Gustafsson, S. Li and T. Sicular (eds.) *Inequality and Public Policy in China*, Cambridge; New York: Cambridge University Press.

Zhou, J. M. (2006) 'Cong xiandai jiating fuwuye de xuqiu yu maodun tansuo goujian hexie shehui de xietiao baozhang jizhi – Shanghai jiazheng lüse lianmeng he shi fulian jinguo jiazheng de tansuo yu shijian' ['From the demand and contradiction of modern domestic service industry to explore the coordination and security system of building up a harmonious society – The exploration and practice of Shanghai Domestic Service Green Association and Shanghai Women's Federation Jinguo Domestic Service'], in *Dagongmei shi zhounian qingdian ji di sijie quanguo dagongmei quanyi wenti yantaohui "Jiazheng Fuwuyuan Quanyi Wenti Luntan" lunwen ji* [*Proceedings of the Forum on Issues of Domestic Workers' Rights and Interests on the Tenth Anniversary Celebration of the Migrant Women's Club and the Fourth National Workshop on Migrant Women's Rights and Interests*], Beijing: The Cultural Centre for Rural Women.

Zhou, Z. (2010, 2 September) *Huajie ruyuan nan ying gongsi bingju* [*Public and private should develop simultaneously to deal with childcare difficulties*]. Online. Available <http://epaper.bjnews.com.cn/html/2010-09/02/content_143236.htm?div=-1> (accessed 12 October 2010).

Zhu, Z. Q. (2004, 22 July) 'Baomu gonghui liangxiang jingcheng' ['Domestic workers' union appeared in Beijing'], in *Zhongguo Laodong Baozhang Bao* [*China Labour and Social Security News*], Zhongguo Laodong Baozhang Baoshe [China Labour and Social Security News Press].

Zuo Ling Domestic Service Company (ZLDSC) (2007) *Suigan* [Casual thoughts]. *Dagongmei Zhi Jia Jiazhenggong Jianbao* [*Domestic Workers' Brief of the Migrant Women's Club*]. Online. Available <http://www.nongjianv.org/web/Html/publishing/> (accessed 25 March 2009).

Author index

Anderson, B. 3, 158n15
Anderson, J. 158n15
Appleton, S. 48
Arat-Koc, S. 35

Bai, L. 122
Baldwin, B. 7
Basu, A. 10
Beaton, J. 158n15
Beneria, L. 12
Berik, G. 14
Bezanson, K. 7, 9
Blacket, A. 127–29, 132, 138
Brodie, J. 9–10
Brodsky, G. 7
Broomhill, R. 8
Bujra, J. 12
Burton, S. 14

Cameron, B. 8
Cao, J.C. 136
Chang, K.A. 9
Chen, H. 52
Chen, L.Y. 49–50, 54, 63, 87,157 (chap 5) n10
Chen, S.Y. 60–62
Chen, W.Q. 121
Chen, Y.P. 41, 52
Chen, Y.X. 13, 52, 89
Cheung, L. 9
Chin, C.B.N. 12
Chow, G. 44–45
Chow, N. 10
Chu, G.S. 5, 22–23
Clarkson, S. 7
Cockburn, C. 4
Cohen, M.G. 7, 10
Cohen, R. 5, 36
Cox, R. 10, 12
Crammer-Byng, J.L. 22

Cranford, C.J. 158n4, n15
Croll, E. 10, 25, 30, 44

Das Gupta, T. 158n4, n15
Davin, D. 28
Day, S. 7
Devasahayam, T.W. 9–10, 133
Dong, X.Y. 12, 48, 58–59, 75
Du, F.L. 48, 71–72

Elson, D. 12, 32
Emerson, J.P. 31
Engels, F. 27–28
England, K. 12
England, P. 85
Enloe, C. 154n6

Fan, C. 39, 135
Fang, Y.Q. 54
Feng, X.N. 119
Folbre, N. 85
Foucault, M. 51, 106
Fox, C. 131
Fraser, N. 8, 143
Frazier, M.W. 61–62
Frobel, F. 5

Gaetano, A.M. 13
Gao, X. X. 28, 40
Ge, S.N. 53
Geiger, S.N.G. 14
Gilbert, A. 5
Glenn, E.N. 10
Granrose, C.S. 54
Gregson, N. 12
Guo, J.P. 63, 87–88
Gustafsson, B. 49, 63, 87

Ha, W. 39
Hamilton, R. 4

Han, H.M. 13, 82, 84
Harding, S. 14
Hardt, M. 85
Hartmann, H.I. 4, 19
Haspels, N. 130–31
He, J. H. 65–66, 74, 76
He, M. 119
Heinrichs, J. 5
Henderson, C. 19
Hershatter, G. 30
Himmelweit, S. 85
Hochschild, A.R. 10, 85
Hondagneu-Sotelo, P. 12
Honig, E. 29
Hou, H.L. 41
Hou, L.M. 67
Hu, A.G. 53
Hu, J. T. 126, 138
Hu, T.W. 61
Hu, X.Y. 11, 53
Huang, A.X. 40
Huang, J.J. 71
Huang, P. 37
Huang, S. 9–10, 12, 133
Huen, W.P. 135
Hussain, A. 59

Jacka, T. 1, 13
Jackson, A. 7
Ji, Y.L. 122
Jiang, M.H. 24
Jiang, Y.P. 65–66, 74, 76
Jin, Y.H. 40, 48
Johnson, K.A. 28
Judd, E.R. 37–38, 155n11

Kelly, L. 14
Kennedy, P. 5, 36
Kipnis, A. 155n11
Knight, J. 48
Koggel, C.M. 12
Kong, R.V. 54
Kou, C.L. 64
Krasner, S.D. 19–20
Kremer, M. 9
Kreye, O. 5

Ladd, D. 158n4, n15
Laderchi, C 155n5
Lan, G. 13
Lang, O. 21, 23, 25
Laxer, K. 158n15
Lee, C.K. 49, 120–21, 129, 139
Lee, P.N.S. 62

Letherby, G. 14
Lewis, J. 60
Li, D.J. 33
Li, J.F. 51
Li, L. 61
Li, L.J. 113
Li, S. 44, 49
Li, X.Y. 45
Li, Y.L. 119
Li, Y.N. 29, 53, 62, 66–67, 72–73, 76–77, 142
Li, Z. 52
Liang, Z. 41
Li-Hsiang, L.R. 21
Lin, K.C. 61
Ling, L.H.M. 9
Liu, B.H. 29, 53, 62, 66–67, 72–73, 76–77, 142
Liu, D.Z. 52
Liu, G.G. 61
Liu, J.Y. 48
Liu, X.D. 53
Liu, X.Z. 61
Liu, Y. 72
Liu, Z. 38, 76
Lowe, M. 12
Lu, D. 26
Lü, M.Y. 24
Lu, S. 22
Lu, X.H. 26, 39
Lu, X.Y. 39
Lu, Y.J. 76
Luxton, M. 9

MacPhail, F. 12
Marchbank, J. 9, 79
Marx, K. 27, 57
McBride, S. 7
McKay, D. 9
Meng, X. 41

Naughton, B. 37–38, 42–44, 47, 62, 155n1
Negri, A. 85
Neysmith, S. 9
Ngai, P. 5–6, 20

O'Brien, K.J. 113
O'Connell, A. 9
O'Connor, J. 8
Orloff, A.S. 8
Ostner, I. 60

Pan, Z.F. 40
Parrenas, R.S. 10

Pei, M.X. 129
Peng, X.Z. 50
Perry, E.J. 41
Pratt, G. 9, 12

Qin, L. 13

Rahman, N.A. 9–10
Ramirez-Machado, J.M. 128–29
Ran, J.F. 121
Ray, D. 39
Regan, L. 14
Reinharz, S. 14
Riskin, C. 44
Ritchie, L. 7
Robinson, D. 7
Robinson, J.C. 70
Romero, M. 12
Rowbotham, S. 10
Rubin, G. 4

Sainsbury, D. 8, 60
Saith, R. 155n5
Sassen, S. 7
Schecter, T. 12
Selden, M. 41
Sen, A. 155n4
Sharp, R. 8
Shaver, S. 8
Si, M. 13, 89
Sicular, T. 49
Sidel, R. 28–31, 65–67
So, A.Y. 5
Solinger, D.J. 49
Song, L.N. 48
Song, S.P. 29, 32
Standing, H. 63, 87,157 (chap 5) n10
Stewart, F. 155n5
Stiell, B. 12
Su, B. 123
Sumner, A. 155n5
Sun, L. 55
Sun, W.N. 13, 135–36
Swenarchuk, M. 7

Tan, L. 51, 63, 87–88
Tan, S. 40, 68
Tang, L.X. 45
Tang, S. 64, 66–67
Tao, C.F. 28
Therborn, G. 59
Tomba, L. 47

Vosko, L.F. 7, 158n4, n15

Waller, D.J. 63
Wallerstein, I. 5
Wang, C.G. 38
Wang, D.J. 51
Wang, F.L. 135
Wang, H. 13, 41–43
Wang, H.F. 13, 134
Wang, J.F. 13, 89
Wang, M.X. 24
Wang, N. 26
Wang, S.M. 11, 53
Wang, W. 123
Wang, W.T. 122–23
Wang, Y.G. 26, 39
Wang, Y.P. 6, 62
Wang, Z.Q. 1, 33, 87, 90–91
Wei, Q.Y. 22
Weisskofp, T. 85
Wen, T.J. 39
White, G. 155n1
Whyte, M.K. 37, 46
Wiggins, C. 7
Wiseman, J. 7
Wong, L. 60, 135
Woo, M.Y.K. 52, 57, 113
Wu, Q.Y 22
Wu, Y. 72–73

Xia, Q.J. 48
Xiang, F.H. 115
Xie, Z.M. 40
Xu, M. 10, 51
Xu, Y. 10

Yan, H.R. 1, 13, 20, 22-23, 31, 140
Yao, Y. 50
Yeates, N. 10
Yeoh, B.S.A. 9–10, 12, 133
Yi, J.J. 39
Young, I. 19
Yu, E.H. 52
Yuen, P. 61
Yuen-Tsang, A.W.K. 48

Zhang, C.H. 53
Zhang, H. 72
Zhang, J.G. 72
Zhang, J.S. 39
Zhang, L.B. 24
Zhang, M.M. 122–23
Zhang, X.M. 45
Zhang, Y. 72–73
Zhang, Y.Q. 62
Zhang, Y.R. 62

Zhang, Y.Y. 29, 53, 62–63, 66–67, 72–73, 76–77, 142
Zhao, Q. 43
Zhao, R.W. 43
Zheng, Y.F. 24
Zheng, Z.Z 40
Zhong, P.R. 52
Zhong, W. 63, 87
Zhou, J.M. 89
Zhou, Z. 75
Zhu, X.J. 63, 87–88, 122
Zhu, Z.Q. 122–23

Subject index

abuse 3, 86, 91–92, 102, 122, 130–34; physical 74, 94–95, 117; sexual 96; verbal 94–95, 103
agricultural sector 42–43, 87; economic reforms 38, 43; labour 37, 39, 46
All-China Federation of Trade Unions (ACFTU) 119–21, 135, 137; Women Workers Committee 48
All-China Women's Federation (ACWF) 52–54, 116, 124, 137

Basic Knowledge for Domestic Service Workers 34
Beijing Administration for Industry and Commerce (BAIC) 80, 92, 133, 136
Beijing Home Service Association (BHSA) 15, 45, 80
Beijing Migrant Women Domestic Workers Cooperative 137
Beijing University Women's Law Study and Services Center (BUWLSSC) 133
brigades, *see* people's communes

capitalism 1, 4–5, 12, 35, 57; class exploitation 27; development of 23–24, 141; feminist analysis of 19; global 5, 140–41, 143
caregivers 7, 11, 30, 59, 79, 85–86, 89, 98–102, 131, 134–35, 141
care-giving work 1, 3, 9–11, 58, 60, 79, 143; aging population 10–11, 59; global care chain 10
Centre for Women's Law Studies and Legal Services of Peking University (CWLSLS) 116, 118–19
childcare 2, 11, 38–39, 58–59, 63–64, 74, 76; crisis in 16, 58, 69; infant/neonatal care 63, 65–66, 76, 85, 151; staff and training 53–54, 69, 74, 85; work hours 67; work units 62, 65, 67, 69, 150; working conditions 16, 76, 78
childcare centers and facilities 29–30, 60–62, 64–77, 79; development of 58, 63–77; fees 157n8, n16
childcare policy 9, 16, 59, 63, 66–67, 77–79, 133; privatization 11, 58, 66, 69–73, 79; publicly owned 11, 29–30, 33, 66, 69–72, 79; rural collectives 29, 63, 67
China Domestic Service Association 136
China Employment Training Technical Institution Centre (CETTIC) 2, 34
China National Occupational Standards for Domestic Workers 2, 136
China National Society of Early Childhood Education (CNSECE) 71
China Women's News 95, 116
Chinese Communist Party (CCP) 6, 25, 48, 64, 137–38, 154n2, 155n9, 156n4
class(es) 12–13, 19, 21–22, 24–25, 27, 32, 43, 67, 125; division 1, 10–12, 22, 31, 33, 80, 141–43, 150; equality 33, 35, 69, 113; 126, 141; exploitation 1, 6, 18–19, 21, 25, 27; inequalities 9, 31, 41, 141; underclass 41, 113, 140, 143; working-class 11–12, 20–21, 27, 34–36, 41, 59, 64–65, 75, 107, 120–21, 125, 136
cleaner(s) 1, 3, 14–16, 82, 86, 98–104, 110, 131–32, 141, 146
Confucianism 21–22, 151
cooking 3, 21, 30, 85. 90, 104, 117, 134, 158n14
Cooperative Medical Systems (CMSs) 63, 87–88; insurance plan 46; rural service 88
Cultural Development Centre for Rural Women 116

Subject index

Cultural Revolution 27–28, 67, 156n7, 150; Great Proletarian 32; 'Iron Girls' 28–29

democracy 24, 155n8
developed countries 7, 9–10, 36, 127, 141
developing countries 5, 7, 9, 36, 127, 141; Third World Countries 9, 12
domestic employment 13, 138, 140; development of 2, 6–7, 10, 12, 18–20, 27, 30, 32–34, 42, 47–48, 81, 104, 112, 130–31, 135–38; occupational mobility 12–13, 41, 47; occupational standards 2, 34, 91, 131; permanent 47–48, 51; rural 135–36; urban 62, 135–36
domestic employment agencies 3, 13–15, 33, 54, 81, 84–85, 91–92, 95–103, 117, 133–36, 147–49; contracts 50, 81, 91–92, 98, 112, 114, 121, 132–34, 146
domestic labour 1–4, 6–7, 9–11, 52, 104, 140; devaluation of 4, 19; paid 2–4, 7, 12–14, 16, 18, 20, 35,52, 126; precarious 3, 7, 16, 18–19, 36, 41, 46, 49, 52, 80–82, 88, 98, 104–06, 138, 140–41, 158n4, n15; unpaid 7–8, 30–31, 36
domestic training programs 53–54, 90–91, 117–19, 127, 134–38, 148, 144, 148–49
domestic work 7, 9–14, 18–19, 28, 32, 41, 46–47, 54–55, 57, 97, 102, 128, 138; demand for 2, 11, 13, 9–12, 33, 35, 54–55, 58; development of 16, 19, 23, 51–56, 85, 137–38; private 18, 50, 140–41; state policy 3, 12, 14, 17, 31–36, 52, 55, 81, 114, 138
domestic worker(s) 1–2, 12–13, 16, 27, 34, 41, 45–46, 54, 58, 80, 82–84, 144, 150, 154 (chap. 2) n3; advocacy interest groups 14–15, 129, 137, 148; discrimination and exploitation 34, 94–97, 102–16, 123, 126–27, 133, 140–41, 149; employer-employee relations 12–13, 14, 17, 80, 85, 91–92, 94, 98, 102, 107–16, 144–47, 149; insurance 88–89
domestic working conditions 13–14, 17, 26, 34, 80, 82, 85–98, 107–34, 139–41, 143–44, 146, 148–49; live-in 3, 41, 82, 86, 92, 110–11, 146; live-out 82, 86, 89, 146; living conditions 13, 80, 86, 92–98, 107, 110–16, 124, 127, 131–32, 140; work hours 14, 86, 89–91, 100, 144, 146; work-related injuries 88–89, 124, 145–46

domestic violence 83, 95
Domestic Workers Network Support Group 117, 119, 123
domestic workers' rights 3, 13, 15, 81–82, 95, 98, 105–07, 110–18, 120, 123, 147–48; development of 26, 36, 107, 127–39, 142
Domestic Workers Rights Project 118

economic reform(s) 5, 12, 14, 16, 32–33, 36–39, 43, 47–49, 52, 57, 78–80, 141; global capital 5, 10, 129, 141; market-oriented 10–12, 18, 20, 37, 43, 58, 67, 70–71, 75, 77, 80, 121, 142–43; rural 37–40, 42–43; social market economy 35, 48, 58, 143; state ideology 9, 33; urban 43
education 39, 41, 43–45, 48, 53–54, 62, 64, 73, 98, 118; early 58, 64, 69, 71, 74, 76–77, 79; rural 29, 46, 63, 84; schools 62, 65; urban 72–73
elder care 3, 59, 85–86, 93, 108, 111, 132; government support 62–63; medical coverage 63, 88; training 134
Employer's Orientation Programme (EOP) 133
employment 10, 46–48, 82, 151; flexible 2, 11, 50–51; informal economic sector 32, 35, 47, 49–51; permanent 42, 47–48, 151; public sector 10, 32, 49, 69, 121; women 2–3, 10, 32, 40–41, 48, 51, 53–55
Employment Ordinance 130
employment regimes 16, 19–20, 35, 140
employment rights 10–11, 53, 82, 126, 128
equality 9, 23–25, 27–28, 31, 33, 42, 50, 82, 106, 113, 129, 143; gender 8–9, 11, 13, 18, 22, 24, 28, 30, 33, 46, 52–53, 56–57, 67, 69, 126, 128–29, 137, 139, 141, 143; inequality 11, 25, 28, 30–31, 41–43, 104, 106–07, 140, 142–43; socialist 11, 18, 25, 27–28, 30–31, 33, 35, 42, 52–53, 56–57, 67, 126, 140–43; women's 25, 27, 128

factory workers 20, 29, 31, 66; labour system 25–26; working sisters 40, 150
family 6, 8, 21–22, 25–26, 28–31, 34–35, 154n4; caregiver/wife 4, 8, 28, 30, 32, 59, 83, 108, 151; male-breadwinner/husband 8, 28, 59–60, 143, 151, 154n3; private/domestic sphere 4, 5, 8, 11, 13, 52, 57, 121, 150

Subject index 187

family service worker 34, 150; *see* domestic worker
farmers 22, 37, 42, 45, 64, 84, 88, 113, 150
Federation of Trade Unions 122
feudal society 19–23, 30, 35, 84, 108, 150
Fu Ping Domestic Service Centre (FPDSC) 83, 134

gender order 4–5, 8, 10, 13, 20, 143
gender regimes 8, 11, 19–20; relations 3–4, 6, 8
globalization 4–8, 16, 56, 79, 140
Great Leap Forward 28–29, 42, 66
Great Proletarian Cultural Revolution 32

health care 7, 11, 39, 41, 44, 47, 62–63, 114, 145–46; privatized 11, 58; rural 86–88; *see also* medical care
health insurance 62, 87
Hebei College of Industry and Technology 55
Household Responsibility System 37–38, 42–43, 87, 141; registration 37, 41–42, 87–88, 141, 155n3, 150
household(s) 1–2, 6, 8–11, 22, 44, 50, 52–53, 81–82, 137–38, 143, 154n3; agricultural 37, 87–88; private sphere of 4, 8–9, 11–12, 16, 52; public housing 29, 47, 60–63, 126; rural 38, 43, 45, 87–88; urban 13, 47, 58, 84–87, 135–36; women 26–27, 29, 31, 150; work 21, 26–27, 33–34, 79, 142–43
housekeeping 3, 30, 85–86, 134; men's participation 30, 143
Hukou System 37, 135–36, 141; Certificate 37
human rights 107, 126–28, 124, 126–27, 141

income 7, 11, 33, 39, 41–45, 50–51, 54, 104, 107, 112, 127, 132, 142, 155n6, n11; cleaners 99, 101–02, 104; differences and disparity 36–37, 41–43, 51, 54; elderly 62; farmers and peasants 37–38, 42–46, 108; inequality 7, 41–42; low-income 33, 43–44, 58, 72, 74–75
International Covenant on Civil and Political Rights (ICCPR) 129
International Covenant on Economic, Social and Cultural Rights (ICESCR) 119, 129

International Labour Conference 127; Declaration on Fundamental Principles and Rights at Work and its Follow-up 127; Resolution concerning the Conditions of Employment of Domestic Workers 127
International Labour Organization 50–51, 124, 128–29, 133, 141; Agenda on Decent Work for Domestic Workers: Rights, Productive Jobs, Social Protection and Representation in Domestic Services 128; Combating Forced Labour and Trafficking in Domestic Workers in South East Asia and Hong Kong 128; Promotion of Equality and Decent Work for Women: Prevention of Human Trafficking, Protection of Domestic Workers and Capacity Building for Gender Equality 128
International Labour Standards 126–28

Jilin Agriculture University 55
job(s) 11–12, 18, 28, 31–32, 38–39, 41, 78, 83–85, 94–95, 98–99, 144–45, 148, 150, 154 (chap. 2) n2; classification 18, 47; creation 49–51, 53, 55–56; loss 28, 39; occupational segregation 13, 30, 36, 41, 51; security 3, 11, 41, 107; stability 14, 97, 104
Joint Project on Domestic Work 135

Keynesian welfare state 7, 143

labour, division of 6, 8, 11, 18, 21, 25, 35, 143, gendered 6, 40, 140, 142–43, 148
labour insurance 61–62, 65
Labour Law 81, 92, 115, 119, 121, 124, 129–31; Labour Contract Law 133, 139
labour market 8, 11, 20, 36, 47, 140; economic reforms 10–11, 16, 47; women's participation 16, 59, 67, 140, 142
labour protections 3, 16, 35, 105, 124, 128, 130, 148
labour rights 11, 82, 114, 124–26, 129, 131, 139, 141
labour standards 11, 126–28, 130–31
law and jurisprudence 113, 115, 123, 130–31, 137–38, 150; civil law 114; labour legislation 128–29; regulation 131, 133, 138
Law Maintenance Group for Migrant Women 117

188   Subject index

Law of the People's Republic of China on Protection of Women's Rights and Interests 119
legal aid 117–18
Live-in Care Program (Canada) 9, 130; Contract 132; Employment Standards Act 130

maids 1, 10, 27, 93
market-based economy 5, 10, 11, 16, 19, 36, 132
Marriage Law 30
Marxism 25, 57, Marxist-Leninism, 27
maternity leave 52–53, 61; paternity leave 53
May Fourth New Culture Movement 25
medical care 2, 44, 62–63, 102; free treatment 62, 88, 124, 132; *see also* health care
medical insurance 46, 61, 87, 117
Migrant Women's Club (MWC) 15, 55, 56, 116, 129, 137, 150
Migrant Women's Right and Interests Conference 117
migration 4, 9–10, 31, 45; global 36; internal 36–40; *see also* rural-to-urban migration *and* rural migrant workers
Ministry of Civil Affairs 54
Ministry of Commerce (MOFCOM) 135–36
Ministry of Education, Act of Tentative Specifications on Childcare 64
Ministry of Finance (MOF) 135
Ministry of Human Resource and Social Services (MOHRSS) 132, 136, 154n1
Ministry of Labour and Social Security (MOLSS) 2, 15, 54, 61, 154n1
Ministry of Manpower (MOM) 133
Ministry of Urban-rural Development 54

nanny 1, 10, 14–15, 82, 86, 89, 93–95, 98–99, 150
National Committee of the Chinese People's Political Consultative Conference 53
National People's Congress 53
neoliberalism 4–7, 52, 56, 58, 141–42
non-governmental organizations (NGOs) 17, 106–07, 116–20, 124, 129, 137–38
Notice of Peasants Entering and Settling down in Town 38

Notice on Further Strengthening Employment and Reemployment 136
Notification on Effectively Safeguarding Rural Migrant Workers' Legal Rights and Interests 121

Oxfam Hong Kong 117, 119–20

patriarchy 6, 12, 19–20, 22, 32–33, 35, 40, 140; family 5–6, 21–22, 30, 33, 140–41; feudal 23, 25; state 4–6, 9, 33, 141
peasants 31, 40–42, 63, 66, 102, 107, 121, 151
pensions 61–62, 87, 145–46
peoples' communes and brigades 29, 37–38, 42, 60, 62–63
People's Republic of China (PRC) 19, 61, 81, 118–19
poverty 9, 26, 41–42, 44, 46, 49, 54; (the) poor 5, 7, 9, 21, 25, 43, 107, 134; rural 1, 41–46, 84, 88, 134
private property 19, 27, 35
public services 29–30, 58, 63; public/social sphere 4, 8, 51, 151

rape 23, 96, 104, 117, 133; sexual harassment 96, 104, 108
Re-employment Service Centres 49, 54; Project 40
Regulation on the Insurance of Workplace Injury 130
Regulations on Protection of Domestic Workers Labour Rights and Interests 119
Regulations on Safeguarding Women's Rights and Interests in Beijing 117
Research Centre for Women's Development and Rights of Northwestern Polytechnic University (RCWDR) 116, 119, 123
resident(s) 10, 41, 65; legal 31, 37; rural 42, 44–45, 62–63, 87–88, 151; temporary permits 38, 56, 137; urban 30, 33, 38, 42–45, 54, 62, 84, 102, 104, 135, 156n19
Rules for the Implementation of the Regulations Governing Labour Insurance 65
rural-to-urban migration 13, 6, 33, 36–40, 97, 99, 107, 121, 136, 141; rural women 31, 40, 83–84, 86
rural migrant workers 9, 13–14, 17, 33, 36, 39, 41, 86–87, 117, 137, 141; migration

controls 31, 37–38, 40, 135–36; women workers 2, 13, 17, 30, 33, 38–40, 106, 141

San Ba Family Service Centre (SBFSC) 33, 83
servant(s) 20, 23, 25–26, 30, 35, 82, 92, 105; aunt 26, 30, 150; bondservant 19–23, 25–26, 35, 150; waged labour 23, 25–26, 35
slavery 21–23, 26
social insurance 61, 87–88, 102, 130–31, 145–46
social justice 127, 129, 139; injustice 142
social reproduction 2, 3; government role in 7–11, 16–17, 29, 52, 58, 75, 77, 141–43; women's role in 7, 10–11, 141–42
social security 3, 13, 17, 49, 59; access to 13, 17, 59, 114, 119, 127, 129, 131–32, 141; employment 3, 51, 81–82; insurance 88–89, 129
social services 42, 44, 58; withdrawal of 16, 44, 78, 142
socialism 1, 6, 10–11, 18–19, 50, 69; ideology 32–33, 35, 42, 52, 140; women's equality, 27–28, 65
socialist centrally planned economy 5, 10, 19, 27, 31–33, 35–36, 56, 122, 140
socialist market-oriented economy 10, 126, 140, 142
Standard Employment Contract for Foreign Domestic Helpers 132
state 7, 22–23, 30, 69, 142; government 6, 10, 36, 137–39, 141–42, 154n2; ideology and policies 5–7, 8, 18, 20, 27–28, 36, 42, 52, 140–41, 143; role of 4–6, 11, 16, 35
State Administration for Industry and Commerce of the People's Republic of China (SAIC) 133, 136
State Administration of Taxation 54
state-owned enterprises (SOE) 1, 61, 123
State Internal Trade Bureau 54

Tai Ji Chang Community Domestic Workers Union 122
taxation 8, 21, 59–60; agricultural 38, 42, 44, 46
Trade Union Law 120–21
trade unions 15, 17, 85, 116, 119–21, 135, 137–38; collective bargaining 121, 127;

unionization 106–07, 120, 124–25, 158n15
transnational corporations 5, 7, 55

unemployment 2–3, 14, 36, 49, 52, 59, 156n19; women 2, 11, 16, 28, 48, 53, 55, 57
unemployment insurance 102
United Nations, Beijing Declaration and Platform for Action 128, 130; Convention on the Elimination of all Forms of Discrimination against Women (CEDAW) 128, 129–30; Declaration on the Elimination of Violence against Women 128; Development Fund for Women (UNIFEM) 116, 118, 120, 133; International Covenant on Civil and Political Rights (ICCPR) 128; International Covenant on Economic, Social and Cultural Rights (ICESCR) 128; International Convention on the Protection of the Rights of all Migrant Workers and Members of their Families 128; Millennium Development Goals 128; Optional Protocol of 1999 128; Thematic Group on Gender (UNTGG) 116, 118, 120; Universal Declaration of Human Rights 128

wages 14, 85–87, 108–09, 114–15, 121, 124, 130–31, 145–46; caregivers 85–86; cleaners 100, 104, hourly workers 98, 151; minimum 26, 86, 100, 131–32, 150; pay ranges and standards 17, 26, 55, 86–87, 92, 115, 151
welfare 11, 63, 130, 141; benefits and services 3, 47, 59–61, 151, elderly 62, housing 29, 61–62, rural collectives 62–63, state 7–8, 20, 29, 37, urban 60–61, 63
women 26–28, 51–53, 106, 137, 151; oppression of 7, 24, 32, 106–07; reforms for 23–24; work undervalued 4, 138, 142
Women's Community Services Program 54
women's federations 30, 33, 54, 83, 117, 119, 124, 137
women's movement 25; feminist revolution 24; liberation 24, 28, 30–31; rights 24–25, 118–19; socialist feminism 4, suffrage 25

Women's Studies Institute of China 15, 52
work 19, 26; decent 127–28, 130, 138; workplace safety 14, 88, 123, 130–31
work unit(s) 29, 58, 60–61, 81; urban, 61–63, 65, 72, 79, 150
worker(s) 32, 42, 51, 107, 120, 127; casual, laid off 13, 48–49, 107, 123, 135, 141, 151; older 26, 31, 48, 82–83, 95, 100

World Trade Organization (WTO) 55

Xi'an Domestic Workers' Trade Union 119, 123–24
Xi'an Women's Federation Re-employment Service Centre 119–20
Xizhen Domestic Service Company 119

Zuo Ling Domestic Service Company (ZLDSC) 108